Food and Identity in a Globalising World

Series Editors
Atsuko Ichijo
Department of Politics
Kingston University
Kingston-Upon-Thames, UK

Ronald Ranta
Department of Politics
Kingston University
Kingston-Upon-Thames, UK

This series aims to overcome the current fragmented nature of the study of food by encouraging interdisciplinary studies of food and serving as a meeting place for a diverse range of scholars and practitioners who are interested in various aspects of food. By encouraging new original, innovative and critical thinking in the field and engaging with the main debates and controversies, and by bringing together the various disciplines that constitute food studies, such as, sociology, anthropology, politics and geography, the series will serve as a valuable source for researchers, practitioners, and students. There will a focus on identities and food; issues such as gastrodiplomacy, settler colonialism, gender, migration and diaspora, and food and social media, while at the same time promoting an inter- and trans-disciplinary approach.

Ronald Ranta • Atsuko Ichijo

Food, National Identity and Nationalism

From Everyday to Global Politics

2nd ed. 2022

Ronald Ranta
Department of Criminology, Politics, Sociology
Kingston University
Kingston-upon-Thames, UK

Atsuko Ichijo
Department of Criminology, Politics, Sociology
Kingston University
Kingston-Upon-Thames, UK

ISSN 2662-270X   ISSN 2662-2718 (electronic)
Food and Identity in a Globalising World
ISBN 978-3-031-07833-0   ISBN 978-3-031-07834-7 (eBook)
https://doi.org/10.1007/978-3-031-07834-7

© The Editor(s) (if applicable) and The Author(s), under exclusive licence to Springer Nature Switzerland AG 2022

This work is subject to copyright. All rights are solely and exclusively licensed by the Publisher, whether the whole or part of the material is concerned, specifically the rights of translation, reprinting, reuse of illustrations, recitation, broadcasting, reproduction on microfilms or in any other physical way, and transmission or information storage and retrieval, electronic adaptation, computer software, or by similar or dissimilar methodology now known or hereafter developed.

The use of general descriptive names, registered names, trademarks, service marks, etc. in this publication does not imply, even in the absence of a specific statement, that such names are exempt from the relevant protective laws and regulations and therefore free for general use.

The publisher, the authors, and the editors are safe to assume that the advice and information in this book are believed to be true and accurate at the date of publication. Neither the publisher nor the authors or the editors give a warranty, expressed or implied, with respect to the material contained herein or for any errors or omissions that may have been made. The publisher remains neutral with regard to jurisdictional claims in published maps and institutional affiliations.

Cover illustration: Contributor: Africa Studio / Alamy Stock Photo

This Palgrave Macmillan imprint is published by the registered company Springer Nature Switzerland AG.
The registered company address is: Gewerbestrasse 11, 6330 Cham, Switzerland

Foreword

Our current historic moment is clearly exposing fraught anxieties and paradoxes about food. We are witnessing a global cultural shift toward ethical and sustainable food consumption that contrasts with unresolved justice issues like the poverty wages of food industry laborers and the slave-like conditions of migrant agricultural workers. We see efforts to grow and integrate markets for food and agricultural products across national borders meeting ardent resistance from populists and nationalists. And we are now observers of the precarity of 'just-in-time' supply chains, as container ships are bottlenecked at seaports and seemingly random supermarket shelves remain empty almost two years after the COVID-19 pandemic began.

Because edibility and morality are intrinsically linked, as anthropologist Mary Douglas once argued, food and culinary practices have long been coupled with political projects, used by those seeking to identify and consecrate the characteristic foodways of nations. Representations of food as 'national culture' are now firmly rooted in public imaginations around the world. And thus far in the twenty-first century, foodways—the varied economic, social, and cultural practices of food production and consumption—have become ever more politically charged, from debates over newly invented food traditions to strategic national branding in global markets to food producers' role in the climate crisis.

Moreover, in an era dominated by conceptions of 'food from nowhere,' vanishing traditions, and the ostensible demise of pastoral, rural landscapes, designating specific foods and dishes as local, place-based, and authentic is an especially marketable idea. Groups, associations, and governments around the world work to promote specific foods and dishes as 'typical' of communities and places, as well as use them as elements of soft power, often with high-profile chefs and cookbook writers serving as their cultural ambassadors, a practice referred to as gastrodiplomacy. Yet this modern-day pride in the 'taste of place' also has a dark side; it can and has easily aligned with xenophobic logics and neo-nationalist political projects that undercut the work of using food for building cross-cultural understanding or social connections, and even the otherwise-universal idea of simply enjoying a good meal. Food can bring people together, but it can also keep them apart. I write these words with one part of my brain focused on planning meals for family and friends for upcoming holidays and another on acknowledging the fact that the arrival of new, food-related elements to the United States, Europe, and elsewhere—companies, workers, plants, and pathogens alongside tasty ingredients and novel cooking techniques—often earns cautious reception at best.

Scholarship on nationalism and food has grown rapidly over the last two decades, detailing and analyzing these dynamic realities, often focusing on case studies of individual regions, countries, or food items. Foodways are now recognized as objectified forms of social belonging and difference, as potential sites of activism, as lenses through which to observe social contestation and change, and even mediums for addressing controversies that are not necessarily about food. Sociologists and others have proffered the importance of examining contemporary 'national' practices around food as relational, as significant, and as embedded in the conflicts that are part and parcel of contemporary globalization. The first edition of this book by Atsuko Ichijo and Ronald Ranta—*Food, National Identity, and Nationalism*—was a meaningful, smart, and systematic engagement of food and nationalism in this vein. It examined a wide range of issues across different levels of politics, from on-the-ground and banal ways of performing the nation through recipes, to nations developing culinary initiatives to promote themselves to tourists, to the inclusion of specific cuisines on UNESCO's list of protected intangible cultural heritage.

Yet, since its publication in 2016, the realm of 'food-and-nationalism' has continued to evolve in leaps and bounds, making this new edition quite a welcome one. They say the 'devil is in the details' and there are many throughout this volume that the authors get just right. Some chapters show, for example, new organizational and categorizational schemas within the recent weaving of populist politics, such as Brexit, into considerations of food identities as well as access. Others account for intersecting trends in social, media, and political discourses with new awareness of what 'belonging' and 'us-versus-them' dichotomies have come to mean in the context of new technologies and controversies, as some people have proven willing to go to extreme lengths to defend 'traditional' food objects, practices, and norms.

Studying the development and ramifications of 'food and nationalism' in contemporary times is humbling. As health and economic crises continue to sweep the globe, we need an approach like this one, one that takes seriously our desire for authentic, meaningful lives without downplaying the tools, trials, and tribulations of national identity and political movements in the global market economy. In sum, this book will help us to further appreciate the idea that foods and cuisines can be producers of both dissonance and pleasure, and that they bring into collision disparate social worlds. This is what makes this new edition valuable—it counters, from the purview of many angles and events, the very notion that food ever exists outside of contemporary politics.

Associate Professor, Department of Sociology and Anthropology, North Carolina State University, Raleigh, NC, USA

December 2021   Michaela DeSoucey

Praise for *Food, National Identity and Nationalism*

"*Food, Nationalism, and National Identity* shows us how nations make food and how food makes nations. It reminds us of the multiple ways in which food and nationalism are intertwined in politics and everyday life, and in so doing it points to the continued relevance of nationalism in our world today. The expanded scope and analysis of this new and revised second edition promises to solidify the book's reputation as a key reference work in the field."

—Professor Jon Fox, *University of Bristol*

Contents

Introduction: Food, Nationalism and National Identity   1

Part I   Unofficial/Bottom-Up: Nationalism and National Identity Through Food Away from the State   25

Chapter One: Everyday Creation of the Nation   27

Chapter Two: When Groups Participate in Defining the Nation   55

Chapter Three: Consuming Nations—The Construction of National Identities in the Food Industry   77

Part II   Official/Top-Down: The Nation-State, Food and Nationalism   103

Chapter Four: Food and Diet in 'Official' Nationalism   105

Chapter Five: National Food in the International Context I—Gastrodiplomacy   131

Chapter Six: National Food in the International Context II—Gastronationalism and Populism 153

Part III Food and Nationalism/National Identity at the Global Level 175

Chapter Seven: Norms, Ethics, Food and Nationalism 177

Chapter Eight: International Organisations, Food and Nationalism 207

Conclusion: From Everyday to Global Politics 233

References 241

Index 273

List of Photos

Introduction: Food, Nationalism and National Identity

Photo 1	Celebrating foods eaten by primary school students	8
Photo 2	Celebrating foods eaten by primary school students	9
Photo 3	Brixton food market	10

Chapter Two: When Groups Participate in Defining the Nation

Photo 1	Examples of Israeli mass-produced 'Arab' hummus	68
Photo 2	Diana Kosher Israeli Grill	74

Chapter Three: Consuming Nations—The Construction of National Identities in the Food Industry

Photo 1	Sainsbury's chocolate range	79
Photo 2	Sainsbury's coffee range	80
Photo 3	Traditional pie and mash shop interior	88
Photo 4	Traditional pie and mash shop menu	89
Photo 5	Pieminister's menu	91

Chapter Four: Food and Diet in 'Official' Nationalism

Photo 1	Coat of arms Petah Tikva	120
Photo 2	Coat of arms of Hadera	120
Photo 3	Coat of arms of Afula	121

Chapter Six: National Food in the International Context II—Gastronationalism and Populism

Photo 1	French Tacos	171
Photo 2	German Doner Kebab	172

Chapter Seven: Norms, Ethics, Food and Nationalism

Photo 1	The menu lists 5 different items (red meat, processed sliced tail fin, bacon, skin and tendon) substantiating the claim that the Japanese do not waste any part of a whale	186

List of Tables

Chapter One: Everyday Creation of the Nation

Table 1	The quantitative outline of extracted recipes	42
Table 2	The coding scheme	43
Table 3	Descriptive statistics of three sets of recipes	44

Chapter Eight: International Organisations, Food and Nationalism

Table 1	The list of elements related to food culture/cuisine in the Representative List of the Intangible Cultural Heritage of Humanity as of December 2021	213

Introduction: Food, Nationalism and National Identity

When we first approached publishers and pitched our idea for a book on food and nationalism in 2013, we were taken aback by some of the feedback we received; important to note that this did not include our publishing editors at Palgrave! One of the main criticisms we had to contend with was that the subject of food and nationalism was no longer relevant; a grant application we submitted roughly at the same time to convene a workshop on food and nationalism received similar feedback. Food, we were told, was increasingly seen not as national but as transnational, regional, local and/or identity based. We were told that nationalism was an important and transformative historic force, but one that was waning in a globalised world.

It is interesting to read these criticisms from our current vantage position. It was clear to us then, as it is now, that *the national* does not have a monopoly over food, and that there are indeed constant tensions, and often conflicts, between the various forces and actors that seek to claim food as their own, or to use, reject and resist the nation as a rallying point. We fully accept that 'the relationship between food and identity is a complex one' (Scholliers 2001: 3). Food can be many things, it can be personal, festive, ethnic, regional, local, gender or generational-specific; for more on this point, see our discussion below. Nevertheless, it is a fact that the politics of the world we live in, and of which food is an integral part, are deeply enmeshed in the nation-state system. We fully acknowledge that this system is being challenged from below, by the forces of the everyday, the local and the regional, and from above, by transnational and international movements and bodies. However, given the time that has passed since our first edition—with the rise of nationalist-populism, the emergence of migration as a global political issue, concerns over global governance, Brexit, the presidency of Donald Trump, the Covid-19 pandemic and vaccine nationalism—it is clear that nationalism is not a waning force. Whether this is just a temporary resurgence or not is hard to tell. What is clear is that nationalism will remain a dominant and transformative force in global politics, at least in the short-term future. In this regard, we would argue, as we have argued in the first edition, that food and nationalism is an important area to study, and that the food-nationalism axis provides a useful prism through which to explore and analyse the world around us, from the everyday to the global, and the ways in which it affects us.

It is an anthropological truism that food holds significance beyond the mere fulfilment of physiological needs; it provides an outlet for people to express 'who and what they are, to themselves and to others' (Mintz 1986: 13). For the purposes of this book, we do not focus on the relationship between food and identity in general, but on how individuals and groups perceive their food culture and how this in turns helps them to imagine themselves as part of the nation. By food culture we refer to the myriad of ways in which food is grown, commodified, prepared, consumed and articulated by a particular society (Ranta and Mendel 2014: 414). The relationship between food, identity and the nation is not a new phenomenon, nor is it limited to particular geographic areas. For example, Avieli (2005) demonstrates the importance of rice cultivation and consumption to Vietnamese identity from the late eighteenth century; Orlove (1997) discusses the importance of beef to Chileans at the beginning of the twentieth century; and Rogers (2003) provides examples, from the arts and literature, of the connection between English and then British national identity, and roast beef from as far back as the late sixteenth century.

There are a number of criticisms to the importance and relevance of discussing food in relation to the nation. As we mentioned above, food can be many different things, it can be regional, local and/or transnational. One could also talk about non-cuisines (baking, seafood, BBQ, etc.), or counter-cuisines (organic, vegan, foraging, slow food movement, etc.), and the apparent non-national aspect of these. This is indeed an important point to address. To start with, the term regional or local is controversial in itself; several authors (e.g., Cook and Crang 1996; Montanari 2004) argue that the term regional is a modern construction that has little to do with historic food traditions. Nonetheless, what has become clear, since the formation and construction of nation-states, is that regional and ethnic differences have been to an extent incorporated into and have become 'subservient to, and part of, the greater national identity' (Edensor 2002: 66). While ethnic or local foods may compete or collide with national food, the former is often incorporated in the latter. Montanari (2004) gives examples of how cookbooks *culinarily* united Italy by disseminating local and regional food knowledge nationally. Additionally, in his discussion on the role of cookbooks in the construction of an Indian national identity, Appadurai (1988) explains how Indian and colonial cookbooks integrated and tied together the diversity of regional and ethnic cuisines to the nation, even though this created strange food 'bedfellows', and reified and inflated historic traditions. According to him, national cuisine, in the case of India, 'has emerged because of, rather than despite, the increased articulation of regional and ethnic cuisines' (Appadurai 1988: 21). The merging of the local and the regional into the nation has also been demonstrated in many other cases (see, e.g., Cwiertka 2006 with regard to Japan; Pilcher 1996, 1998 with regard to Mexico; and Simpson Miller 2021 with regard to Ghana). The same can also be seen in the way ethnic- and identity-based foods have been incorporated into national food culture: for example, in the case of Britain (Panayi 2008), Israel (Prieto-Piastro 2021) and the US (Gabaccia 1998; Harris 2012).

There is no denying the strong relationship food has to geography, land and locality. The point to emphasis here is that increasingly this has been and is viewed and interpreted through the prism of the nation; this is not to say that we argue that food is national, but rather that it is imagined and constructed as such. A good example to illustrate this point is the concept of *terroir*, which was for a long time mostly associated with wine and has now increasingly been used in reference to food. *Terroir* is not an easy concept to define and can mean different things, from qualities of natural geography (soil, temperature, precipitation, elevation, etc.) to methods of production and cultural practices. Although the term has been used for centuries, in more recent times it has been used to differentiate between foods that might be considered modern and industrial and those that reflect artisanal and local history, knowledge and tradition. This has been partly a result of the increasing emphasis on *terroir* by the private sector to denote difference, authenticity and quality: a process that we define as 'terroirism' and which is often simply a crude marketing strategy. Nevertheless, the ideas behind *terroir* have increasingly been used either in the context of particular nations (most famously with regard to France: see Ferguson 2006, 2010; Trubek 2008) or as a site for national contestation. A point illustrated in recent work on wine and the way in which *terroir* is intertwined with debates over borders, sovereignty, history, national identity and even indigeneity and cultural appropriation (Monterescu 2017; Monterescu and Handel 2019); we will return to these debates in "Chapter Six: National food in the International Context II—Gastronationalism and Populism".

In terms of other cuisines, these too are, to some extent, discussed within the boundaries of nations. Thus, vegetarian and vegan cookbooks might reference Indian food and extol its virtues, while advocates of healthy eating might discuss Japanese food and its reliance on fresh produce, soybeans and fish. Overall, although it is possible, it is hard to escape the persistent reference and allusion to nations and nationalism in food. Additionally, many food items and practices are so closely linked to the idea of nations that it is a challenge to find a cookbook that has no references to nations or national qualities in it, even though this is not something many cookbooks set out to do. One can also see this focus on nations in mainstream television and streaming services: from Netflix's *Chef's Table* to different manifestations of the popular *MasterChef* series, food is constantly discussed through the prism of the nation.

This is not to argue that the relationship between food and nations/nationalism is self-evident or unproblematic. It is wrong to take for granted that there is always a relationship between food and nations/nationalism, and if such a relationship exists, it is always contested and challenged. As demonstrated by several authors (see, e.g., Ichijo et al., 2019, King 2019), the relationship between food and nations/

nationalism or the association of specific food items and practices with a particular nation is complex and at times heavily contested from within and outside the nation. As we have shown elsewhere (Ichijo et al. 2019), while it is possible to generalise and demonstrate parallels among cases, the relationship between food and nations/nationalism is often context dependent. For instance, in several settler colonial states, it is hard to discuss or even identify the idea of national food/cuisine. However, in the age of nation-states, we always find attempts to forge such a link between food and a nation, as seen in the invention of Israeli salad, the use of kangaroo meat to differentiate Australian culture from other English-speaking ones and the promotion of maple syrup as a quintessentially Canadian product. In these attempts, we find a variety of power relationships laid out and, as such, the 'food-and-nationalism' axis help us grasp the politics of these societies.

Building on the above points, our second edition has three main aims. First, it aims to continue shedding light on an under-investigated area in the study of nationalism, that is, the relationship between food and nationalism/national identity. As we will elaborate further below, while the centrality of food in and to human life is well acknowledged, the relationship between food and nationalism has not been systematically investigated in the study of nationalism despite the recent rise in interest in 'everyday nationalism'. In our first edition we argued that the subject of food and nationalism had not been systematically addressed and was largely neglected. While we still stand by our argument that the subject had not been systematically addressed, in many ways we were unfair to those who had written about the subject before us and upon whose shoulders we were standing. In that regard our scholarship clearly benefited from and built on the work done by others, among them: Appadurai (1988); Avieli (2005, 2013); Cwiertka (2006, 2012); DeSoucey (2010); Ferguson (2006, 2010); Gabaccia (1998); Pilcher (1996, 1998); and Wilk (1999, 2006).

Secondly, the second edition continues to draw the reader's attention to the relevance of the 'food and nationalism' axis for studying and understanding politics, political economy and international relations. Needless to say, nationalism is an integral aspect of politics, political economy and international relations, and food is one of the essential commodities with which political powers at various levels are concerned. As such, neither nationalism nor food in itself constitutes a novel aspect to investigate *the political*. What this edition aims to illuminate is that food and nationalism can serve as an axis to bring together analyses of the political at different levels.

Thirdly, looking at the first edition, it is clear that we did not pay sufficient attention to a number of important areas. In this edition we try to fill in many of the gaps and lacunas identified and include some of the new scholarship on food and nationalism that has come out since. In particular, we include and discuss the relevance of food and nationalism to diasporas, social media, transnationalism, tourism, food security, populism, technology and *terroir*. We have also included additional discussions of definitions and methodologies, and have revised and updated our previous case studies, as well as added a number of new ones.

Food and Nationalism: Areas for Investigation

In the first edition, we proposed to approach the link between food and nationalism/national identity in three areas: unofficial/bottom-up, official/top-down and the global level. This was because while not conflating nationalism as an ideology with the nation-state as an apparatus of power, we wanted to acknowledge the importance of the nation-state in making nationalism an enduring and all-permeating ideology in our life (Malešević 2013). Consequently, we proposed these divisions in reference to the nation-state.

In investigating the official/top-down aspect of food and nationalism, the analyses will focus on phenomena which are ostensibly not controlled by the nation-state. What to be analysed is therefore approached by way of banal nationalism and everyday nationalism (Billig 1995; Edensor 2002; Fox and Miller-Idriss 2008a, b; Skey 2011). The second aspect, the official/bottom-up one, is where the relationship between food and nationalism is directly mediated by the nation-state in the form of national branding, standardisation of 'national' cuisine, protection of agriculture or restrictions on trade of certain food items. This can be seen as part of a growing trend of asserting national rights to food, which has

Introduction: Food, Nationalism and National Identity   7

been described as 'Gastronationalism' (DeSoucey 2010: 446) and 'Culinary Nationalism' (Ferguson 2010: 102). The nation-state, however, is increasingly compelled to take into account forces that operate beyond the nation-state framework in this globalising world as it is widely recognised (e.g., see Beeson and Bisley 2013). It is therefore logical for the volume to proceed to examine the relationship between food and nationalism at the global level in which the mundane life, the nation-state, international organisations and global norms, economic and political forces come together to create particular dynamics in respect to food. These three areas are elaborated further below.

Unofficial/Bottom-Up

'Why do *we* ... not forget *our* national identity? The short answer is that *we* are constantly reminded that *we* live in nations' (Billig 1995: 93). We all notice the waved national flags, but rarely observe the many unwaved flags, or for that matter other banal national symbols, such as coins, buildings, spaces and monuments. These banal national symbols are a constant reminder of the nation. For the most parts, the food images we are exposed to on a daily basis, from food labelling and marketing strategies used by governments and corporations to advertisements and restaurants, constantly remind us that we live in a world dominated by nation-states, with particular characteristics. We are introduced to the idea of nations and nationalities at a very young age, often in a seemingly non-ideological (banal) manner. The two photographs below were taken at a UK primary school. They showcase and celebrate some of the foods eaten by students, which are associated with nation-states.

Despite, or maybe because, of the rapid advancement of globalisation, we are now encountering not less but more manifestation of banal nationalism in food. Most of the restaurants we frequent and the cookbooks we read are related to a particular nation. Whereas two decades ago that would have meant a selection of Chinese, French, Indian and Italian cookbooks, the range today spans the globe from Jamaica to Colombia and from Ethiopia to Lebanon (see Photos 1, 2 and 3). Additionally, the national branding and labelling of food are literally found everywhere,

Photo 1 Celebrating foods eaten by primary school students

conveying particular images of the nation, constructing and reproducing it in our everyday lives. As a consequence, we have become almost oblivious to the fact that the food is routinely constructed and reproduced as national. From Thai or Mexican seasoning to pure Canadian maple syrup to Turkish coffee and English mustard, these constructs convey particular images of what the product and the nation are. This is even more so when people encounter, discuss or consume nationally recognised cuisines or dishes. According to O'Connor, national cuisines are 'never perceived as value-free, symbolically-neutral source of nutrition that has come haphazardly into being' (2009: 157).

Banal nationalism is also prevalent in discourses about food, which include, but are not limited to, the writings of food authors, historians and critics, everyday talk as well as advertisements. These discourses, using Fox and Miller-Idriss' (2008a) terminology, 'discursively construct' and reproduce the nation as well as other nations, highlighting real, perceived or imagined qualitative differences and significance. The qualitative differences these discourses point out provide the nation with

Photo 2 Celebrating foods eaten by primary school students

food-related boundaries, which remind us of who we are and who we are not. It is true that most of the information in these discourses relates to ingredients, nutrition, processes and measurements. Nonetheless, they also construct and reproduce what nations are, not only in terms of produce and dishes but also in terms of images, traditions, scenes, people and geography, through, for example, the choice of language, context and photographs.

Banal representation of the nation in food discourse is not the only method for experiencing the nation through food and reminding us of who we are. Food culture, through routine and mundane activities, such as the procurement and consumption of food, also helps construct and reproduce the nation. Using Edensor's terminology and concept of nationalism in everyday life (2002), food culture 'institutionalises' our lives and identities by providing common structuring and normalising patterns of 'how things are' and 'how we do things', and, we would add,

Photo 3 Brixton food market

how we talk about things. These normalising structures and patterns can be viewed as social and cultural food 'rules'.[1] These 'rules' explain how we eat, what we eat, when we eat and where we eat. They thus help define and characterise the nation through its particular food culture. From the spaces in which we produce, procure and consume our food to the timings and traditions of our meals, these banal and mundane food activities help sustain and build a familiar sense of time, space and being. Food culture enables us, on the one hand, to imagine the nation by providing it with particular food-related boundaries, patterns and characteristics,

---

[1] The concept of food rules is borrowed from Ashkenazi and Jacob (2000).

while, on the other hand, reproduce and sustain the nation through mundane and routine images and practices. Taken together with the banal representations of the nation in food, our food culture constructs the time and space of our national identity while conveying meaning and symbolism to it. What these banal and taken-for-granted social and cultural 'rules' bring about is a passive, though reflexive, sense of one's national identity. The reflexive part of our national identity is thus prompted when we travel abroad or encounter 'other' food cultures that challenge our familiar settings. In fact, we would argue that one of our first encounters with other nations occurs through food. In short, food culture locates what is familiar and ours from what is not.

So far the role of food in constructing and reproducing familiar settings as well as the food-related boundaries of the nation, through among other things daily experiences, discourses and banal nationalism, has been highlighted. There are, however, two additional elements that need to be addressed with regard to how we experience the nation, namely, practising and asserting the nation through our food culture. Practising and asserting national identity through food means making choices and decisions which provide direct links to, among others, the nation's perceived or imagined history, social traditions, culture and geography. Through these decisions and choices, people get to 'perform the nation'.

The nation, however, is not a monolithic entity; it is indeed made up of a variety of groups and people who at times promote competing perceptions and images of what the nation is, based on gender, class and ethnicity, among others. This can be seen most dramatically in *counter-cuisines* and *cuisines of resistance* (more on this below). It is also important to note that food culture is not static; through their food choices people decide whether to observe particular food traditions, rules or cultures, reproduce them, reinvent them, discontinue with them, or invent and construct new ones. Indeed, examining national food culture it is noticeable how it changes in accordance to various factors, such as migration, climate, globalisation and the economy.

The nation, as performed by individuals, is about practice, routine and repetition. When groups of people make choices, for whatever reason, on a regular and repetitive basis, whether once a year or once a day, it affects the way they and others view the nation. These food-related choices instil and reinforce an abstract, reflexive, yet particular image of what the nation is and what its boundaries are. This promoted and projected image, whether the result of changing diets, climate, corporate marketing or national policies, allows us, through practice and repetition, to imagine ourselves as part of the nation. The individual sees themself as part of a larger community of people who have similar values and sensitivities, or for the purpose of this article make similar food-related choices. This is not to argue that all members of a particular nation make the same choices or eat the same food (far from it; food choices and preferences are often based on a variety of reasons). In other words, food culture enables us to imagine the nation by projecting a particular image of what the nation eats and what are its food-related boundaries. An example of the process is given by Avieli on the role of rice cakes, within the context of the Vietnamese new year's celebrations, which help develop and sustain Vietnamese cultural and national identity: 'in terms of the *imagined communities* analytical framework, this food item serves as an important means for practicing and *concretizing* national identity' (2005: 167). Another way in which these performances assert national identity is through cuisines of resistance. Providing the example of Israeli-Palestinians, Gvion explains how 'culinary knowledge becomes a means of identity creation that strengthens' communal boundaries, 'redefines their political identity, and forms a culture of resistance' (2006: 309). In this way, performing the nation through food can also serve as a means of resisting national hegemonic practices (Cesaro 2000).

It does not have to be a specific food item, in many cases performing the nation through food means taking part in food-related events, traditions or rituals. This could be a national event or holiday or a tradition such as having a BBQ on Israel's Independence Day (Avieli 2013; Shoham 2021) or on Australia Day in Australia (Newling 2022); important to note that these traditions can also be sites and space for contesting the nation. These food-related events, traditions and rituals might be, in reference to Hobsbawm, invented or constructed, yet they have in many cases become part of the cultural hegemony of the nation, they are flexible to various interpretations, but they endure. These events and traditions provide not only an opportunity to perform the nation but also, in the words of Foster, an opportunity for 'anchoring the imagined national community in daily practice' (1991: 250).

Performing the nation does not only occur at national events and spaces. These performances also include 'invisible' spaces, such as the home. Thanksgiving feast, an American national holiday, is a family event that takes place largely at the home. This in turn implies a large measure of interpretations and variations among those celebrating, based on class, ethnicity and gender. However, the basic traditions of Thanksgiving, involving the consumption of roast turkey, potatoes, cranberries, pumpkin pie and corn and providing an abundance of foods, have been practised by an overwhelming majority of Americans (Wallendorf and Arnould 1991). The feast, though performed at an 'invisible' space, provides a direct link to the nation's imagined history and traditions, through what is a widely participated food cultural practice. It situates the individual within a larger community, which shares similar food traditions and practices. Performing the nation also occurs during mundane and everyday situations. For example, in England, having a full English breakfast, consuming curry with lager, Sunday roast, going to the pub and afternoon tea are all examples of everyday performances of the nation (Brown 2019).

Official/Top-Down

National identity is not only experienced and performed by individuals through their food culture in their daily lives but also engineered by a powerful apparatus called the nation-state. Food choices are not simply about individual taste and identity. According to Warde and Martens, there are various 'material, cultural, and social constraints that might limit our Freedom to choose' (Ashley et al. 2004: 59). As explained by Belasco, what people decide to eat is, for most parts, 'based on a rough negotiation between dictates of identity and convenience, with somewhat lesser guidance from the considerations of responsibility' (2008: 8). In other words, food choices are based on complex negotiations between myriad factors, which include the food images people have as a result of their surroundings and upbringing. These food images, of which banal nationalism plays an important part, help influence choice, and are, to some extent, constructed and reproduced from above. In fact, a wide range of agents, from social entrepreneurs to the media to the private and public sectors, but of which the nation-state is the most important and dominant, engage, for a variety of reasons, in constructing and reproducing food images, which have, in many occasions, a national element to them.

In order for individuals to experience their national identity through food, there, first of all, needs to be a nation. How and why are nations constructed and then reified and reproduced through food? The appearance of national food cultures, either in practice or in writing, appears to go hand-in-hand with the appearance of national narratives and movements. The construction of a national food culture can thus be seen as part of the process of constructing, establishing or reifying nations. In fact, we argue that it is an important element of this process. Constructing, reifying, asserting and at times inventing, a common food culture is a useful method by which national entrepreneurs and movements try to bring different groups of people (divided by ethnicity, religion, geography or class) together; this process is made easier if it taps into existing or imagined shared food practices and traditions. By establishing a common food culture and demarcating the food-related boundaries of the nation, national entrepreneurs and movements enable the creation of an imagined community. Additionally, national movements use food as a means of asserting the uniqueness of their nation while, at the same time, placing it on par with other nations, who, it is perceived, have unique food cultures.

The construction of a national food culture often takes place in opposition to the spread of, what are perceived to be, foreign, or in some cases opposing national influences. This is especially true with regard to postcolonial states, where the construction and reproduction of a common food culture enforces and instils the idea of the nation in relation to the colonial power (Cusack 2004; Pilcher 1998). This could also be seen in terms of promoting 'national', 'local' or 'traditional' food as a reaction to the growing abundance of 'foreign' foods (Caldwell 2002; Cesaro 2000; Eum 2008). The nationalisation of food thus provides a method of defining what is 'ours' from 'not ours' and 'authenticating' the nation (Caldwell 2002).

What are the means by which food culture is constructed and reproduced? We have seen examples of how in Italy and India, cookbooks and food literature have been used as a means of instilling national unity through the incorporation of ethnic and regional cuisines, in addition to demarcating the food-related boundaries of the nation. Food literature provides a great number of examples of this phenomenon, some of which date as far back as the eighteenth century.[2] This is true not only with regard to 'established' nations; according to Cusack (2000, 2003, 2004), constructing, or at times inventing, national cuisines and then disseminating the knowledge through education, media and literature, appears to be an important way for ruling elites to bring people together in many African states; see also the example of Ghana (Simpson-Miller 2022). The construction and emphasis on the nation can also be part of distancing groups from or opposing hegemonic ideas of the nation. This can be seen in examples from Catalonia (Johannes 2019), Quebec (Fabien-Ouellet 2019) and Scotland (Fraser and Knight 2019).

Constructing and reproducing the nation through food is not limited to the dissemination of ideas through literature and the media. Many national movements have attempted to construct or reify nations by actively changing dietary and/or consumption habits. According to Takeda (2008), the Meiji government, in the late nineteenth century, in an effort to establish Japan as a strong-military nation and instigate rapid industrialisation, undertook measures to promote a common, but also modern and healthier Japanese food culture. This was done by, for example, introducing 'western food' as well as meat and dairy products. These steps were taken through national campaigns as well as education at school and the military. In recent years, in response to food security as well as health concerns, public campaigns have been launched promoting Japanese food under the slogan of 'healthy Japanese food contributes to building a healthy Japanese nation' (Takeda 2008: 24). What is interesting about these examples from Japan is not the promotion of healthy or nutritious food, but the attempts to educate individuals about the virtues and health qualities of national food, as opposed to, one could postulate, 'foreign' food.

---

[2] For example, Ferguson (2006), Jacobs (2009), Montanari (2004), Pilcher (1998) and Rogers (2003).

The importance of national food images and brands to national claims of qualitative difference and significance can also be demonstrated in the events surrounding the 'mad-cow disease' and its impact on relations between Britain and the EU (Billig 1995); a similar process is now underway regarding Brexit. The importance of beef to first English and then British national identity and heritage has been argued to go back as far as the sixteenth century (Rogers 2003; Spierling 2007; Edwards 2019). Therefore, European, in particular German and French, calls to boycott British beef, in response to the outbreak of mad-cow disease, were perceived as attacks on Britain and British national identity and heritage. British tabloid media were quick to praise the virtues of British beef in comparison to French beef—which, it was claimed, was fed on sewage. It was also argued that the abysmal form of the French national football team was in response to switching the players' diet from British to French beef (Rogers 2003). One tabloid went as far as using specific nationalist language relating to World War II, in calling on its readers to 'burn German flags' and shout at German tourists 'we shall fight them on the beaches' in response to Germany's boycotting of British beef (Ashley et al. 2004).

The importance of national brands and images, which signify and provide evidence of national qualities, is also behind the rise of what *The Economist* (2002) describes as 'Gastrodiplomacy'. The term can be roughly defined as the construction and reproduction of national food brands and images by the nation-state for political, diplomatic and commercial reasons. The most well-known example of this is that of the Thai government's investment in establishing Thai restaurants around the world, providing cooking classes, disseminating information regarding and exporting, what is claimed to be 'authentic' Thai food. These actions are taken in order to improve the image of Thailand internationally, but also domestically. However, these actions also entail the standardisation and homogenisation of Thai food culture, as well as the promotion of a specific image of Thai food and national identity. As you will see in "Chapter Six: National food in the International Context II—Gastronationalism and Populism", the subject of gastrodiplomacy has not been extended to many countries and has become a specific field of study within the food and nationalism axis.

At the Global Level

While no society has ever existed in absolute isolation, the level of interdependency has undoubtedly deepened in recent decades. The emergence of the global level as a focus of politics is one of the major features of the contemporary age. The development of inter-governmental/supranational organisations such as the European Union, the entrenchment of human rights norms, the emergence of global civil society and the calls for stronger global governance to tackle climate change are challenging the conventional notion of the Westphalian system in the study of politics and international relations (Cenry 2013). The now-tired description of the nation-state 'under attack' from two directions, one from below and one from above, summarises the recent concern in the study of politics.

This idea of perceived threat from multiple fronts can be seen in recent moves by states, as well as national food producers, to defend particular food practices, ingredients and dishes, by asserting national rights to them. These actions are taken against attempts to appropriate what are seen as national food brands and/or images and are viewed as direct attacks on the nation's heritage and culture. This is most evident in recent food 'wars'; we discuss two specific examples in "Chapter Six: National food in the International Context II—Gastronationalism and Populism", namely, hummus and kimchi.

The debate over national food rights and issues of authenticity, especially with the advance of globalisation, traverses the boundaries of the nation-state and includes a myriad of actors: from individual consumers and local producers to nation-states and multinational corporations. As a consequence, discussion and mediation over food labelling, safety, origins and rights have been increasingly taken on by international organisations and are now also part of most multi-lateral trade negotiations. In the EU, the 'Protected Geographical Status' framework has been put in place to ensure that only food items that have originated or are produced in a particular region can be identified as such. Currently over a thousand food items are protected, these include vegetables, dairy products, alcoholic beverages, meat and even pastries. For example, Balsamic vinegar must be produced in Emile Romagna (Italy), Feta cheese in Greece and Spettekaka (cake baked on a spit) in Sweden.[3] Another example of this phenomenon is the inclusion of food and cuisine among UNESCO's list of 'intangible cultural heritage' in need of recognition, support and protection. So far UNESCO has included Japanese Washoku, Turkish Coffee, Korean Kimchi, Mexican Cuisine and the Mediterranean diet, which is listed as encompassing the nation-states of Greece, Italy, Spain, Morocco, Portugal, Croatia and Cyprus. These measures and others have been advanced as supporting national agricultural and food sectors as well as rural and local communities against unfair competition, and are based on economic, cultural and environmental as well as other factors. Nonetheless, these measures also demonstrate how food links the everyday to matters of state sovereignty, international political economy and global cultural rights.

As this volume suggests, the food-and-nationalism axis provides a helpful channel through which to understand the dynamics of political forces at various levels in a way that is relevant to our everyday life. The nation-state may behave as if it had monopoly of the image of nationhood, but its success also depends on reception, how other countries/peoples would receive and perceive the message and the receivers are not monolithic. What food item is appealing or acceptable to eat is increasingly an issue, not just because of accelerated movement of people across the globe but also because of the development of human rights discourse and continuing struggle for fairness and equality in the world. Is eating dogs acceptable? If every culture is equal, then, eating dogs should be respected as part of someone's culture. When it is acceptable to hunt, kill and eat whales and when it is not? These questions also increasingly relate to how we grow and produce our food, including the use of technology and man-made chemicals.

---

[3] One of the general concerns the business world had with Brexit has been how to ensure the protection afforded by the EU's GI scheme to the British produce. This has been dealt with by the EU-UK Trade and Cooperation Agreement (TCA), concluded in 2020, by ensuring GIs with UK origin 'protected under the EU scheme as at 31 December 2020 will continue to have effect in the 27 member states of the European Union. GIs with EU origin protected under the EU scheme have been granted equivalent UK protection under the new UK GI scheme' (Khwaja and Elkin, 2021).

The debate over food, identity and human rights extends at the global level to food aid. When you are dependent on food aid, is it ethical to force you to eat what you normally avoid? And according to whose ethics? There is more confrontation of different ethnical frameworks—local, ethnic, national and international—in thinking about food on the world stage. The discussion over food aid and human rights also touches upon food security and sovereignty. Here again, the local, the national and the 'universal' often collide spectacularly with a diverse mix of actors: consumers, producers, big capitals, civil society organisations, the nation-state and international organisations in efforts to safeguard the rights to food. It also demonstrates how the link between food and nationalism sheds light on the complexity of the issue at this level, making the link a useful tool to comprehend the enormously complex dynamics of political forces.

The Plan of the Book

The volume consists of three parts which correspond to the three areas of investigation identified above. The first part, 'Unofficial/Bottom-up: Nationalism and National Identity Through Food Away from the State', investigates the relationship between food and nationalism/national identity which is not directly controlled by the nation-state.

"Chapter One: Everyday Creation of the Nation" focuses on the mundane and daily acts performed by individuals away from the ostensive influence of the nation-state. The chapter first investigates the theoretical framework of everyday/banal nationalism and analyses the ways in which the seemingly mundane behaviour of individuals on an everyday basis contributes to or disrupts the maintenance of 'nation-ness'. Everyday action of the individual can reinforce the dominant idea of the nation; it can also contest the official version and lead to an emergence of an alternative view. The chapter then carries out empirical investigation into everyday/banal nationalism in the field of food with a case study of the evolution of Japanese-style pasta sauce. It examines the process of making a foreign food item—pasta—into an item that is widely recognised as Japanese through accumulation of ordinary people's participation. Following the analysis of the evaluation of the Japanese-style pasta source drawing from material available on the Internet, the chapter concludes with a brief discussion of netnography, an emerging method of carrying out qualitative research in cyberspace and how it has been applied to the study of the relationship between food and nationalism.

"Chapter Two: When Groups Participate in Defining the Nation" shifts the focus of analysis from the level of the individual to that of groups. Here, the ways in which 'nation-ness' is constructed, contested and maintained by various groups through collective action, which seemingly takes place away from the nation-state's direct influence, are investigated. The chapter first reviews theoretical issues regarding collective action and nationalism paying particular attention to the role of symbols and rituals in maintaining group cohesion. It then investigates the relationship between group identity, food and the nation, and the importance of food as a way of symbolising and performing the nation, including by diaspora (an issue neglected in the first edition) through three case studies: the Burns Supper, the Bulgarian Diaspora in the UK and the Arab-Palestinian citizens of Israel. The chapter demonstrates the importance of food as a means of solidifying group identity and also as a means for constructing, maintaining and contesting national identity.

Through their actions, food retailers and suppliers construct and define national characteristics and boundaries, and thus promote the banal reproduction of nations, as well as provide, what is for many, the first encounter or point of contact with other nations. "Chapter Three: Consuming Nations—The Construction of National Identities in the Food Industry" looks at the construction and reproduction of 'nation-ness' through food by profit-seeking entities which are ostensibly independent from the nation-state's ideological work. It therefore focuses on the food industry, broadly defined, and seeks to understand in what ways the commercial entities contribute to the creation, contestation and maintenance of national identity and in so doing how they interact with individuals, groups and the nation-state as an actor. The chapter examines two cases: the ways in which the consumption of pie and mash has evolved in reference to the idea of English/British cuisine. The chapter argues that the rise and fall of pie and mash as a stereotypical English/

British food has been conditioned by a combination of forces including demographic change, commercialisation and globalisation. The second case study investigates the ways in which the Scotch whiskey industry negotiates between Scottishness and Britishness. Both case studies highlight the increasing importance of the private sector in understanding, negotiating and changing ideas concerning national identity and the nation-state.

Part II 'Official/Top-Down' examines the link between food and nationalism/national identity when the nation-state is actively involved.

In the second part, the analytical focus shifts from a 'bottom-up' to a more conventional 'top-down' one. "Chapter Four: Food and Diet in 'Official' Nationalism", highlights what the 'food and nationalism' angle can bring into the study of 'top-down' nationalism. It investigates the reasons why food and diet can be a powerful tool for the state and the state-sponsored organisations in pursuing a nationalist programme by examining the issue of food in modernising Japan in a comparative context. After supplementing the analysis of the Japanese case by looking at the recent changes in the ways in which the Japanese government tried to control rice, the chapter looks at the case of the Zionist movement in Israel/Palestine to explore the role food plays in a nationalist project in detail.

The relationship between food and nationalism and its importance to the nation-state extends far beyond the borders of the state. Food is not only used for domestic purposes and as an internal and banal symbol of the nation, it is also used internationally by the state in its diplomatic engagements. "Chapter Five: National Food in the International Context I—Gastrodiplomacy" and "Chapter Six: National Food in the International Context II—Gastronationalism and Populism" investigate the duality of national food: on the one hand, it can be used to indicate the attractiveness of the nation and increase its appeal, while, on the other hand, it can also be seen as a 'contested medium of cultural politics that demarcates national boundaries and identities' (DeSoucey 2010: 433). This means that what is viewed as a national food item or tradition can be used in branding and marketing the nation internationally but might also require state intervention and protection from foreign claims. "Chapter Five: National Food in the International Context I—Gastrodiplomacy" focuses on the growing use of gastrodiplomacy by a wide range of states and investigates the relationship between the national and the transnational in the promotion of the New Nordic Cuisine (NNC). It also adds a discussion on the role of food and nationalism in tourism, an issue neglected in the first edition.

Building on chapters "Chapter Four: Food and Diet in 'Official' Nationalism" and "Chapter Five: National Food in the International Context I—Gastrodiplomacy", "Chapter Six: National Food in the International Context II—Gastronationalism and Populism" examines the assertion of national rights over food (gastronationalism). The chapter starts by investigating the complexities of gastronationalism in an increasingly interconnected and interdependent world. It then examines, and historically contextualises, the rise of nationalist-populism as a political movement and its relationship with food security and food populism, including discussion on the Trump presidency. The UK's withdrawal from the European Union (Brexit) is then used as the main case study to further explore the rise of nationalist-populism and its relationship to gastronationalism and food populism. Lastly, as gastronationalism invariably leads to contestation between states, the chapter concludes by investigating the phenomena of food wars, using the examples of hummus and kimchi.

Part III, 'Food and Nationalism/National Identity at the Global Level', moves our investigation to the global level and see what dynamics the food and nationalism axis can disentangle.

As widely acknowledged, food could be an emotive issue in the contemporary world and sometimes the discussion extends to the normative level. Is it right to eat x/y/z? Is it barbaric to eat x/y/z? Is it criminal to eat x/y/z? Who says, according to what? "Chapter Seven: Norms, Ethics, Food and Nationalism" investigates normative concerns related to food in reference to nationalism making the most of the highly symbolic nature of food. The chapter is not about food taboos as widely investigated in anthropology but focuses on the question of who decides what is appropriate to grow, produce and eat in the international arena. The chapter illustrates the ways in which a shift in norms leads to a new form of friction between values and norms that often assumes a nationalistic hue. It aims to demonstrate the effectiveness of the 'food and nationalism' angle in investigating different levels of politics. The chapter opens with an examination of the case of whale meat eating to review how the question about resource management has developed into a contestation of values with nationalist tinge. It then places the whale problem in a comparative context in reference to the issues of dog meat, foie gras consumption and the growing international debate over the use of technology in food, with a specific reference to genetic modification and the fears it raises not only with regard to food safety but also the 'contamination' of national food, tradition and heritage. Using these examples, the chapter highlights the dynamic relationship between changes and shifts in dominant norms and the strengthening of the demand for the particular. The chapter concludes with an investigation into veganism in its capacity to transcend nationalism. The cases discussed in the chapter demonstrate the tension that is inherent in the national assertion of norms and values in a globalising world.

The last chapter, "Chapter Eight: International Organisations, Food and Nationalism", focuses on the way in which international organisations as the global norm/standard setter influence nationalism in reference to food. Unlike in the cases of international disputes about human rights where international organisations appear to have some power to be the ultimate judge of what is right and what is wrong, in relation to food, they appear to be more likely to be used by the nation-state and other groups in order to reinforce national identities and claims rather than being able to set global norms and standards. The chapter investigates UNESCO's intangible cultural heritage list and the issue of geographical indications in international trade and shows that in these cases, international organisations play a contradictory role of promoting universal values and norms while protecting the particular and strengthening the national. The chapter is updated to consider the implications of Brexit to the EU's GI scheme.

The volume concludes with a chapter which pulls together different themes discussed in the preceding chapters and shows how these issues, which manifest at different levels, are inter-related. Because food is such an essential item, it permeates every level and aspect of human life and therefore can serve as an entry point to various issues. This in turn suggests that food can function as a point of integration of different levels and aspects of politics. These insights are then placed in the context of politics and international relations to show why food and nationalism matter to students of politics broadly defined.

Part I

Unofficial/Bottom-Up: Nationalism and National Identity Through Food Away from the State

Chapter One: Everyday Creation of the Nation

Tell me what you eat and I will tell you what you are. (one of the founding fathers of French cuisine and modern gastronomy: Jean Anthelme Brillat-Savarin)

The chapter investigates the ways in which the nation is created, given meaning and maintained by everyday/banal acts of cooking, writing, blogging, talking about and consuming food. The chapter pursues its aim by exploring the parameters of everyday nationalism, in particular talking, writing and choosing the nation, and through the case study of Japanese-style pasta. In this case study, the creation, revision and maintenance of 'Japaneseness' is examined with data collected from two recipe sites to which interested members of the public submit their recipes for collective evaluation without explicit commercial motive. By analysing the ways in which the Japaneseness of Japanese-style pasta is constructed, claimed and evaluated, the chapter charts the process of making a foreign food item—pasta—into an item which is widely recognised as Japanese through accumulation of ordinary people's participation.

In the current edition, the analysis of the everyday creation of Japaneseness is complimented by a brief discussion of netnography, an emerging research method, which is of particular use to food scholars, and its use in an examination of everyday creation of the nation. We will do that through a focus on how comments made by restaurant visitors and tourists help construct and shape what is meant to be a national food.

Food and National Identity: The Theoretical Context

The importance of food in constituting *the social* is widely acknowledged to the point that stating 'food plays an essential role in facilitating and maintaining social relationships' would be met by a blank stare. The significance of food in the investigation of human society, history and various aspects of politics has been well articulated. For instance, Fischler (1988: 277) identifies two important dimensions of human beings' relationship with food as the 'omnivore's paradox' and the 'incorporation principle' and states:

> Because we are omnivores, incorporation is an act laden with meaning. Because of the principle of incorporation, identification of foods is a key element in the construction of our identity. Finally, because identity and identification are of both vital and symbolic importance, man has "invented" cuisine.

Cuisine in this context is understood to represent the most fundamental aspect of human life. Another anthropologist, Emiko Ohnuki-Tierney (1999: 244), uses a less value-laden concept of food and describes food as 'a unique metaphor of the self of a social group'. In elaborating the mechanisms of assigning power to food, she adds: 'when each member of the social group consumes the food, it becomes a part of his or her body. Thus this important food becomes *embodied* in each individual and functions as *metonym* by being part of the self' (ibid., 244).

Lien (2004: 6–7) not only notes 'the immediate biological implication' of food but also acknowledges food as 'a convenient medium for the expression of social and economic distinctions, and for naturalising relations of community and hierarchy' as well as its link to nutritional science which interacts with interests of science and business. In a similar vein,

Grew (1999b: 6–7) points out the two major dimensions that a focus on food would bring: first, food can be a tool for an investigation of a society's political economy because its production is embedded in a particular labour system and its consumption in an ever-evolving trading pattern. Second, food has the symbolic function which works as 'an aesthetic, cultural and semiotic code' in defining and reinforcing group membership.

This brief review of literature is sufficient in reiterating the relevance of focusing on food in investigating social relations. Given that much emphasis has been placed on food's symbolic power in relation to group membership, the relationship between food and the nation is no doubt a legitimate topic for research. In investigating the relationship between food and the nation, in particular, national identity, this chapter draws from the theoretical approach called everyday nationalism. The use of the approach is merited based on the fact that food represents a routinised everyday practice (Lien 2004: 6).

The goal in studying everyday nationalism is to understand how ordinary people make sense of and enact nationalism, nationhood and national belonging in their everyday life. By ordinary people we mean those acting outside of elite structures and not for commercial gain. The focus on everyday nationalism is articulated as a critique of conventional macro-focused analyses of nationalism which tend to prioritise the elite's behaviour propagated through the state and other formal structures in understanding nationalism. The conventional focus, according to the advocates of research into everyday nationalism, does not tell the whole story because it is a 'top-down' approach which tends to treat ordinary people as passive recipients of messages transmitted from the above with little room for exercising their agency. The 'top-down' approach also portrays the experience of nationalism as homogenous; it ignores the great diversity that exists in the manners in which nationalism, national identity and national belonging are experienced and understood by individuals in their everyday lives. Ultimately, therefore, the urge to study everyday nationalism corresponds to the inherent tension between agency and structure in social sciences and continued efforts to strike the right balance between the two in any investigation into social phenomena.

Interest in what is now termed as everyday nationalism has been observed in different guises. In particular, Michael Billig's focus on the permeation of nationalism as a discursive form into the everyday in his *Banal Nationalism* (1995) and Tim Edensor's work on the routinised nature of national identity (2002, 2006) appear to have inspired a large number of scholars to investigate the everyday-ness of nationalism and nationhood more closely. One of the works on food and national identity inspired by the idea of banal nationalism is by Catherin Palmer (1998) in which the link between the body, food and the landscape on the one hand and national identity is explored focusing on its banality. The perspective of everyday nationalism can be argued to have synthesised research concerns on banal nationalism and routinised practice of national identity to propose distinct research areas.

Jonathan Fox and Cynthia Miller-Idriss (2008a) have identified four areas of research into everyday nationhood: 'choosing the nation', the nation implicated in people's choice; 'talking the nation', the discursive construction of the nation through routine talks; 'performing the nation', the ritualised enactment of nationhood through symbols; and 'consuming the nation', expression of nationhood and belonging to the nation through daily consumption habits. Looking into these four areas, Fox and Miller-Idriss contend, would provide insight as to how the nation is produced and reproduced by ordinary people and hence can address nationalism 'from below'.

Choice[1]

> What we do with food, therefore, how we think about it and use it, inheres in what we are, as societies and as individuals. (Ferguson 2006)

The definition provided by Fox and Miller-Idriss regarding choosing the nation narrows it down to mainly institutional choices people make, for example, which school to enrol in. We propose a broader and more

---

[1] Below we build upon the ideas of Fox and Miller-Idriss with regard to the first two areas identified: choosing and talking the nation. 'Performing the nation' is dealt with in "Chapter Two: When Groups Participate in Defining the Nation", where the discussion is focused on the role of food items as symbols in rituals, while 'consuming the nation' is discussed in "Chapter Three: Consuming nations—The Construction of National Identities in the Food Industry", where individual food consumption is related to the private sector's construction of national brands and nationality.

expansive way of understanding this area that includes a wide range of mundane choices and decisions made by ordinary people in their everyday lives and what these mean with regard to the nation and national identities. In particular we focus on the decisions and choices of what and how to eat and cook as well as on the manner in which people categorise and classify food in everyday life.

Peoples' first encounter with issues concerning national, religious and/or ethnic identity is normally through their palates. The food people eat is directly linked to where they grow up, the groups they belong to and the cultural and social space they inhabit. In other words, the food people eat and cook conveys a lot of information about who they are. It is, therefore, not surprising that there is a strong correlation between peoples' acquired taste and food preference and their national identities; though it is not clear whether taste fosters or expresses this identity (Ferguson 2011). In reference to Levi-Strauss, Barthes notes that taste 'might well constitute a class of oppositions that refer to national characters (French versus English cuisine, French versus Chinese or German cuisine, and so on)' (Barthes 2019). Though we agree with Mintz (1986) that food items and ingredients cannot be easily or neatly divided into national categories, it is widely accepted that certain foods are closely linked to particular images of nations, for example, rice and Japan, pasta and Italy and corn and Mexico. One would not, for example, expect to find chilli, lime and ginger in French cuisine or chickpeas, cumin and cinnamon in Japanese cuisine. It is important to note, however, that the relationship or association between certain foods and images of nations is constructed over time and is not inherent to any particular context (see, e.g., Gentilcore 2010 on the history and journey of the tomato in Italy). Additionally, with regard to staple foods, many nations show a particular preference for certain types of grains, for example, rice or wheat (Oum 2005). The preference for certain types of staple foods cannot be explained by reference to geography alone. This is particularly noticeable in settler colonial countries, where settlers had a strong desire to replicate their previous food culture rather than adopt local foodways (Ranta et al. 2022). It leads from this that the correlation between certain foods and national identities is such that adding or removing ingredients from nationally recognised dishes would transform and change them.

The choices individuals make in the everyday regarding how and what to eat and cook, therefore, are directly related to how they view and engage with their national identity; by choosing whether to eat or cook specific foods people are engaging with and communicating who they are. Oum (2005) demonstrates how the choice of whether to include specific dishes, such as *kimchi*, which is seen as a Korean national dish, in the family meal choice, is strongly correlated to expressions of Korean and/or American national identity within the Korean Diaspora in the US. These choices are directly related to where Koreans in the US situate themselves within the Korean-American spectrum; Oum accepts that these choices also relate to other factors such as gender and class. Additionally, he notes that the inclusion or exclusion of specific ingredients can in turn help bring rise to hybridised foods and identities, for example, Hawaiian *kimchi* (with the addition of pineapple) and *bulgogi* (meat marinated in a soy sauce blend) burger. These innovations relate to levels of cultural diffusions, desire for integration and family relations. They might, for example, arise in mixed marriages. It is interesting to note that the idea of creating cultural food hybrids is also used by multinational food corporations as a way of making their brands more appealing: in its South Korean restaurants, McDonald's offers the choice of *bulgogi* burgers. As demonstrated, the meanings assigned to food dishes and ingredients are not static or immutable. By adding or removing ingredients, and changing and adapting recipes, individuals transform and manipulate not only flavours and textures but also meanings, which can be used as a vehicle for engaging with and expressing national identities.

Talking the Nation

What is meant by the discursive construction of the nation and how do ordinary people participate in it? Discourses are means of constructing meaning and of representing ideas. For example, sociologist Uri Ram argues that nationality can be viewed as a discourse: 'a story which people tell about themselves in order to lend meaning to their social world' (quoted in: De Cillia et al. 1999: 155). National discourses, which may be presented in a variety of different forms—oral, from speeches to stories, and textual, from books to newspaper articles—convey ideas about the dimensions and particularities of the nation and help bring about the idea of the nation as an imagined community: a community with shared values, culture, boundaries and history.

Much of the study on food discourses and nationalism has tended to focus on texts and in particular on the relationship between cookbooks and the formation and maintenance of national identity (see, e.g., Appadurai 1988; Montanari 2004). This is because cookbooks are among the most published and accessible forms of food discourses. Nowadays most of the cookbook writing is done by professionals working in the food industry. However, this was not the case in the past. Many of the best known and most influential cookbooks were written by middle- and upper-class women as a way of sharing or providing useful housekeeping and culinary information with fellow women. Cookbooks, such as *Mrs Beeton's Book of Household Management* (1861) and Amelia Simmons' *American Cookery* (to use its shortened title) (1798), go beyond discussing matters relating to measurements, procedures and nutrition. They contain additional information relating to history, tradition, geography, values and identities. For example, in the introduction to her book Simmons (1798) writes that the book has been written for 'the improvement of the rising generation of females in America' and that the recipes provided had been 'adapted to this country' (US); even the book's title conveys the idea that the recipes and advice given are related to a particular nation. Cookbooks do not only help construct and maintain national identities. They can also be written in order to contest and/or resist particular national ideas (see, e.g., Harris 2012 on African-American foodways and Kitchings 2022 on the evolution of Hawaiian cookbooks).

The focus on ordinary people, however, and the way in which they discursively construct the nation through food in everyday life brings up a number of methodological difficulties. Ordinary people rarely write cookbooks, so accessing how they engage with nationalism/national identities within the context of food discourses is not straight forward. Additionally, as noted by Fox and Miller-Idriss (2008a), the nation is not a constant or regular topic of everyday conversation but context dependent. How then should one go about collecting and analysing how ordinary people talk about and discursively construct the nation?

Most of the research done on the everyday discursive construction of the nation has been limited to interviews, focus groups, surveys and ethnographic research. A particularly innovative and useful way of examining how people discursively construct the nation is through the study of recipes and in particular those that members of the public upload to popular cooking websites. Recipes are, first and foremost, a discursive product, which identifies, describes and gives meaning to a dish. Recipes tend to be viewed as instruction manuals. To some extent this is correct: recipes provide lists of ingredients, measurements and instructions to be followed. However, as will be demonstrated below, these ingredients and instructions also contain information regarding how members of the public perceive issues regarding taste, identity, geography, authenticity and tradition. Moreover, the focus on recipes uploaded to popular food websites provides additional tools for studying how people engage with food in the everyday.

The methods and ideas suggested by Fox and Miller-Idriss limit the study of everyday discursive construction of the nation to how people talk about the nation. The study of online recipes allows for a wider engagement with how ordinary people also talk *to* the nation. In effect, ordinary people influence one another through their food discourses, and observe, through the comments and feedbacks generated, how others perceive and/or react to these. What is particularly interesting about these exchanges is that they allow the researcher to observe how ordinary people experience and engage with the nation in everyday life in, what used to be, the hidden space of *home*, and in an apolitical context. To give a brief example, AllRecipes is one of the most widely used international food websites. Launched in 1997, AllRecipes now has several different language sites and is visited tens of millions of times a month; it was sold to Meredith Corporation for $175 million in 2012 (https://meredith.mediaroom.com/2012-03-01-Meredith-Completes-Acquisition-of-Allrecipes-com-From-Readers-Digest). AllRecipes has tens of thousands of unique recipes, which are provided free of charge by members of the public. The first step in uploading a recipe is providing it with a title and placing it within one of the categories provided. Many of the titles proposed and the categories provided are related to the idea of nations and national cuisines. By uploading a recipe and either characterising it or categorising it based on national cuisines, people are engaged in choosing the nation; the act of writing these recipes and titling them is part of the discursive construction of the nation. For instance, a search for 'Moroccan chicken' on its main site, allreceipe.com returns 9476 results as of 6 December 2021, all of them uploaded by the users. These recipes provide an indication to what members of the public in different parts of the world define and consider as Moroccan. By way of recipes, ordinary people transform a list of raw ingredients that correspond to ideas of taste and textures to a nationally consumed culinary artefact. In these recipes the Moroccan elements correlate to the addition of cumin, coriander and cinnamon to either the chicken marinade or sauce and the serving of the dish with cous cous.

Japanese-Style Pasta

As demonstrated above, a focus on recipes is particularly appropriate for an investigation of everyday nationhood in food. In our case study, this will be pursued through an in-depth analysis of recipes of Japanese-style pasta. In relation to the four areas suggested by Fox and Miller-Idriss, by identifying a dish as a 'Japanese-style pasta', people are involved in an active process of choosing the category of 'Japanese' in their routine of categorising and giving meaning to their surroundings; creating and sharing a 'Japanese-style pasta' recipe is an act of performing the nation, enacting what is meant to be Japanese food; cooking a Japanese-style pasta according to the recipe and consuming it as such represents an act of consuming the nation, a process through which the nation becomes part of the body through food. Since the concern of this chapter is to capture what meaning people attach to a nation, in this case, the Japanese nation, through creating, talking about and sharing recipes and through cooking a dish, the question can only be approached qualitatively.

There are some critiques to the idea of everyday nationalism/nationhood. In a debate between Fox and Miller-Idriss on the one hand and Anthony Smith on the other (Fox and Miller-Idriss 2008a, b; Smith

2008), Smith alerted the audience to a possible neglect of the socio-historical context in a research agenda that is focused on the 'here and now'. He further pointed to an inherent limitation of the study of everyday nationalism or 'cold' nationalism in that the proposed research agenda is necessarily confined to the study of developed western democracies. There are also needs to elaborate further the definition of ordinary people and to problematise the relationship between the elite and the non-elite more precisely (Smith 2008).

Some of these shortcomings can be addressed by making efforts to situate the study of everyday nationalism and nationhood in a wider socio-historical context. In our case study, the evolution of the idea of Japanese cuisine, which is entwined with modernisation of Japanese society since the nineteenth century offers such a context. Smith's second point is not tackled in this chapter: the chapter looks at 'cold' nationalism in a largely westernised democratic society. This does not mean that everyday nationalism cannot be investigated in a context where 'hot' nationalism is dominant; on the contrary, a study of everyday nationalism in such a context would be an insightful way of finding a way of resistance or subversion mounted by the non-elite.

The Evolution of the Idea of Japanese Cuisine

On 4 December 2013, *washoku* (Japanese cuisine) was inscribed on UNESCO's Representative List of the Intangible Cultural Heritage of Humanity, an event which recognised the status of Japanese cuisine as one of the defining elements of Japanese culture officially and internationally.[2] In the inscription, *washoku* is presented as 'traditional dietary cultures of the Japanese', which implies *washoku*'s timelessness quality. However, it is widely acknowledged among scholars studying food culture in Japan that the term and idea of *washoku* are very modern having emerged and developed in the process of modernisation starting in the mid-nineteenth century (Cwiertka 2006, Harada 2005). Enhanced exposure to foreign cuisines

---

[2] For more details, see UNESCO's website: http://www.unesco.org/culture/ich/en/news/Seventeen-new-elements-inscribed-on-the-lists-of-the-Convention-00072. This will be further investigated in "Chapter Eight: International Organisations, Food and Nationalism".

due to the end of the so-called closed country policy is one of the impetuses for differentiating what Japanese were cooking and eating as Japanese cuisine. Another driving force was the push for homogenisation which accompanied the processes of industrialisation and modernisation, in particular, in terms of building modern military forces. Cwiertka (2006: 79) singles out the institution of conscription as an important step in forging a cuisine that would bridge the regional differences. It is in the army made up with conscripts from across Japan in which the ideas of rice as staple and of soy sauce as *the* seasoning were established (helped by increased standardisation of soy sauce due to industrialisation), and the idea was brought back to different corners of Japan when conscripts completed their duty. It is also in the army where western food items were introduced including meat. *Nikujaga* (potatoes cooked with shredded meat in soy sauce-based broth), now a typical 'mother's taste' dish that is supposed to go with a bowl of rice, was devised in the army which was intent on improving the conscripts' physique in order to realise a 'strong military'.

The Evolution of Japanese-Style Pasta[3]

Pasta is one of the food items introduced to post-Meiji Restoration Japan from the West. Prior to this period, except for a short period in the sixteenth century, when Christian missionaries and traders from Europe were actively engaged with Japan and introduced new food items (*tempura*, widely seen as a typical Japanese dish, is said to have been introduced by the Portuguese during this period), the major sources of influence on food in Japan were China and Korea. Pasta is a food item which is clearly marked and recognised as foreign in contemporary Japan. It took a long while for pasta to gain popularity as everyday food. Domestic pasta production started in the 1920s, but pasta was an exclusive food item served at western-style hotels and top-end restaurants. Pasta started to become familiar to ordinary Japanese in the 1960s when all-automated pasta-making machines were introduced from Italy. Helped by an Italian food boom in the mid-1980s, the consumption of

---

[3] For the history of pasta in Japan, see the Japan Pasta Association's website: http://www.pasta.or.jp/content/dictionary/index.html.

pasta grew. The domestic consumption of pasta jumped from 95,000 tons in 1975 to 265,000 tons in 2009 although in terms of average consumption per head, the average Japanese lags behind (unsurprisingly) the Italian whose consumption is about 14 times that of the Japanese and by the Canadian who consumes three times as much as the Japanese (Japan Pasta Association 2013). Of late, the domestic production of pasta has been stable at around 150,000 tons a year and the import at around 120,000 tons a year (Japan Pasta Association 2013).

The origin of Japanese-style pasta is obscure, but it is widely believed that a restaurant in Tokyo called 'Kabe-no-ana (a hole in the wall)' was one of the major players in devising Japanese-style pasta. The restaurant owner claims to have created *natto* pasta, cod roe pasta and soy sauce-flavoured clam pasta in the 1950s and 1960s as a way of promoting consumption of pasta in Japan (https://macaro-ni.jp/99493?page=2 accessed on 17 February 2022). Japanese-style pasta gained its popularity in the Italian food boom in the 1980s and it is now an established dish.

Data

Data were collected from two websites. The first one, Cookpad (http://cookpad.com/), is the biggest recipe site in Japan with more than 1,610,000 recipes available (as of January 2014). The site was set up in 1998 as a site where members of the public can submit their recipes and where they can search for recipes. As of December 2013, the site is said to be used by 80–90 per cent of women in their 20s and 30s who cook, and by more than 20,000,000 users per month (https://info.cookpad.com/outline_of_service, accessed on 30 December 2013). The basic functions of the site are offered free of charge, but in order to use all functions, the user needs to register for its 'premium service' (at the cost of 294 yen per month) to access extra information such as suggestions from professional cooks, nutritious experts' advice on dealing with allergy, the recipe ranking, use of the 'my folder' facility to save recipes and so on. In order to submit a recipe, the user needs to register with the site and acquire an ID, which is free of charge.

The second one is the official site of the Japan Pasta Association (http://www.pasta.or.jp/index.html). The Japan Pasta Association, a non-profit body, was set up in 1972, originally under the name of the Japan Macaroni Association, in order to improve the quality of Japanese-made pasta and to promote the consumption of pasta in Japan, and it was renamed the Japan Pasta Association in 2002 (http://www.pasta.or.jp/association/greeting/index.html, accessed on 30 December 2013). The association continues to carry out research for the purpose of improving the quality of Japanese-made pasta and is engaged with promotion and marketing activities in relation to pasta so as to contribute to the general improvement of quality of food life in Japan. The Association's website serves as a repository of recipes; there is a collection of recipes provided by cooking professionals and there is another set which is made up with the recipes submitted by members of the public. In order to submit a recipe, the user needs to register with the site to acquire an ID, which is free of charge.

These two sites were selected for the following reasons: Cookpad was selected because it is the largest recipe site in Japan which collects recipes from the public and, as such, can be seen as the most representative of those who are engaged with recipe producing and sharing activities, which makes this site ideal for investigating everyday nationalism. The Japan Pasta Association's site was selected because of its 'official' status and because it offers two sets of recipes: one provided by the professional (in other words, 'official' recipes) and the other by members of the public who are conscious of the site's 'official' status. It is therefore expected that meaning making on this site is more intentional. By comparing and contrasting data from these two sites, the scope of investigation of everyday nationalism in relation to Japanese-style pasta sauce is enhanced.

The two sites were accessed on 30 December 2013 and a search was made for 'Japanese-style' pasta recipes. Cookpad returned 710 'recommended' recipes for 'Japanese-style' pasta (out of a total of 4036). The Japan Pasta Association's site returned 628 recipes as 'recommended by the Association', that is, recipes proposed by the 'professional' and 519 as 'everyone's pasta', that is, submitted by the public. Data for analysis was extracted from the first 50 recipes of each data set and the following categories of information were extracted: the name of the dish and description of and comments on the recipe.

What Makes a Pasta Dish Japanese?

There is an immediate issue to be solved at this stage: what makes a pasta dish, a dish revolving around a foreign food item, Japanese? Both sites allow the user to select the category to upload their recipes to, which suggests that both websites expect the users to have a pretty good idea as to what makes a pasta dish Japanese. Nonetheless, Cookpad's blurb in the 'Japanese-style' pasta section says: 'An exact fit for Japanese taste. *Mentaiko* (cod roe marinated with chilli), cod roe, soy sauce, miso paste, pickled plums and *natto* (fermented soy beans). Let's keep creating new pasta recipes by using these Japanese food items' (http://cookpad.com/category/133, accessed on 30 December 2013).[4] This suggests that the Japaneseness of Japanese-style pasta is defined by the inclusion of food items that can be clearly identified as Japanese. This is confirmed when a total of 100 recipes extracted from the Japan Pasta Association's website were investigated. With very few exceptions[5] these recipes appear to be defined as Japanese because of the inclusion of food items which are widely seen as Japanese including Japanese soup stock, seaweed, dried small fish, Japanese vegetables and herbs, Japanese pickles, in addition to the items listed on Cookpad's site. It is the inclusion of these Japanese items that appear to define the Japaneseness of Japanese-style pasta rather than the absence of clearly western items or a particular way of cooking. In fact, many recipes very happily use non-Japanese food items such as olive oil, mayonnaise and butter. But when, for instance, butter is combined with soy sauce or mayonnaise with cod roe, it becomes Japanese in these recipes.

Harada (2005: 8–9) points out there are two aspects to what makes a dish Japanese: (a) the presence of certain ingredients such as soy sauce or *miso* paste and (b) the rice-*miso* soup-pickles combination. While the

---

[4] There are five sub-categories under 'Japanese-style pasta' on this site: *mentaiko*/cod roe (152 recipes); soy sauce (321 recipes), miso paste (58 recipes), pickled plums (62 recipes) and *natto* (117 recipes) making a total of 710.

[5] One was described as 'tropical' using *nam pla* (fish sauce) and bitter squash (*goya*) despite being listed under the Japanese-style pasta and the other was explained as 'not really Japanese' because of the main ingredient, botago. The recipe creator was aware that botago was a European food item but categorised it as a Japanese-style past because botago was commonly thought to be a Japanese food item under the name of *karasumi*.

second criterion cannot be applied to the case of Japanese-style pasta, the recipes investigated for this chapter largely satisfy the first criterion. Cwiertka (2006: 176, 10) also refers to soy sauce as 'the dominant flavouring agent' in defining Japanese-style cuisine (*washoku*) and names soy sauce and fresh seafood as the two most important signifiers of the Japaneseness in the context of food to the contemporary Japanese. Cod roe and *mentaiko* in Japanese-style pasta recipes can be seen as corresponding to Cwiertka's 'fresh seafood' category. The collection of recipes analysed in this chapter seems to suggest overall congruence in the understanding of what makes food Japanese among the elite and ordinary people.

At the same time, the 150 recipes do not represent a totally homogenised understanding of the Japaneseness of Japanese-style pasta. There is some fuzziness about the boundary of the Japaneseness. For instance, some recipes use Chinese or Korean ingredients such as *zha cai* (Chinese pickled mustard plants), chicken soup stock which is widely associated with Chinese cuisine and *kimchi* (Korean pickles usually made with chilli) but are still presented as Japanese in contrast to the two recipes (the 'tropical' and 'not really Japanese' ones) alluded above. This is an interesting point to consider. On the one hand, these food items are now part of everyday diet of contemporary Japanese although their 'foreign' origin is widely acknowledged. In this sense, these items share a similar position with curry rice and ramen; they are both 'foreign' in their origin but fully assimilated into Japanese food culture, and possibly they are on their way to become 'Japanese'.[6] After all, many scholars with interest in Japanese society and culture tend to single out 'appropriation' or 'selective adoption' of foreign ideas, practices and items in the Japanese context as a major characteristic of Japanese society and its culture (Kramer 2013, Gluck 2011, Garon 1994).[7] On the other hand, Cwiertka (2006: 176)

---

[6] For an insightful study of the development of ramen in Japan and its implication to politics, see Kushnar (2012).

[7] Kramer (2013) suggests the adoption of 'shukyo' as translation for religion in Meiji Japan was a case of appropriation rather than transplantation based on pre-Meiji discussions of politics and religion. Gluck (2011) describes social change in Japan that took place since the arrival of Commodore Perry in 1853 as 'blended modernity' rather than 'Westernisation' recognising the element of agency on the part of Japanese society.

emphasises the importance of drawing clear boundaries among Japanese, western and Chinese cuisines so as to form a tripod structure in the development of the idea of Japanese cuisine. If a stricter separation of three traditions has been key to the establishment of Japanese cuisine, then conflation of Chinese/Korean food items as Japanese one can be seen as a process of reversal. The scope of this investigation goes beyond the current chapter, which means a separate study is needed to pursue this point.

Everyday Nationhood in the Japanese-Style Pasta Recipes

In order to capture a general outline of the extracted recipes, quantitative characteristics of the data for analysis are summarised in Tables 1 and 2.

First, the amount of textual information of each set is counted by the character. Because a heavy use of graphic characters such as ♪ in contemporary, informal Japanese writing is common, these are separately counted. Table 1 highlights the different nature of the three data sets. Recipe set B consisting of 'recommended' recipes from the Japan Pasta Association is clearly more 'serious' in that it hardly uses graphic characters. What are counted as graphic characters in the recipe set B are Roman characters such as 'C' in 'vitamin C'. In contrast, recipes in the recipe sets A and C, which are submitted by members of the public, make frequent use of graphic characters indicating the recipe creator's positive evaluation of the product to render the description and comments more

Table 1 The quantitative outline of extracted recipes

		Name	Description	Comments
Recipe set A	No. of characters	742	1817	2237
	No. of graphic characters	40	61	31
Recipe set B	No. of characters	724	1090	4753
	No. of graphic characters	0	1	11
Recipe set C	No. of characters	665	1260	2314
	No. of graphic characters	10	19	26

Notes: Recipe set A, 50 recipes from Cookpad; recipe set B, 50 'recommended' recipes from the Japan Pasta Association; recipe set C, 50 submitted recipes from the Japan Pasta Association

Chapter One: Everyday Creation of the Nation 43

Table 2 The coding scheme

	Content
Self-reference	Any direct reference to 'Japan' or 'Japanese'
Convenience	References related to convenience: 'easy', 'quick', 'time saver', 'uncomplicated', 'not much washing up' and so on
Health benefits	References related to health benefits: 'light', 'refreshing', 'low in calories', 'nutritious', 'xxx prevention', 'anti-fatigue', 'promoting apatite', 'good for xxx' and references to nutrients (DHA, calcium, vitamin C, etc.)
Comfort	References related to comfort: 'comforting', 'relaxing' and references such as 'My mother used to make this for me', 'introduced to me 30 years ago by my husband's brother' to suggest family continuity
Left-over	References related left-over: when comments are made on the recipe as a means of using up left-over
Seasonality	References to a particular season or 'in season'

informal, thus, accessible. Second, the comments in the recipe set B are much wordier than those in the other two. Efforts are clearly made to present a story about the recipe in the recipe set B, while in the recipe sets A and C, the intention is less on presenting a story but to convey the recipe creator's excitement. This suggests that comparing these three sets of recipes helps elucidate characteristics of everyday nationhood expressed in these recipes.

Next, the extracted textual information was coded according to the following coding scheme.

A few words on the coding scheme are due. In order to investigate manifestations of everyday nationalism, it was felt necessary to look for direct references to 'Japan' or 'Japanese' as expression of awareness of the national framework in proposing a recipe. The rest of the codes represent different positive aspects that can be associated with recipes. The importance of positive quality in meaning making is well established, and in this investigation into articulation and re-articulation of Japaneseness in preparing and consuming food, four aspects have been chosen as relevant: convenience, health benefits, comfort and thriftiness. Convenience can be a positive quality in recipes in busy modern life which makes recipes accessible and therefore more attractive. Its implication of defining Japaneseness is whether being Japanese is complicated/inaccessible or uncomplicated/accessible. Health benefits are usually positive in any situation, and they constitute a particularly appreciated positive aspect in recipes. Japanese cuisine has increasingly been associated with being healthy, although this association emerged in the second half of the twentieth century (Kushuner 2012; Cwiertka 2006; Takeda 2008). Being Japanese is therefore associated with a universally positive quality through food. The power of food as a source of comfort is also well established (cf. Holtzman 2006). In articulating and maintaining the sense of being Japanese, a sense of comfort can be reasonably speculated to have positive, therefore encouraging effects on maintaining and enforcing identification. The category of thriftiness relates to the use of left-over. Avoiding waste by making clever use of left-over is often seen as a positive attribute in recipes although it has a whiff of austerity around it. It has been repeatedly pointed out that the idea of 'being a good wife and a wise mother' has been behind the development of the idea of Japanese cuisine and there is a historical connection between being thrifty by not allowing any left-over going to waste and being 'modern' Japanese (Harada 2005, Cwiertka 2006). Finally, reference to seasonality is deemed to be important in defining the Japaneseness because of the frequent association of Japanese cuisine with seasonality (Cwiertka 2006). The first analytical step was therefore to collect descriptive statistics of the three data sets extracted. The initial coding has yielded the following results (Table 3):

The above table neatly summarises the characteristics of the three data sets. The recipes from Cookpad (recipe set A)—all submitted by the public—are mostly concerned with 'convenience', which arguably reflects

Table 3 Descriptive statistics of three sets of recipes

Code	Recipe set A			Recipe set B			Recipe set C		
	Name	Des.	Com.	Name	Des.	Com.	Name	Des.	Com.
Self-reference	13	13	5	4	17	17	10	7	0
Convenience	10	37	21	0	2	10	1	8	3
Health benefits	1	8	2	0	11	42	2	11	4
Comfort	0	1	3	0	4	4	1	0	0
Left-over	0	4	9	0	1	2	0	0	2
Seasonality	0	0	0	1	9	22	4	7	2

Notes: Des., the description given to the recipe by the creator; Com., comments given on the recipe by the creator ordinary people's concern in their daily life: they want to cook uncomplicated but reasonably nice dishes. In terms of reflecting 'real life' concerns, the number of references to making use of left-over is higher in this data set than the rest, which reinforces the impression that Cookpad is a site which is ideal to investigate everyday nationalism. At the same time, the recipe creators are also aware of the 'Japanese' aspect of their products. The professional recipes from the Japanese Pasta Association (recipe set B) reveal their educational zeal by being very concerned with emphasising the various health benefits of their recipes. That Japaneseness is also frequently acknowledged suggests that the association of being healthy with Japanese cuisine is maintained and reproduced in this collection of recipes. There is also a marked emphasis on seasonality, one of the recognised features of Japanese cuisine, which is absent in recipe set A. The ordinary people's recipes from the Association's website (recipe set C) are marked by their lower level of commitment to meaning making; the number of references to any of the five codes is smaller than those in the other two data sets. Still there is a faint echo of the characteristics of the other two data sets: there is concern for convenience and seasonality and the association of Japanese cuisine with being healthy.

In What Ways Is the Japaneseness Articulated and Communicated?

Of the three recipe sets investigated in this case study, recipe set B cannot be described as embodying 'bottom-up' construction: they are the recipes proposed by an industry body to promote consumption of pasta trying to maximise their effects by utilising popular discourse about Japanese cuisine. The recipes contain more textual information, and there is ample and explicit reference to health benefits and seasonality, the two major qualities widely associated with Japanese cuisine. For example, recipe 4 named '*mentaiko* spaghetti with cabbage' is 'a spring *mentaiko* pasta combined with soft cabbage', and its Japaneseness is flagged up by *mentaiko* and its seasonality is emphasised by a direct reference to spring and the evocation of spring by the use of the word 'soft'. The comment is elaborate: 'We have added spring cabbage, which is in season, to popular *mentaiko* pasta. The spirit of spring is conjured by cabbage's soft texture and sweetness, and its pastel colour. It is easy to make because all you have to do is to mix *mentaiko* with butter or some alternative, and combine it with cooked spaghetti'. The comment includes references to the season, comfort and convenience as well as repeated mention of *mentaiko*. The reader is reminded that sensitivity to the season is important in Japanese cuisine and that seasonality signals comfort—comfort of home, being at one with the environment.

Recipe 13, 'Japanese style spaghetti with *komatsuna* (a leafy vegetable), fried tofu and *jako* (dried small fish)', is described as having 'a comforting taste produced by *kombu* (seaweed) *dashi* (soup stock)'. The comment runs: 'Several familiar food items are combined with pasta. A comforting and relaxing taste is created by *dashi* from *kombu* and *jako*. *Komatsuna*, which is in season, is rich in calcium and β-carotid. This is also good for preventing cold in a cold season'. The Japaneseness of the dish is signified by ingredients clearly identifiable as Japanese especially through its emphasis on *dashi*. The recipe contains reference to the season (winter), potential health benefits and the dish's comforting effects, thus providing a more complete discursive picture of Japaneseness expressed in cooking.

In these two examples, a story of 'Japanese' dishes is carefully presented with the use of ingredients clearly marked as Japanese, which is in turn reinforced by the explicit association with health benefits and seasonality, which then brings a sense of comfort. Japanese cuisine is kind to the body and lets you feel the season deeply, and consequently, Japanese food brings you comfort reminding you of your mother, family and Mother Nature. One can clearly see very conscious attempts are made to tell a complete and comprehensive story about the Japaneseness of the dish in these examples. In this regard, what emerges from recipe set B resembles what Arjun Appadurai (1988) and Igor Cusack (2000, 2003, 2004) have found: a conscious attempt to define nationhood by utilising widely circulating discursive building blocks on the part of the creators.

Compared to this polished storytelling found in recipe set B, discourse presented in recipe sets A and C is rough and not very comprehensive. There is less conscious effort to delineate the Japaneseness in the recipes which rely on what is taken for granted.

Chapter One: Everyday Creation of the Nation   47

Some recipes articulate the Japaneseness by naming ingredients which are widely understood to be Japanese. Recipe 2 from recipe set A is a typical example. The dish is named 'Easy, rich and tasty *natto* spaghetti' and it does not make any direct reference to 'Japanese'. The recipe is described as 'By adding oyster sauce, a *natto* pasta with a very rich body and lots of *umami* is born. Chopped *takuan* (pickled *daikon* radish) sparkled over adding a lovely accent to the dish'. The creator explains the genesis of the recipe as follows: 'When eating rice with *natto*, I happened to notice a bottle of oyster sauce. When I added it as a joke, it turned out to be very tasty and that's why I have applied this to pasta'. This Japanese pasta is associated with 'richness' which is often seen as the major property of western dishes, and its novelty lies with the use of oyster sauce, a clearly Chinese ingredient. Still, the dish's Japaneseness is beyond doubt due to its use of two unambiguously Japanese food items (*natto* and *takuan*). In addition, there is a reference to '*umami*', often seen as the fifth basic taste and widely seen as a Japanese concept, in the description. Moreover, the inspiration comes from a rice dish. A closer scrutiny of the recipe reveals that it uses the defining ingredient, soy sauce, as well. In this case, the discursive strategy, which is most likely taken by the creator unconsciously, is to reinforce the taken-for-granted Japaneseness by repetition. Because what is widely seen as Japanese is repeatedly mentioned, the dish described in the recipe becomes Japanese and can then be freely associated with a variety of meanings that are linked to Japanese cuisine.

Recipe 5 of recipe set A also pursues the same strategy of repeatedly making reference to ingredients that are unambiguously seen as Japanese in order to highlight the Japanese aspect of the recipe. Named 'Japanese style pasta with crispy *gobo* (a root vegetable) *tempura*', it is 'delicious Japanese style pasta born out of collaboration between crispy *gobo tempura*, succulent prawns and crunchy *mizuna* (a leafy vegetable)'. The comment runs: 'The *udon* bar I often go to serves *gobo tempura*. I thought combining this with pasta and *mizuna* would be fantastic and created this Japanese style pasta'. The main seasoning ingredients are soy sauce and fish *dashi*. As in the case of recipe 2, the Japaneseness of the recipe is highlighted by reference to a large number of ingredients clearly identifiable as Japanese: *gobo tempura*, *mizuna*, soy sauce and *dashi*. There is no explicit reference to health benefits or seasonality, or to convenience. The association with the Japaneseness is therefore established solely by the use of Japanese ingredients. At the same time, the recipe draws from the inspiration gained from a Japanese noodle bar, which enhances the Japaneseness of the recipe.

There are two aspects to the Japaneseness that emerges from recipes 2 and 5. Firstly, it is defined by uniquely Japanese ingredients; being Japanese is therefore using/eating uniquely Japanese food items. Secondly, the Japaneseness of these recipes is further underpinned in its close connection to everyday activities, as the source of inspiration, which are, nonetheless, largely seen as uniquely Japanese. The inspiration for recipe 2 comes from an everyday activity of eating rice with *natto*. That for recipe 5 comes from a visit to an *udon* bar, part of everyday activity of any Japanese. These recipes are Japanese because they are firmly embedded in everyday, familiar life of ordinary Japanese, not because any particular meaning is invested in the recipe.

Other recipes flag up their Japaneseness by doing something similar to what the Japan Pasta Association does in their recipe: by clearly associating themselves with (a) being 'light' and 'refreshing', terms associated with health benefits, (b) comfort which is linked to family and (c) enhanced seasonality.

The creator of recipe 2 from recipe set C, named 'A citrus-flavoured, simple pasta with courgette', advises the reader 'to keep seasoning to the minimum' because this is 'a light pasta with a refreshing aftertaste'. The creator then says 'if you do not have courgette, it is OK to use whatever you have in the fridge. *Yuzu* (a citrus fruit) is good for preventing cold. When added to pasta, it is very refreshing'. The recipe differs from the previous two in that it gives a nod to the notion of minimising waste; if courgette, which is not a very common vegetable in Japan, is not available, anything in the fridge would do, so this recipe can also be read as one to appealing the idea of 'good wife, wise mother'. At the same time, courgette can also be seen as dispensable because it is not a recognisably Japanese ingredient. What is important in this recipe is *yuzu*, a Japanese variety of citrus fruits, which makes this pasta dish Japanese. Soy sauce is also used, so the Japaneseness of the recipe is first and foremost established by these two quintessentially Japanese ingredients and it is rooted in everyday life. *Yuzu*, however, sharpens the contour of being Japanese in this recipe because it makes the dish 'light' and 'refreshing', and because being a citrus fruit, it contains vitamin C which is widely believed to help the prevention of colds, and its benefits are clearly spelt out in the recipe. The Japaneseness in this recipe is outlined in two ways: the use of Japanese ingredients and reference to the widely held association of Japanese cuisine with being light and health promoting. It should be noted that this discursive construction works within an even wider discursive context of renowned Japanese longevity. The recipe mobilises available discursive building blocks to describe what is meant to be Japanese and works to reinforce existing discursive formulations about being Japanese.

Evocation of 'home' in depicting the Japaneseness of the dish is seen in recipe 6 from recipe set A. The dish is named 'Japanese style pasta with *komatsuna* and bacon, *yuzukosho* (citrus flavoured chilli paste)-flavour'. Both Japanese and non-Japanese ingredients feature in the name of the dish, and the recipe's Japaneseness is further elaborated by its evocation of the idea of 'home' in the description: 'mixing well with chop sticks, this smooth Japanese style pasta is the best. This is a taste of home, a comforting Japanese style pasta which you will never get tired of even if you eat it every day'. The major quality of the dish is its comforting nature: it reminds you of home, your mother's cooking and it is so familiar that you will never become tired of. The Japaneseness which is conveyed through direct references to 'Japanese' is now closely linked to the terms that evoke familiarity: 'chop sticks' and 'a taste of home', an 'everyday reality' of ordinary Japanese. The 'homely' feel is further emphasised by two kinds of onomatopoeia ('mazemaze' describing the act of mixing and 'tsurutsuru' describing the smooth surface) used in the description because they remind the reader of children's tottering speech. The creator comments: 'I wanted to eat an easy, delicious Japanese style pasta which I can make every day. So I tried it with *yuzukosho* which I love, which turned out to be a great hit'. As seen in other recipes, the Japaneseness in this recipe is first established by the use of Japanese ingredient (*yuzukosho*) and utensils which are very, if not exclusively, Japanese (chopsticks) in addition to direct references to 'Japanese'. Then, the Japaneseness in this recipe is presented as something to do with home, one's own family, which is familiar and a source of comfort. In this case, the Japanese nation is a source of 'ontological security' (Skey 2011) rather than having a particular quality. As in the case of recipe 2 from recipe set C, the Japaneseness of the recipe is firmly embedded in *the familiar* and closely linked to 'everyday'.

Japanese cuisine is held to be sensitive to seasonality and some of the recipes of Japanese-style pasta make reference to seasonality. For example, recipe 15 from recipe set C makes a clear reference to seasonality in its name: 'pasta with seasonal mushrooms and grated *daikon*'. The Japaneseness of the recipe is flagged up by the use of grated *daikon* and the use of *mentsuyu* (soy sauce-based noodle dip). The creator describes the recipe as 'using seasonal mushrooms generously, and to your surprise, grated *daikon* is cooked before it is combined with pasta'. Grated *daikon* typically accompanies Japanese dishes as a refreshing condiment and is usually served raw. The recipe is therefore challenging a conventional way of using grated *daikon* but its Japaneseness is in no doubt. The comment runs: 'plenty of seasonal food items of autumn are used. Cooked grated *daikon* creates harmony making this dish well-balanced and complete'. It is not just mushrooms but other seasonal ingredients that are used in this recipe, which in turn highlights the Japaneseness of the dish. Because the dish is in tune with the season and because of the innovative use of grated *daikon*—a very Japanese ingredient—the dish is 'well-balanced and complete'. The recipe, just as other ones examined in this chapter, makes use of existing discursive frameworks about being Japanese and appears to affirm them.

What the Japanese Case Study Reveals

Several insights have emerged from the investigation of Japanese-style pasta recipes created by members of the public from the angle of everyday nationalism. First, the recipes testify that ordinary people take part in the creation and maintenance of national identity through their everyday acts. By proposing a recipe for the category of Japanese-style pasta, they actively take part in defining and redefining Japaneseness in food. The major determining element of the recipe's Japaneseness is the use of ingredients clearly identifiable as Japanese and in particular the inclusion of soy sauce appears to be important. These recipes however tend to play on existing discursive devices in describing the Japaneseness and giving meaning to it. They refer to the light or health-promoting qualities of the dish which is linked to the well-known fact of Japanese longevity; they emphasise seasonality, taking a cue from the dominant idea that Japanese cuisine, and Japanese people in general, is sensitive to the season. The sensitivity to the season implies being in harmony with one's environment, being at ease with Mother Nature. In contrast to the recipes created by the professionals, what is noticeable in the recipes created by members of the public is that the articulation of Japaneseness is firmly embedded in 'everyday' life and is built on the familiar. These Japanese-style pasta dishes are Japanese because they are rooted in what an ordinary Japanese person would do: eating rice, going to the *udon* noodle bar, using chopsticks and using Japanese ingredients. The recipes investigated here are focused on evoking the familiar, the feel of home, implying comfort and security.

Netnography and Its Use in Everyday Construction of Nationhood in Food

The case study above, which draws data from online recipe submission sites, shows the growing importance of data available in the cyberspace even in investigating 'ordinary people'. In fact, what is happening in the cyberspace has taken over this observation; the importance of social media in creating, shaping and maintaining discourses both by the professional and the lay people is increasingly recognised and the cyberspace as a site of ethnography is gaining recognition. This has led to the emergence and development of netnography as 'specific sets of research positions and accompanying practices embedded in historical trajectories, webs of theoretical constructs, and networks of scholarship and citation: it is a particular performance of cultural research followed by specific kinds of representation of understanding' (Kozinets 2015: 20.8). Simply put, netnography is a set of methods and rules of investigating what people are doing in cyberspace. Christine Hine (2011) highlights 'unobtrusiveness' as the advantage of Internet research, which allows the researcher to collect data that could shed light on the ephemeral aspect of everyday life as well as reduces burden on the 'research subject'.[8] Netnography is being refined day by day. According to Robert Kozinets (2020: 5), one of the driving forces behind establishing netnography as a research method, the emphasis is now on 'a qualitative research approach to social media data, encompassing interviews, data scraping, archival work, online observation, and active engagement with new forms of data collection, visualisation, thematic analysis and field-level rhetorical representation'. Netnography has already been applied in the study of consumer behaviour in marketing, studies of tourism (Tavakoli and Wijesinghe 2019), sexuality and gender research, nursing, addiction research (Kozinets 2015), and there are some works investigating the creation of national food using it.

Within the context of the elite's active promotion of national diversity in post-dictatorship Chile, Isabel Aguilera Bornand (2019) has employed netnography to investigate how restaurant customers/diners are formulating the idea of Chilean food through reviews posted on TripAdvisor. After the long period of dictatorship, new Chilean elites were engaged with emphasising multiculturalism as an important principle for Chilean society and many professionals have begun producing a discourse of Chilean cuisine as culturally/ethnically diverse, in particular in the context of cultural diplomacy. While the elite level is engaged with the production and promotion of an idea of culturally diverse, heterogeneous and, thus, inclusive Chile, consumers visiting restaurants to consume 'Chilean cuisine' are developing a different take. Aguilera Bornand (2019: 111–114) has identified three major themes, none of which echo the official elite discourse: Chilean food as rural food; as working-class food; and as urban and popular, mostly expressed as the 'guachaca', 'a way of life linked to poverty and vulgarity, as well as a fondness for alcohol'. Those visiting TripAdvisor planning their time in Chile are told that, for instance, *El Hoyo*, a restaurant located in the suburb of Santiago, Chile's capital city, is the only place they can experience authentic Chilean

---

[8] Costello et al. (2017) have argued that non-participatory netnography represents missed opportunities in many cases as participatory netnography could contribute values to online spaces. However, detailed discussions of pros and cons of netnography as a method are out of scope of the current chapter.

cuisine because of its association with the *guachaca* without scant attention to the elite version of authentic Chilean cuisine. Here, diners are choosing, talking and performing the nation, the portrait of which does not closely match what the elite is trying to propagate, and this version of the Chilean nation is captured through the use of netnography.

While not focused on 'national' food, Muchazondida Mkono (2013) has also employed netnography to investigate what makes African dining experiences authentic for tourists visiting Victoria Falls on the border of Zambia and Zimbabwe. While the study's focus is on how to create authenticity as a way of enticing tourists rather than on the construction of Africanness, it makes use of its unobtrusiveness in data collection because data are extracted from blog posts by tourists which are 'self-interpretive expectations, meanings, and perceptions of tourism experiences for their blogsphere uploads' (Mkono 2013: 186–187). From these blog posts, Mkono (2013) has found that African dining experience and the food provided in the selected restaurants have been made more authentic for the tourists by an augmentation with cultural entertainment, which typically involves some performative elements such as putting on the local costume or face painting and eating insects as 'traditional/authentic' dishes. The diners who have partaken in the performance of African dining experiences would then report their impression of 'authentic' African food on the blog, thus contributing to the strengthening of Africanness proposed by the restaurateurs and tourism promoters through performing their selves.

Concluding Remarks

The top-down method of analysing nationalism/national identity treats ordinary people as passive receipts of the national message and their experiences as fairly homogenous. However, through the examination of seemingly mundane activities, such as cooking and eating, and everyday discourses, such as conversations and recipes, the chapter demonstrates that this is not the case. In an ostensibly apolitical context, members of the public participate in the collective endeavour to define, redefine and give meaning to the nation. The nation is thus more than just an elite idea, it is a way of viewing, talking and acting in everyday life. In this regard, Michael Skey's (2011) suggestion that national identity provides 'ontological security' in a fast-changing world appears to apply very well. Accumulation of everyday acts such as cooking, eating and writing recipes contributes to the maintenance of the nation as a source of security for individuals.

The chapter has also discussed the emerging method of netnography as a way of capturing 'everyday nationalism', and seen that netnography can reveal an emergence and development of an idea of nationhood which is independent from the elite version. The African dining experience goes beyond the national frame, but it still shows some of the strengths of netnography as a method of researching the 'everyday' in identity formation.

Chapter Two: When Groups Participate in Defining the Nation

"Chapter One: Everyday Creation of the Nation" investigated the relationship between individuals and the nation through food using the frameworks of banal and everyday nationalism. These frameworks have enabled us to address Anthony Cohen's concern that the largely structuralist and often uncritical assumption that individuals 'by default' derive their identity from their membership of a group would undermine the individual's agency in discussing national identity (Cohen 1996). In this chapter, we continue to apply banal and everyday nationalism frameworks to our exploration of the relationship between food and nationalism/national identity, but the focus shifts to groups. It is truism that the nation comprised not only individuals but also a vast number of groups which mediate their members' experience of the nation. However, the chapter does not subscribe to the assumption that the nation is a homogenous entity with all sub-units falling neatly in line, but it adopts a pluralistic view that the nation consists of diverse class, ethnic and cultural groups who are in constant competition in their claims to nationhood. In other words, we take the view that the nation is a 'zone of conflict' (Hutchinson 2005), a dynamic space where a variety of identities interact in the daily act of formation, revision, maintenance and resistance of the nation-ness.

Group Identity and the Nation

The construction and contestation of the nation through food by various groups is not a new phenomenon; as documented by food historians, it has been going on for several centuries. Ben Rogers (2003) has investigated the emergence of roast beef as the national symbol of England/Britain in the seventeenth and eighteenth centuries paying attention to the impact of the French revolution, the activity of elites and the symbolism of blood which meat invariably suggests. Rogers argues:

> [E]ighteenth-century Englishmen identified their national culinary traditions not just as one set of tastes and techniques among others, but as the encapsulation of home and hearth, Church and nation. It bound their world together. And like modern-day French and Italian patriots, early Englishmen naturally found in the threat to their culinary tradition a ready representation of larger, more elusive threats to all these ultimately important things. (Rogers 2003: 55)

Looking at France, Kolleen Guy (2003) reviews the ways in which champagne, originally a regional product, became a national one by studying the social history of the late eighteenth to early twentieth centuries, paying close attention to the forces of capitalism and industrialisation. While Guy does not pretend to contribute to a theoretical exploration of the relationship between food and national identity, she hints that the idea of *terroir*, a pivotal concept in wine making which combines soil, topography and climate, could have fostered an organic understanding of the French nation as a response to urbanisation and the development of the capitalist marketplace. Both historians place the association between food and national identity in particular historical context, and therefore their arguments are more concrete than abstract. Rogers points to elite men as the prime agency for establishing roast beef as a symbol of England/Britain, and Guy provides insight into the ways in which different groups responded to social change in France by making a linkage between food and national identity.

A different approach to the study of how groups construct and contest identities, including national identities, is presented by food anthropologists. They examine the way food serves as a means of forming and cementing group relations as well as a boundary-setting mechanism. This is because food and specific food items are not meaning and value neutral but can be viewed as symbols that represent particular values, ideas and sensibilities. Inspired by Mary Douglas' work, some anthropologists have introduced categories of clean, polluted, edible and inedible in discussing the power and hegemony of food in society (Cowan 1991). As a result, and throughout the ages, food—in particular specific food items, practices, taboos, regulations and methods of consumption and preparation—has been used to define and express group identity internally and externally (see, e.g., the role played by food in relation to group identity throughout history, Civitello 2006; Higman 2012; for a study of food and social memory, see Sutton 2001). The use of food to define and express group identity is particularly evident with regard to religious identity. For example, food prohibitions, regulations regarding food and personal hygiene, and preparation and consumption rules have differentiated and separated Jewish communities across the world from their neighbours (on the history and traditions of Jewish food, see Roden 1999). The importance of food in delineating religious groups and negotiating relations between different groups within the nation is also discussed by Avieli with regard to Buddhist, Catholic and Protestant communities in Vietnam (Avieli 2009). Additionally, food can be used to signify differences within groups based on, for example, gender, age and lineage. Chan provides the example of the Southern Chinese village banquet fare *poonchoi* that 'consists of a variety of food items which are cooked separately but served together afterwards in a large basin' (2007: 53). The dish, which is mostly consumed by invited male village elders, serves to mark out status differences relating to gender and age. As noted by Palmer (1998), food culture also serves to define and demarcate group boundaries within and often in opposition to the nation, for example, separating particular minority, ethnic or sub-national groups within the state from the dominant and majoritarian core national group (this is also true with regard to migrants and diasporas, as we will demonstrate below). In these cases, through their food choices, discourses and performances, groups imagine, contest, maintain and engage with their own identity as well as that of the dominant national group.

What is of particular interest is that the meaning and values attached to food items and practices, which in turn help define group identity and boundaries, are not static. As demonstrated in the previous chapter with regard to Korean-Americans, specific food items can be manipulated and utilised to create new meanings and values and to redefine group membership and boundaries. Narayan (1995) in her study of the British colonial experience in India demonstrates how the imperial setting brought about a manipulation and 'fabrication' of Indian food, in particular the concept of 'curry'. This encounter also led to the adoption and incorporation, through modification and appropriation, of Indian food traditions and ideas into British food culture, resulting in hybrid 'British' dishes such as 'chicken tikka masala' and 'mulligatawny'. This adaptation and incorporation of food is present in many other settings as well, for example, Takeda (2008) discusses how adapted foreign food items, such as *sukiyaki* and *tempura*, became representative of the Japanese nation.

Performing the Nation

Building on the insights offered by preceding works on food and identity, some of which have been briefly reviewed above, and being mindful of the dynamic and heterogeneous nature of the nation, the chapter uses the angle of 'performing the nation' as a way of investigating how groups relate to the nation through food. Fox and Miller-Idriss (2008a) have described performing the nation as the ritualised enactment of nationhood through symbols. As it has been noted, food is widely used as a symbol of the nation in ritual performances. Through the use of national symbols, members of the nation learn what it meant to be part of the nation (Kolsto 2006). National symbols help define and express what the nation is, and although the nation is a subjective experience, the interpretation of national symbols is not arbitrary, but dependent on education, history, culture and tradition (Elgenius 2010). In terms of everyday life, national symbols are used as means of practising, engaging with and performing the nation (Edensor 2002). These routine and mundane daily performances, though 'dull, rote repetition, performed mindlessly and dispassionately', play a part in rooting and ingraining the nation (Fox and Miller-Idriss 2008a: 549).

More often than not the importance of performing the nation is linked to specific social events and/or spaces in which individuals come together as a group to stress their belonging to the nation. For instance, Bell and Valentine (1997) provide a number of examples of drinking communities which are categorised by their membership, social structures, the type of drinks consumed, the spaces in which these are consumed and the specific rituals attached. Though they do not discuss these drinking communities in the context of the nation, the examples provided depict particular national settings, in this case Britain and England.

Though the sense of national belonging can be expressed through everyday and banal performances (Edensor 2002), it is most visibly and dramatically done in public on particular days, utilising specific symbols and through learned rituals. Just as one cannot separate the ideas and practice of the nation from national events, such as memorial and independence days, one can also not play down the importance of the symbols that accompany such events, from monuments, flags, banners, uniforms and so on.

Burns Supper

As an example of 'performing the nation', the chapter briefly investigates Burns Supper or Burns Night. This ritual to commemorate the birthday of Robert Burns (1759–1796), a Scottish poet, is an ideal material for the chapter's purpose on several grounds. First, Burns Supper is not a state-sponsored event but voluntarily organised, although it is now increasingly associated with the promotion of tourism (Brown 1984). Second, as the name 'Burns Supper' suggests, food and sharing a meal are at the centre of this ritual to affirm Scottishness; no Burns Supper is complete without haggis and Scotch whisky, and as such food is an indispensable part of performing the Scottish nation. Third, while Burns Supper celebrates Scottishness, the ritual has developed after 1707 when Scotland was united with England and Wales, under a wider framework of Britishness, and not necessarily as a venue for demanding separate

Scottish statehood. As an example of a ritual to articulate and affirm national identity, Burns Supper has at least two layers: Scottish and British. This is in line with the chapter's view that a nation is a dynamic and heterogeneous entity with competing claims.

Today, Robert Burns is globally known as the national poet of Scotland. Burns Supper, which takes place on his birthday, 25 January, is held in Scotland and a variety of places, with the tradition of Scottish migration. The get-togethers to commemorate Burns are said to have started shortly after the poet's death and by the nineteenth century they were widely practised.

As it is widely acknowledged, Burns had become a symbol of Scotland by the mid-nineteenth century (Brown 1984: 141), and Burns Supper, in which food items such as haggis, whisky, neeps and tatties (mashed turnips and potatoes) are served, is an unmistakable example of performance voluntarily pursued by a group of people to articulate and affirm Scottishness. The power of these food items as symbols of Scottishness was observed, for instance, in nineteenth-century New Zealand. Haggis, neeps and tatties, and shortbread became widely popular among the Scottish community in Otago, for they 'facilitated a culinary journey home and an affirmation of the past' and 'helped to foster a sense of solidarity' when the Scottish migrants were trying to find their place in the new world by organising Burns Supper (Bueltmann 2012: 84). Food items, seen from this angle, form an integral part of performing the nation by virtue of being part and parcel of rituals.

Symbolism of food items associated with Burns Supper is, however, highly contextualised. Haggis, a sausage made from sheep's liver, heart and lungs mixed with minced onions, oatmeal, suet, salt and spice, occupies the centre stage of the occasion because Burns himself addressed it as 'Great chieftain o' the pudding-race!' in *Address to a Haggis* (Calder and Donnelly 1991). The poet's address to the haggis is the reason it is seen as representing Scottishness, rather than any inherent symbolic meaning. Whisky, on the other hand, can be seen as inherently Scottish because, under current legislation, only whisky made in Scotland can be considered Scotch whisky, as we shall see in the following chapter in more detail. However, when Burns Supper was instituted after the poet's death, the Scottishness of whisky was not clearly established, which means the symbolism of whisky as inherently Scottish is retrospectively invested. This in itself is an interesting observation that testifies the living and evolving nature of any ritual; however, as a route through which a group of people seeks connection to the nation, whisky's importance is context dependent.

Examination of the evolution of Burns Supper in British colonies further supports the context-dependent symbolism of haggis and other 'Scottish' food items. Alex Tyrrell (2011) reports that Scottish settlers in Melbourne, Australia, in the second half of the nineteenth century complained about the clannish feel of the choice of foodstuff at the commemorative events of Robert Burns. While these events, presented as Burns Festivals, were popular and played an important role for the Scottish settlers to assert their distinctive Presbyterian identity, which was in competition with Catholic Irish settlers, food items seen as essential in Burns Supper were pushed to the back stage. The festivals were noted for speeches made by members of the Scottish settlers who drew on the legacy of Burns as the champion of freedom in their efforts to promote the group politically in Melbourne. In New Zealand, where a craze for Scottish foodstuff was observed, the focus of Burns Supper gradually shifted to dancing: Burns Supper's entertainment value was increasingly found in its dancing rather than its speeches, haggis and whisky whose fume would be 'distasteful' for the ladies (Bueltmann 2012: 89). In this episode, haggis appears to have lost its symbolic power of representing Scottishness by way of association with Burns and to be downgraded to a 'distasteful' status. This suggests that haggis did not have inherent symbolic value as such. The fact that haggis was the highlight of the menu of St Andrew's Day dinner in the 1900s in Calcutta, India, also confirms the contextualised nature of haggis as representation of Scottishness (Buettner 2002). St Andrew is the patron saint of Scotland and St Andrew's day is Scotland's national day. However, St Andrew's Day celebration does not have an explicit link to a specific food item, although it has generalised association with anything Scottish, from Scottish dancing, Scotch whiskey, tartan and so on. The fact that haggis was the centre piece of the celebration among expatriates in Calcutta at the beginning of the twentieth century can only be explained by the close association between haggis and Scottishness which had been established through a nearly two-century-long history of Burns Supper.

Banitsa

While the case of Burns Supper does not illustrate the inherent symbolic power of food in the articulation of national identity, there are some studies that suggest that food items are important in rituals not only as an integral part of the ritual but also for their inherent meanings. Though it might not seem important at first sight, food and specific food items are directly linked to and are an important feature of national events, festivals and experiences; see, for example, the importance of BBQs (barbecues) to the national days of several countries, the 4th of July in the US, Australia Day (Newling 2022; Spillman 1997), Israel's Independence Day (Avieli 2013) and Heritage Day in South Africa. Moreover, as demonstrated by Deborah Lupton (1994), food and specific food items are often central to our memories of national events and settings. This is because there are differences between how national or important events are celebrated in various states. This is particularly noticeable within states among diaspora and migrant communities.

In recent years, a number of studies have explored how migrants and diaspora communities use food not only during special occasions but also in their daily lives to mediate their relationship with their host and home communities and anchor their sense of belonging (Rabikowska 2010). For example, Gasparetti (2012) has demonstrated how tie bou jenn, a popular Senegalese food item, helps foster a sense of belonging among the Senegalese community in Turin, Italy. Johnson (2016) has shown how food helps demarcate and transcend ethnic, religious and national boundaries among Guineans in Lisbon. Interestingly, Hubbell and Van Beukering (2022) have looked at the ways food and food memories (real and constructed) have helped maintain and construct a sense of identity and belonging among the Pied Noir community in France. An identity that 'called upon a nostalgic version of Algeria as a lost paradise, filled with scenes of sun, beach, and harmony between the Europeans and the Arab majority' (224).

Banitsa provides another interesting example of the inherent symbolic power of food, but also its malleability, in the mediation and articulation of national identity. For many Bulgarians, Banitsa is a popular dish that signifies the nation; its name derives from the verb 'to fold' ('gibanitsa'). It comprises folded sheets of pastry stuffed with cheese and eggs, to which other elements could be added, for example, spinach. In Bulgaria it is eaten throughout the year but is also associated with national and religious holidays. For example, it is customary to hide written notes, known as *kusmeti* (lucky charms), between the pastry sheets for the New Year (Maeva 2017).

In their study, Ranta and Nancheva (2019) highlight two particularly interesting aspects of banitsa among the Bulgarian diaspora in London. First, they demonstrate how Bulgarians in London perform the nation and anchor their identities through preparing, eating and talking about banitsa. Their research shows that banitsa is 'literally found everywhere', from children's birthday parties and breakfasts to special occasions and even to being offered to the interviewers on several occasions. The importance of the dish is in the fact that for most Bulgarians memories of banitsa are 'interwoven with memories of childhood, long summer breaks from school and Christmas holidays' (Ranta and Nancheva 2019: 69).

The second interesting aspect of their study is that the importance of banitsa as a signifier of Bulgarian identity is not related to what it is made of, but to how it is made and by whom. When asked what cheese she used for her banitsa, one of their interviewees confessed to using Greek feta rather than the traditional Bulgarian sirene cheese. It appears that most of the ingredients used in the preparation of banitsa were not Bulgarian (from the type of the cheese and pastry to the various fillings used). This, however, did not diminish its association with Bulgaria and Bulgarianness. In other words, it is the practice of preparing and consuming the dish that is important rather than the raw ingredients and their origin (Ranta and Nancheva 2019).

So far, the chapter has examined food and nationalism/national identity through literal performance of the nation. While the example of Burns Supper emphasised the contextual nature of symbolic power vested in food, the banitsa example has shown that food can have symbolic power in its own right, which is further enhanced by virtue of being part of rituals. However, the example of banitsa also demonstrates that mundane, quotidian acts can also be seen as 'performing the nation' and that it is often the performance that is the crucial element in linking food to the nation.

The rest of the chapter expands the scope of performing the nation, and of food as a symbol of the nation, through the case study of the Arab-Palestinian citizens of Israel. The case study considers the inter-related examples of hummus in the context of Arab-Palestinian and Jewish-Israeli relations, and the dual processes of 'Palestinianisation' and 'Israelisation'. The case study further illustrates the political nature of food in performance as well as contestation and subversion of the idea of the nation.

Arab-Palestinians in Israel

This case study looks at the role of food as a means of evaluating and exploring the ways in which groups, in our case Arab-Palestinian citizens of Israel perform the nation, but also engage with, contest and subvert the dominant idea of the nation. This is a particularly interesting case study primarily because of the complex relations between Arab-Palestinians and Jews in Israel, a state that was created for Jews and that is defined by the majority of its population as Jewish. According to Smooha (1989), Israel can be described as an ethnic democracy: a state that is based on the identity of and ruled by a majority national group. Others, such as Yiftachel, have gone even further by arguing that Israel is an ethnocracy: 'a particular regime type [that] … facilitates the expansion, ethnicization, and control of a dominant ethnic group over contested territory and polity' (2006: 11).

Arab-Palestinians are the largest national minority in Israel; they currently (2022) constitute around 21 per cent of the population. They are mostly decedents of Arab-Palestinians who remained within the boundaries of the state of Israel in the aftermath of the 1948 war; many of them were internally displaced as a consequence of the war. The 1948 war is described in Israel as its war of independence, while for Arab-Palestinians it is the *Nakba*, the catastrophe in which over 700,000 Arab-Palestinians became refugees. From 1948 until 1966 Arab-Palestinians in Israel lived under a military rule and their movement and political activities were restricted (Louer 2007).

The relationship between Arab-Palestinians and the Israeli state has been and still is a complex one. The state was envisioned and established as a national home for Jews. The Jewishness of the state is reflected in the official symbols, including the state's anthem and flag, official narrative and leading institutions. The position of Arab-Palestinians in the state is further complicated by the ongoing Israeli-Palestinian conflict and the importance attached to the role of the military in Israel; related to this there have been recent calls within Jewish-Israeli society and among several leading Jewish-Israeli political parties for Arab-Palestinian citizens to declare their loyalty to the Jewish state and accept its Jewish nature.

How then do Arab-Palestinians engage with the state and its dominant Jewish cultural and political hegemony? On the one hand, advancement and social mobility depend on accommodation, at time subservience, and acceptance of the state, its institutions and social and economic forces. On the other hand, Arab-Palestinians have to navigate complex cultural and national issues, such as the wider Israeli-Palestinian conflict, the Israeli control over the Occupied Palestinian Territories (the West Bank and the Gaza Strip) and the Palestinian refugee problem.

It is probably not surprising that the complexity of these relations is manifested in Arab-Palestinian food culture in Israel. In general two distinct processes have been observed. First, in line with Bhabha's (1997) ideas on mimicry, it is evident that Arab-Palestinians have adopted, internalised and adapted certain Jewish-Israeli culinary traits and habits. Either because of their desire for social mobility or as a result of grander processes, such as modernisation and globalisation, there is a movement among Arab-Palestinians towards Israelisation. Second, there has also been an increasing movement among Arab-Palestinians in Israel to assert and emphasise their Palestinian identity, a process which can be described as Palestinianisation. The assertion of a Palestinian national identity has gained more prominence in recent decades. The two processes are not mutually exclusive and demonstrate the shifting nature and complexity of national identities.

A Short Introduction About Hummus

The fact that food items and practices can be used to represent group identity while, at the same time, they can be manipulated and transformed opens up a range of possible points of debate and contestation regarding the place of the nation and national identity. An interesting example to illustrate this point, and as a way of introducing our case study, is by looking at the place of hummus in the context of Jewish-Israeli and Arab-Palestinian societal relations.[1] What is of particular interest to us is to examine how a food item can not only be viewed as a national symbol for more than one group but also provide a means of performing the nation as well as contesting and challenging prevailing attitudes regarding the nation in everyday and banal settings.

Hummus (a puree made of chickpeas, which is normally served with olive oil, lemon juice and *tahini*) is arguably Israel's national dish (Hirsh 2011). Though the origins of the dish are unclear and it has been eaten across the Middle East for over several centuries, Jewish-Israeli writers have described it as the embodiment of the nation and Israel as the land of hummus (Galili 2007). The history of hummus in the context of Jewish-Israeli and Arab-Palestinian relations is one of fascination and adaptation leading to appropriation and nationalisation (Hirsh 2011). The history and place of hummus in Israel, as well as the journey it has taken, was illustrated to us by Sallah Kurdi, the head chef of the Jamila restaurant in Jaffa. Kurdi grew up in Jaffa, which is a mixed Jewish-Arab city. Though as an Arab-Palestinian he grew up eating hummus, it was not a dish he ate frequently. Occasionally he was sent by his mom to get some hummus for the family from local Arab-Palestinian artisan producers as a quick and cheap way of having lunch and to give his mom a rest from cooking. As he grew older he decided, like many Arab-Palestinians in Israel, to enter the food industry. The food industry in Israel, and the hospitality sector in particular, is one of the few to provide Arab-Palestinians with opportunities for social mobility and progression

---

[1] We will come back to the complexity of hummus as a national symbol in our discussion of the Israeli Lebanese 'hummus wars' in "Chapter Six: National Food in the International Context II—Gastronationalism and Populism".

(Gvion 2014, 2019). Kurdi worked as a chef for several Jewish-owned Mizrahi (a term used to denote Jews from the Middle East and North Africa) restaurants that catered mostly to working-class Jewish-Israelis. Most of the food served in these restaurants, despite being labelled as Mizrahi food, was a mixture of different food cultures loosely based on Arab and Arab-Palestinian mezzes. In these Mizrahi restaurants he also learned to make and serve hummus.

A few years ago Kurdi decided to open a modern Arab restaurant in Jaffa specialising in Arab-Jaffan food, and in order to stress his departure from more traditional Arab and Arab-Palestinian foods, or at least the Jewish-Israeli perception of these foods, he decided not to serve hummus in any shape or form. At roughly the same time, the Israeli food industry, which had mass-produced hummus from the early 1950s, started to label some of its hummus as Arab in order to increase its perceived authenticity. If you go to any of the large Jewish-Israeli supermarkets, you will find these Israeli mass-produced 'authentic' Arab hummus ranges (see Photo 1). We thus have a case of Jewish-Israelis producing hummus, mostly for Jewish-Israelis, marketed as 'Arab' in order to increase its perceived quality and alleged authenticity, clearly linking, what is seen as a Jewish-Israeli national symbol, with its Arab-Palestinian roots. Closing the circle, Kurdi complained that now, when he goes back home, he is confronted head on by the journey that the hummus has made from his childhood in Jaffa into his refrigerator: seeing his wife and kids prefer to eat the Jewish-Israeli mass-produced, allegedly 'Arab', hummus (Ranta and Mendel 2016).

Palestinianisation

Over the past three decades there has been an evident movement among Arab-Palestinians, as a national minority group in Israel, towards stronger identification with and assertion of their Palestinian national identity. This can be seen in their growing assertiveness in Israeli cultural and political life, for example, the formation of independent Arab-Palestinian political parties. This movement can be argued to have begun during the first Palestinian popular uprising, known as the Intifada, in 1987, with Arab-Palestinian citizens of Israel closely identifying with the

Photo 1 Examples of Israeli mass-produced 'Arab' hummus

Arab-Palestinian struggle in the West Bank and the Gaza Strip against the Israeli occupation (Ghanem 2001).

This movement, which can be defined as Palestinianisation, is clearly manifested in Arab-Palestinian food culture. Through specific food-related actions, Arab-Palestinians attempt to assert their national identity in distinction or in opposition to the Jewish-Israeli hegemonic national discourse as well as emphasise their own link to the land of Israel/Palestine and their history as the native population.

For example, in order to assert and emphasise their separate national identity, some Arab-Palestinian women choose to collect and cook with wild herbs and plants. Foraging is used by Arab-Palestinian women in Israel as a means of strengthening and symbolising their national connection to a land they view as their own. The choice of foraging relates to the idea of 'nature loving' as a form of romantic nationalism that emphasises the importance and knowledge of the land, its produce and the right to access it, but also of country and rural life, which include the reviving of folk traditions (Dahl 1998). Interestingly enough, in recent years Israel has started to restrict the foraging of wild herbs and plants. A political decision, argued by Eghbariah (2017), by the Israeli state which specifically targets its Arab-Palestinian women citizens. The choice of foraging for wild herbs and plants, such as *Malukhiyah* (jute leaves), *hindibah* (chicory) and *hubeisa* (mallow/malva), is partly a result of prevailing socio-economic circumstances, that is, cuisines of poverty. However, the action should also be seen as a reflection of a distinct and conscious desire among Arab-Palestinian women to perform the nation. In addition to foraging, the importance of cooking, what are seen as, traditional dishes, and the restriction on the entry of Jewish-Israeli food are also stressed. Through their actions they participate in a particular national culture and discourse, draw links to a particular geography and historical narrative and sustain their own food resources as a way of resisting Israeli cultural and social hegemony and its mass-produced food industry (Gvion 2006).

The performance of the nation and the movement towards Palestinianisation is also evident among Arab-Palestinian chefs as well. In interviews conducted with several Arab-Palestinian chefs,[2] a constant theme emerged of cooking food that is based on the distinct products of Israel/Palestine. In contradistinction to many Jewish-Israelis, Arab-Palestinian chefs made it clear that they were mostly not interested in imitating and in utilising foreign or Jewish food ingredients. They wanted to cook food that represented their own national identity and heritage using ingredients they perceived as belonging to their homeland and *terroir*. This also entailed, at least in some cases, and similarly to Arab-Palestinian women, performances of the nation through collecting and foraging wild herbs and plants (see also Ranta and Monterescu 2022). Lastly, many chefs also talked about preserving traditional recipes or refusing to serve certain foods for fear that these would be appropriated by Jewish-Israelis.

---

[2] Between 2012 and 2014, and 2016 and 2019, several field research trips to Israel were undertaken. During the trips a number of leading Arab-Palestinian chefs were interviewed, including, among others, Sallah Kurdi (Jamila restaurant), Hussam Abbas (Al Babur) and Habib Daoud (Izbah). In addition, a number of leading chefs were interviewed online in 2020, including Fadi Kattan and Reem Kassis.

Another way in which Arab-Palestinians assert and emphasise their national identity and their rootedness and connection to the land is through challenging the Jewish-Israeli hegemonic discourse. For example, Ashqar, one of the few Arab-Palestinian wineries in Israel, has launched its latest wine 'Iqrit', named after a village which was destroyed and whose inhabitants were expelled by the Israeli Defence Forces (IDF) as part of the 1948 war and in relation to Israel's 'security needs'. The Arab-Palestinian inhabitants have not been allowed to return to the village since; however, the Israeli state allows those born in the village to be buried there (Vered 2013). By labelling their wine 'Iqrit', and by using grapes grown on land that used to be part of the destroyed village, the winery, which is owned by descendants of those expelled from the village, draws attention to the continued discrimination of Arab-Palestinian citizens of Israel and to their own national heritage and claim to the land. It also links Arab-Palestinian identity in Israel with Arab-Palestinian elsewhere and with the wider Arab-Palestinian refugee problem.

Arab-Palestinians also perform the nation by discursively challenging attempts by Jewish-Israeli chefs and groups to appropriate what are perceived to be Arab-Palestinian national food dishes. There has been a long history of adoption of Arab-Palestinian food by Jewish-Israelis and its appropriation and transformation into becoming symbols of Jewish-Israeli national identity. This can be seen in food items such as falafel and hummus, among others, but also the Israeli salad and breakfast (Ranta and Mendel 2014, 2016). This phenomenon is not limited to early group interaction but is an ongoing and continuous one. For example, in recent years, one of the most well-known Arab-Palestinian desserts has been discussed and presented as Jewish-Israeli. The apparent attempts to appropriate *knafeh* (a cheese pastry with noodles soaked in sugar syrup), which is associated with Arab-Palestinian food and with the city of Nablus in particular, have given rise to an online campaign through social media to reclaim the dish as Palestinian (for discussion on the appropriation of the *knafeh*, see, e.g., Abunimah 2014; Vered 2014). The struggle over the *knafeh* adds to a number of additional Arab-Palestinian social media campaigns to reclaim symbolic foods as well as to assert the nation through the boycotting of Israeli food products.

Process of Israelisation

Living in Israel, a state that is dominated politically, economically and culturally by Jewish-Israelis, raises a number of issues for Arab-Palestinians regarding, among other things, living in mixed Jewish-Arab cities, integration, economic opportunities and social mobility. For example, a number of scholars have pointed out the importance of Hebrew language proficiency for Arab-Palestinians as an avenue for social mobility. The importance of Hebrew as the main language of higher education and economic life has also brought about the hybridisation of the Arabic spoken by Arab-Palestinians in Israel (Mar'i 2013). In other words, the Arabic spoken has become Israelised. The incorporation of Hebrew into their spoken Arabic is part of a wider process of Israelisation that is based on acquiring and adopting Jewish-Israeli traits and habits. This process should not surprise us, after all, and despite the fact that they see themselves as a part of a wider Arab-Palestinian nation, they have lived in Israel and have had daily contact with Jewish-Israelis since 1948. This process can be seen on the one hand as a tactical decision by Arab-Palestinians to successfully navigate life in Israel. On the other hand, the process is also about reinterpreting what it means to be an Arab-Palestinian but also an Israeli; through their actions Arab-Palestinians are undermining and challenging the Jewish nature of Israeli national identity (Regev and Seroussi 2004: 23–24). The process of Israelisation can be seen in a number of food-related areas.

To begin with, it is clear that Arab-Palestinian citizens of Israel have to a certain extent adopted and acquired Jewish-Israeli food items, dishes and eating habits. The Israelisation of Arab-Palestinian food culture is partly related to the dominance of Jewish-Israeli food companies and media, but also to the impacts of modernisation and globalisation. The last two factors are relevant in understanding Arab-Palestinian adoption and consumption of fast food and frozen food, for example. As argued by Gvion the importance of modernisation is not so much with regard to a 'break from traditions' but rather as a 'means to improve living conditions and access to higher standard of living' (Gvion 2012: 164). In short, the need to practise a modern lifestyle, win acceptance in Israeli society and become more socially mobile has caused Arab-Palestinian women to cook less traditional food and consume and prepare more food items that are seen as Israeli (Gvion 2019).

No other Jewish-Israeli food item exemplifies the process of Israelisation better than the schnitzel. Schnitzel, originally a central European breaded veal escalope, often referred to in Europe as Vienna Schnitzel, was brought to Israel by European, mostly German and Austrian Jewish immigrants. Schnitzel was quickly established as one of the most widely consumed and popular national dishes, though in Israel schnitzel is made of either turkey or chicken. In Israel there are even several restaurant chains that specialise in gourmet schnitzel (they are colloquially known in Israel as *schnitzelia*, plural *schnitzeliyut*).

Over the past few decades, schnitzel has become increasingly popular and today it is widely consumed by Arab-Palestinians in Israel. While many Arab-Palestinians do not necessarily perceive the consumption of schnitzel as part of becoming Israeli, they nonetheless recognise the dish as coming from the Jewish-Israeli food culture. According to Gvion (2012), there are a number of reasons why the schnitzel was adopted by Arab-Palestinians; these include the growing importance of frozen and readymade food, which are often how schnitzel is sold in Israel, and the similarities between Jewish kosher and Islamic halal regulations regarding meat products. In general, most of the food items and practices that have entered Arab-Palestinian kitchens from the Jewish-Israeli food culture either fit in with the halal regulations and meal structure or are those that can be adapted and transformed.

A different side of Israelisation is occurring with regard to the presentation and marketing of Arab-Palestinian food, restaurant and chefs. In the previous section we discussed how Arab-Palestinians are emphasising and performing the nation through food. At the same time, however, Arab-Palestinian chefs, restaurant owners and food company executives are also moving in a different direction: they are trying to present their food as Israeli.

For many Arab-Palestinian chefs, working in the Jewish-Israeli food industry, in particular in Mizrahi restaurants, provided them with their first steps in the industry and main opportunity for advancement towards opening their own restaurants. The restaurants they subsequently opened relied to a certain extent on Jewish-Israeli food suppliers and clientele; this is true with regard to many Arab-Palestinian restaurants in mixed cities and in Arab-Palestinian cities and towns. As a result, many Arab-Palestinian chefs openly discussed their difficulty in presenting their food as Palestinian. A move to emphasise or market their restaurants, cookbooks and food as Palestinian might alienate their Jewish-Israeli customers, hinder their careers and make it harder for them to make further inroads into the Jewish-Israeli food market. As a result, Arab-Palestinian food is often represented as Levantine, Middle Eastern, regional (e.g., Jaffan or Galilean, which helps tie in with similar regional movements among Jewish-Israelis) and also Israeli or Mizrahi. This is particularly true with regard to Arab-Palestinian businesses that market themselves to Jewish-Israelis.

A good example of this phenomenon is the story of the Nazareth-based Diana restaurant chain. Diana is an Arab-Palestinian restaurant chain owned by Dukhul Al-Safadi, whose family are linked to the former mixed city of Safed that after 1948 was mostly emptied of its Arab-Palestinian population. The restaurant was named after the first Arab cinema in Nazareth. The restaurant's success in Nazareth, an Arab-Palestinian city frequented by tourists and Jewish-Israelis, prompted the opening of Diana franchises in several mixed and Jewish cities. In many of these the Arab-Palestinian aspect of the restaurant and the Al-Safadi family has been downplayed and instead the food has been presented as Israeli: flashy neon signs declare the restaurant to be 'An Israeli Grill Restaurant' (Ranta and Mendel 2016). This phenomenon can also be observed in restaurants that operate in mainly Arab-Palestinian cities, but which attract Jewish-Israeli clientele; for example, many Arab-Palestinian restaurants in Nazareth market themselves as serving Mizrahi food (Photo 2).

On the one hand, this story indicates how Arab-Palestinians have had to compromise over their food cultural heritage and national symbols in order to successfully operate in Israel and appeal to a mostly Jewish-Israeli clientele. On the other hand, however, the process of presenting Arab-Palestinian food as Israeli, though not necessarily as Jewish-Israeli, opens up new possibilities and avenues with regard to what constitutes Israeli national identity. A somewhat similar issue is raised by Azri Amram (2021) regarding the strategies adopted by some Arab-Palestinian food business in Israel in relation to incorporating Jewish dietary rules (*kashrut*).

Photo 2 Diana Kosher Israeli Grill

This last point regarding the subversion or reinterpretation of Israeli identity needs to be elaborated on. The importance of food items as symbols of the nation is very apparent in Israel. However, because many of these symbols, such as falafel and hummus, are shared and/or contested their reinterpretation raises the possibility of a more inclusive way of looking at Israeli national identity. For example, and as a way of coming back a full circle to the example used at the beginning of this case study, the idea of hummus as either an Arab-Palestinian or a Jewish-Israeli national symbol is contested. Partly as response to the rise of Arab-Palestinian chefs, restaurants and food companies, and partly to do with Jewish-Israeli consumer demand for more authentic and better quality products,[3] leading Jewish-Israeli food companies are marketing some of their hummus products and brands as Arab. These hummus products are

---

[3] The relationship between national identity, product quality and consumerism will be discussed in depth in the following chapter.

often based on recipes of leading Arab-Palestinian chefs and/or related to specific Arab-Palestinian towns and concepts. As a result of this, and a number of related factors, Jewish-Israelis consumers perceive Arab-Palestinian hummus as better, tastier and more authentic. This raises the question of whether hummus is now perceived solely by Jewish-Israelis as their inclusive national symbol. The hummus example is repeated with many other food products, for example, *tahini* (sesame paste) and *baklava* (sweet pastry).

Conclusion

In this chapter we examined the relationship between group identity, food and the nation, and the importance of food as a way of symbolising and performing the nation. The case studies and related examples presented demonstrate the importance of food as a means of solidifying group identity and also as a means for constructing, mediating, maintaining and contesting national identity. Additionally, and as shown, food is not merely used as a banal symbol of the nation but also used as a way for groups to negotiate and express their national identity through performance. These performances, which range from official national events and festivals to more mundane settings and occasions, help increase and solidify the sense of group and national belonging. The case studies also raised important questions with regard to how minority and diaspora groups engage with the nation and/or with dominant national hegemonic cultures and discourses and demonstrated some of the conflicting pressures that exist. Food in this regard opens up possibilities for groups to mediate, contest and subvert the nation, but also new avenues for researchers to examine the relationship between different national groups.

Chapter Three: Consuming Nations—The Construction of National Identities in the Food Industry

This chapter sets out to examine the ways in which the private sector engages with food and nationalism. In particular, the chapter looks at the ways in which food is articulated, constructed and reproduced as national by the private sector. Despite, or perhaps because of, the advance of globalisation and the spread of multinational food corporations, there has been an increase in the articulation and promotion of food as national by the private sector over the past two decades. This has in turn helped to construct and reproduce food images, values, tastes and qualities as belonging to or originating from particular national settings.

In the first edition we stated that despite the increase in attention towards banal nationalism, by and large, the private sector's role in constructing and reproducing nations through food has not received enough attention in the mainstream literature, which has tended to focus on the state-driven and top-down nationalism and, in recent years, everyday nationalism (Prideaux 2009). What was mostly examined in the literature was the relationship between food consumption and nationalism and/or how nationalism affected consumers and their perspectives on national and foreign brands: see, for example, Balabanis et al. (2001) on the impact of nationalism, patriotism and internationalism on consumers in Turkey and the Czech Republic, and Watson and Wright (2000) on consumer ethnocentrism in New Zealand. We argued that the reasons for this relative lacune were varied and partly to do with the general shift towards everyday nationalism from banal nationalism. We lamented that given the potential of the everyday nationalism approach to capture the messy and complex reality of the world (Jones and Merriman 2009: 166–7), it was unfortunate that the private sector's involvement has not received sufficient attention.

Since the publication of the first edition, however, there has been a growing scholarly interest in the ways in which the private sector engages with, produces and promotes nationalism in general, which is often referred to as corporate or commercial nationalism (see, e.g., Volcic and Andrejevic 2016; or Kania-Lundholm 2014 for 'commercializing the national'), and specifically with regard to food. The scholarly interest has gone beyond banal representations of the nation by the private sector, to studies of how the private sector affects everyday nationalism and how it engages with nationalism and national identity through food. This chapter will discuss and elaborate on the above themes through a number of examples and two main case studies. The first case study looks at the recent decline in traditional pie and mash shops in the UK as well as the emergence of upmarket pie restaurants and brands. In doing so the case study examines the ways in which the private sector engages with, constructs and defines a modern sense of English and British national identity, through, for example, the incorporation of regional and ethnic culinary traditions. The second case study focuses on the Scotch whisky industry. Because the basis for the product's identity and brand coincides with the geographical framework of a nation, the industry is inevitably engaged with defining, maintaining and promoting the idea of a Scottish nation in its pursuit of profit, highlighting the entrenchment/permeation of the nation-state framework in the everyday life. In other words, the private sector unwittingly acts as nationalists in maintaining and reinforcing the framework of the nation while pursuing apolitical activities such as profit maximisation.

Food, Nationalism and the Private Sector

Walking down any high street in the developed, and increasingly also in the developing world, and the banal reproduction of nations through food is evident almost everywhere. Most restaurants and cafes, which are increasingly part of global chains, either market themselves as part of a particular national food culture (Thai, French, American, etc.) or display, construct and reproduce nationalities in their menus, décor and products. Global coffee chains sell and advertise many of their coffees and teas, but also chocolate and other products, as coming from and/or belonging to particular nation-states, for the purpose of conveying ideas regarding taste, value and quality. This increase in the articulation of food as national is clearly present in food labelling and can be seen on the shelves of most food stores and supermarkets; see, for example, the increased use of country names for chocolate and coffee products among many others by UK supermarkets (Photos 1 and 2).[1]

This is partly a result of national and international regulations that require food retailers to provide increasingly more information—from

Photo 1 Sainsbury's chocolate range

---

[1] Even though the image is taken from a UK supermarket, the phenomena can be found in most developed countries.

Photo 2 Sainsbury's coffee range

country of origin and producer/grower details to nutritional values—regarding the food they sell (for more on country of origin and geographic designation, see "Chapter Eight: International Organisations, Food and Nationalism"). What is particularly interesting for our purposes is that much of the geographic and national labelling by the private sector is done out of choice and not required by law. In some cases, this is done to signal potential consumers that the company is in tune with prevailing ethical norms, for example, that the produce is organic and sustainable and/or complies with fair trade practices. However, the emphasis on providing geographic indication on food, often to the point of it becoming a fetish—all food items now seem to require some geographical information, however spurious[2]—is also done because, as Cook and Crang pointed out almost three decades ago (1996: 134), 'diversity sells' and that 'adding meaningful knowledges about food commodities and their geographies' has become a 'crucial means of adding value'.

Another important reason has to do with the promotion of the nation, as food products are also blatantly labelled and/or advertised as national as part of campaigns to promote national produce or for the purpose of national branding, which tap into consumers' national or ethnocentric preferences. According to Aronczyk (2008), national branding by companies has become a global trend since the 1990s. The association of

---

[2] In a very similar way to the process of *terroirism*.

products with certain images, values and qualities of nations is seen as providing some competitive advantage. The idea of the private sector promoting the nation and/or establishing national brands has also been acknowledged in other fields, such as tourism (see, e.g., Shaffer 2001), where the private sector expects to increase profits and benefit from a stronger and more appealing national brand.

Aronczyk (2008) points out that national branding should be seen as a particular and deliberate strategy to convey ideas, images and values regarding national identity through the branding and marketing of products. A good example of commercial nationalism and the promotion of the nation—or a particular idea of the nation—can be seen in how dairy companies in Sweden and the UK package their products. The research done by Andersson (2019; and with Smith 2021) examines how the private sector engages with national discourses and narratives through its labelling, packaging and advertising campaigns. Demonstrating how 'banal flagging' of the nation is 'not always so banal' (Andersson and Smith 2021). The companies examined promote and convey particular ideas of what and who the nation is and what are the national values. For example, in the case of Sweden consumers are reminded of the 'national' values of openness and equality. Though it is also clear that hidden behind these often mundane narratives and images are more traditional discourses concerning race and gender.

Selling national brands or relating products to the nation helps in sustaining a culture of national belonging and taps into the idea of ethnocentric consumption exhibited by some consumers. Selling the nation also links in well with the romantic ideals of cultural nationalism regarding the national landscape and heritage (Andersson 2019; Andersson and Smith 2021) and with alternative food movements, such as 'slow food', organic and 'local' (on the interplay between food corporations and alternative food movements regarding issues of nationality, locality and authenticity, see, e.g., Leitch 2003; Pratt 2007). The construction and promotion, as well as support for national brands and images, contributes to national claims of qualitative difference and significance. These actions help and enable the 'authentication' of the nation on a regular basis. As argued by Fox and Miller-Idriss, with regard to the idea of consuming the nation, 'consumers don't simply buy national commodities;

they constitute national sensibilities, embody national pride, negotiate national meanings, thus making nationhood a salient feature of their everyday lives' (2008: 551). The idea of promoting national products also taps into consumers' sense of national belonging and, to use Skey's terminology, provides some security and comfort (Skey 2011). These national images and claims of value and quality provide consumers with familiar settings which reminds them who they are and which food culture, and/or national identity, they are part of. This can be useful during times of political, social and/or economic change. Caldwell (2002) provides the example of how the private sector in Russia, alongside the state, promoted a 'Buy Russian' campaign. Domestic food producers, store clerks and customers helped to classify foods and other products as either 'Ours' (Nash) or 'Not Ours' (Ne Nash) and describe local goods as superior to foreign goods in terms of taste, quality and healthfulness. A more recent study by Yormirzoev et al. (2019) further demonstrates the importance of nationalism in evaluating domestic and foreign brands in Russia. In this case the consumption and perception of local and foreign dairy products in response to western sanctions on Russia, following the Ukraine crisis, and the subsequent Russian import ban on certain western food products, including dairy.

Another interesting feature of commercial nationalism occurs when a business becomes a national symbol and part of national discourses and narratives. A good example of this phenomenon is Tim Hortons, a Canadian coffee chain, which also has a number of international outlets, particularly in the US. For a country that is argued to lack a clear and identifiable cuisine and/or national dish (see, e.g., Fabien-Ouellet 2019 on Canadian cuisine and whether Poutine should or could be seen as the national dish), Tim Hortons provides not only a food-related national symbol but also a space in which to experience and consume the nation, metaphorically and physically. The chain, which interestingly is owned by the American fast food company Burger King, itself part of a global subsidiary, was founded in 1964. One of the original founders Miles Gilbert (Tim) Horton was and still is considered one of the greatest Ice Hockey players of all time, which partly explains the chain's long association with ice hockey, arguably Canada's national sport (Cormack 2008).

Cormack (2008) demonstrates how the chain helps project and construct an image of Canadian national identity by supporting and promoting national sports (in particular ice hockey), causes and events and by addressing, through its advertisements, Canadian issues and concerns. This is particularly noticeable in its 'true stories' ads which have focused on ordinary Canadians and their everyday lives. Emphasising 'cliched versions' of what Canadianness is, for example, highlighting the qualities of ruggedness, endurance and civility. In its drive to define itself as Canadian, the chain celebrates being 'un-American' and juxtaposing Canadian and American national identities and values. Abu-Laban (2020: 19) argues that 'Tim Hortons is a part of Canadian popular culture, stands for the nation, and is a way to even literally consume the nation in both official languages through its food and beverages'. Despite this appealing and apparently benign image, Abu-Laban (2020) also notes that Tim Hortons' appeal is partly a result of tapping into particular discourses and images of Canadian national identity and history, while suppressing others, such as persistent social inequalities and Canada's foundation and history as a settler colonial state and nation.

The role of the private sector in constructing the nation through focusing on particular discourses and images, while suppressing others, such as race and history, is also present in other settler colonial states. Engaging with the ongoing debates over national food and cuisine in Australia, Newling (2022) examines the emergence of lamb, rather than an indigenous animal, such as kangaroos, as the 'national celebratory meat' on Australia Day. Australia Day, which is celebrated on the 26th of January, marks the official founding of the colony in 1788 and is designated a national holiday. Over the past two decades, Meat and Livestock Australia, a private sector trade body, has focused on the promotion of lamb for Australia Day through its national campaigns and advertisements. It has claimed that it is 'un-Australian' not to eat lamb on Australia Day and that lamb was an inclusive meat that had the potential for uniting Australians. Its advertisements, which are presented as light-hearted, have caused controversy 'for insensitive cultural and religious stereotyping, ridiculing vegetarians and vegans, and more recently, trivialising the impact of colonisation', a 2017 advertisement featured 'Aboriginal Australians barbequing lamb on a beach while welcoming boatloads of colonisers and immigrants who all party once ashore' (Newling 2022: 185). The insensitivity is striking given that Aboriginal Australians have designated the 26th of January as a 'Day of Mourning' and the fact that it ignores the negative environmental and social consequences of the introduction and cultivation of lamb.

A different side of this debate also demonstrates the heterogeneous nature of the private sector's engagement with national identity and nationalism. As noted by Newling (2022) and Craw (2008), there has been a movement by the private sector, as well as by local, state and federal governments, to try and promote kangaroo meat as national food. The early European settlers in Australia relied on kangaroos as a source of protein, but with the introduction and spread of European techniques of farming and the introduction of farm animals, mostly sheep/lamb, the consumption of kangaroo meat plummeted (at least among the settler population). From the 1980s, upmarket restaurants started to serve kangaroo meat and its consumption has been increasingly supported by a variety of Australians. The consumption of kangaroo meat is now framed in a multi-layered discursive context. Eating kangaroo meat can be presented as an act of correcting ecological damages brought by the European farming style. The ecological benefit of eating kangaroo meat can also be presented as a means of pest control, which ultimately contributes to kangaroo conservation. It is also a way of getting to know the country better and of being integrated with the natural environment. Kangaroos are seen as embodying what Australia is and illustrating the defining 'otherness' of Australia, and eating it literally ensures the maintenance of Australian distinctiveness on the international stage. It is not a coincidence that it is used, along with other indigenous animals, as a national symbol (Craw 2008).

Before we turn to our two main case studies, which also explore the ways in which food businesses construct and engage with the nation, it is important to note that there are other important private sector actors. One of the main areas that are still relatively unexplored is the role of the media. By media we are referring to a wide range of actors including social media, publishers and TV and streaming food programmes. A simple visit to a bookstore, with shelves upon shelves of cookbooks dedicated to specific nations, or scrolling through cooking programmes, from

Masterchef to Netflix's *Chef's Table*, illustrates the power of the media to construct and reify national qualities through food (see, e.g., Leer 2019). Taking the example of *Chef's Table*, most of the episodes are in-depth accounts of ground-breaking chefs and the ways in which they engage with their traditions and perceived national food culture.[3]

Pie Loving Nation[4]

There is an ongoing debate over what constitutes English or British cuisine, notwithstanding a wider domestic and international discussion over the quality of food on offer in the British Isles. What is less in doubt is that there are many food items that are clearly identified in the UK with the nation, such as fish and chips (Panayi 2014), roast beef (historically seen as the embodiment of the nation: Edwards 2019; Rogers 2003) and English breakfast (O'Connor 2009). Another food item that is perhaps less well known internationally, but is seen as quintessentially English and British, at least in the UK, is pie (Brown 2019; Ranta 2020), which will be the focus of this case study. What we aim to highlight is not only the important role played by the private sector and market forces, in promoting, and in some cases downplaying, particular food items, food cultures and traditions, but more importantly the role played in constructing and defining national identity through food. The case study also illustrates the changing nature of national food cultures and foodways, which are forever in a state of flux, evolving and responding to changing social, economic, political and environmental conditions.

A pie is a baked pastry dish with a sweet or savoury filling, though there is some debate over whether a stew with a pastry lid, or indeed a potato crust lid, qualifies as well. It is not clear when pies were first invented or eaten, some scholars point to ancient Egypt, but there is clear

---

[3] Important to note that the use of national themes in TV programmes is not limited to the private sector. Indeed, since the end of World War II, cooking programmes have been used by a wide range of national broadcasters as a way of constructing, maintaining and engaging with ideas concerning national food culture (see, e.g., Tominc's edited volume 2022)

[4] Most of the research presented in the case study is based on fieldwork conducted by Ronald Ranta between 2018 and 2021, some of which have been published (Ranta 2020).

evidence of pie recipes and reference to their preparation and consumption across several regions during Antiquity. Pies were probably introduced to the British Isles by the Romans, though written accounts of their widespread consumption and first recipes appeared much later, in the thirteenth and fourteenth centuries. Since then, pies have become a central part of English and British diets, food cultures and traditions; for example, mince pies, which are filled with dried fruit and spices, have been a national Christmas tradition since the Middle Ages. Another example of the historical relevance of pies and their place in the nation's consciousness is the Woolton pie, served during the rationing period of World War II and named after Lord Woolton, the British Minister for food during the war. The official Woolton pie recipe consisted mostly of diced potatoes, cauliflower, swede and carrots and was an attempt to demonstrate what could be culinary possible with the rations provided (Sitwell 2016). There is even a British pie week, celebrated each year at the beginning of March, with awards for the best national pies. It is not a surprise, therefore, to those living in the UK, that the British have been described as a 'pie loving nation' (Ranta 2020). To further illustrate this latter point, food writer Pete Brown states that 'Britain does pies better than anyone else in the world and has done since pastry was first perfected by chefs working for the Tudor monarchs' (2019: 9).

In 2018, A. J. Goddard, a pie shop in East London that had operated for 128 years, closed down. The closure was the latest to occur across the country; over the past three decades, traditional pie shops, alongside traditional cafes, fish and chip shops, and local pubs, have been closing in increasing numbers. Though there are many reasons for these closures, in the UK's post-Brexit social and political environment, the closure of so many traditional eating establishments, many of which catered for white working-class neighbourhoods, has been interpreted as part of a wider decline in traditional English culture and identity in the face of globalisation and changing demographics (Ranta 2018).

In the period around the two world wars, pie shops, which were mostly family owned, and employed people from the local community, were very popular. They offered calorie-rich, satisfying, affordable and transportable food to working-class families. Alongside traditional fish and chips shops, cafes and local pubs, pie shops dominated the culinary scene of many English neighbourhoods, where they became closely associated with English white working-class food culture, tradition and identity (Ranta, 2018). It is important to note that there were regional variations on the pie shop, including their fillings and what they were served with, to which we will return below. This raises an interesting question, if pie shops were so popular, why have they declined so rapidly, with only a small number of traditional shops still in operation?

There are many reasons for the decline of traditional pie shops, including changing business environments, demographics and national diets. Many shops have struggled to adapt to the highly diverse and competitive restaurant market and to rising costs and rents associated with the gentrification of urban areas. The demographics of the neighbourhoods most traditional shops operated in dramatically changed in recent decades, with newly arrived residents from within the UK and immigrants from further afield, bringing with them different food cultures, preferences and traditions. Nationally, tastes and food fashions have also changed considerably, partly because of the arrival of immigrants (Panayi 2008); the fact that most traditional pie shops did not cater for vegetarians and vegans also had an effect. Many of the surviving traditional shops have become anachronisms in a diverse modern Britain, resembling living museums, using decors, recipes and menus that have not changed in decades (see Photos 3 and 4).

While the above might indicate a decline in pie eating in the UK, the reality could not be more different. While traditional pies shops have been in decline, pie eating and the pie trade in the UK have been booming; one could make the argument that the UK is going through a pie renaissance period. Walking through UK supermarket aisles, one cannot but be amazed at the number and variety of pies on offer, including those aimed at vegetarians, vegans and gluten-free consumers. Most gastropubs, bistros and modern British restaurants offer at least one pie, if not more, on their menus; sweet and savoury pies are also found in most staff canteens and school menus. Over the past two decades new pie businesses have emerged across the country, including several new 'trendy' and upmarket pie restaurant chains, such as Piecaramba, Piebury and Pieminister. The UK has also moved to protect its pie industry and brands, with protected geographical indications given to two of the most

Photo 3 Traditional pie and mash shop interior

widely known pies, Melton Mowbray Pork Pie and Cornish pasty. The latter, though associated with Cornwall, a region in southern England, has emerged as one of the most popular nationally, with Cornish pasty chains operating across the country, and internationally.

The expansion of the pie industry in the UK points to the transformative power of the private sector and its ability to construct and redefine national food. In the process the private sector has not only reinvented pie eating in the UK but has also directly engaged with new ideas about English and British national identities and food cultures. They have done so through a number of different ways, including the fusing of regional culinary traditions; the incorporation of foreign and migrant food cultures, and traditions; and the emphasis on British traditions and produce. The end results are profit-seeking endeavours and establishments that manage to reach a wide audience while engaging with, reinventing and promoting English and British national identities.

Photo 4 Traditional pie and mash shop menu

There are a number of different English culinary traditions associated with pie eating; we have mentioned one example above, the Cornish pasty. In the North of England, the traditional way of eating pie has been with mushy peas (soft-cooked dried marrowfat peas) and gravy, while in the South, particularly in and around London, it has been with mash and liquor, a parsley sauce, historically alongside jellied or stewed eels—a tradition that is rapidly disappearing. Most pie shops today offer a choice of either mash or mushy peas, or both, alongside either liquor or gravy; some have also added chips and baked beans as an offering. In most supermarkets and food retailers, pies and Cornish pasties are placed together on the shelves, obscuring any difference between them. The fusing of different regional food cultures helps contextualise them as national. This parallels many other historical case studies of national food cultures and cuisines emerging through the incorporation of ethnic and regional foods (see, e.g., Appadurai 1988). It is important to note, though, that the term regional is a complicated one. As argued by several scholars (Cook and Crang 1996; Montanari 2004), regional is a modern construction which has little to do with historic food traditions.

Beyond the incorporation of regional food traditions, most new pie restaurant chains, as well as many retail pie brands, have also redefined and broadened the concept of pie eating and traditional and national food, through the provision of greater choice and the incorporation of ethnic and migrant food cultures. The pie chain Pieminister, for example, offers over a dozen different pies, two of which are vegetarian and three vegan (for comparison, many traditional pie shops offer only around half a dozen varieties). The new pie chains also demonstrate greater awareness of a wide range of food issues that are important to consumers, from ethically and sustainably sourced products, particularly meat, to the provision of gluten-free pies and allergy charts (see Photo 5).

As the 2021 UK census demonstrates, England and Britain are more ethnically, religiously and nationally diverse than ever before. One could hypothesise that the decline of traditional pie shops, and the emergence of new 'trendy' pie chains, is to an extent related to their willingness or unwillingness to accept and embrace the changing nature of the nation. The new pie chains have broadened and redefined the concept of traditional and national food by adding ingredients, which are not usually seen as or used in British and English food, such as maple syrup, chorizo, quinoa and goat cheese. More importantly, they have included ethnic and migrant foods and flavours. A good example for this is the chain Pieminister. It offers a selection of Jamaican patties, a type of flat pie brought over to the UK by migrants from the Caribbeans, with filling that include jerk chicken (another Caribbean influence), and chickpea curry (see Photo 5). Other chains offer many similar ethnic and migrant pie fillings, with curries proving particularly popular, such as sag aloo and chicken tikka masala; the latter was famously argued two decades ago, by the then British Foreign Secretary Robin Cook, to be the British national dish. These examples of incorporating migrant and ethnic flavours and food traditions follow a long history in the UK and point to the important role played by migrants and their food cultures in the creation of British food culture (Panayi 2008). As Brown notes, the history of food in the UK is consistent with one generation's concept of foreign food

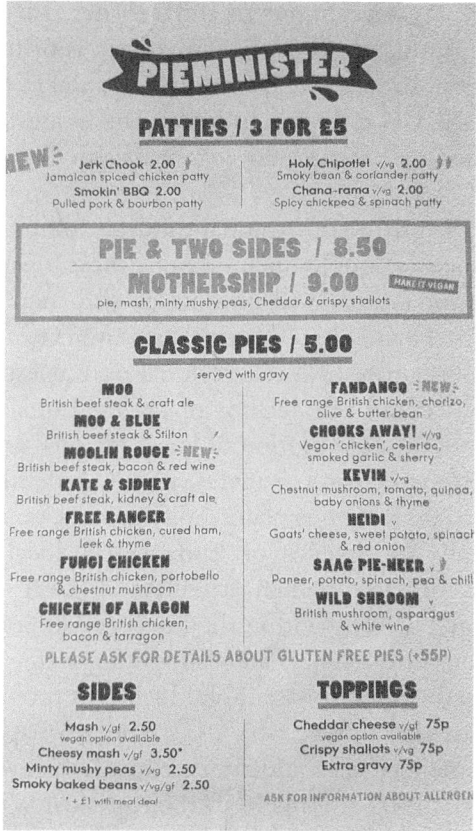

Photo 5 Pieminister's menu

being transformed into 'the next generation's traditional British' (2019: 31).

The incorporation of ethnic and migrant flavours and food traditions by pie restaurant chains and retailers does not suggest a move away from emphasising national food traditions and qualities. Indeed, one could argue that the English or British pastry shell is a necessary vehicle to integrate what might be seen as foreign. More to the point, while ethnic and migrant influences are present, there is also a clear emphasis on the promotion of the nation in a more traditional sense. There are a number of different aspects to this. First, English and British regional produce is mentioned often on restaurant menus and websites. This is done through stressing that the produce used, particularly meat, is British, often including the Red Tractor Label (which informs consumers that the product was produced in the UK to high standards), and alongside other qualitative statements, such as 'organically reared British beef' and 'free range British chicken'.

Second, English and British regional produce is emphasised, particularly cheese and meat: examples include game meat from Hampshire and Devon pork. Regional and local produce is also mentioned regarding artisanal crafted beers and ales. Through stressing the quality, authenticity and sustainable nature of local, regional and artisan produce helps construct, reproduce and reify claims of national qualities and importance. This idea, that the promotion of local, regional and artisanal food promotes, or to some extent articulates, national identities, is also suggested by Leitch (2003). She explains how, in the case of the slow food movement in Italy, its defence of 'endangered' local—and therefore national—artisan produce helped articulate a larger debate over the meaning of national identity within the European Union.

Third, pie chains and retailers are also reinterpreting and reinventing traditional national dishes, for example, Piebury's provides a scotch pie with haggis, neeps and tatties, which is a take on haggis, the Scottish national dish. Some have also added other iconic British dishes, such as fish and chips or bangers and mash, to their menus. What these actions do is further cement the traditional and national aspect of pies by associating them with other iconic national dishes. Lastly, most pie chains and retailers also resort to traditional banal nationalism. They state, for example, on their menus and websites that they sell 'award winning handmade British pies'.

There is no denying the rapid decline in what was once a traditional English and British national working-class food culture. However, it is also clear, how pie eating has been transformed and expanded to provide a new way of understanding national food culture. In many ways, the case study demonstrates the important role played by the private sector in engaging with, constructing and reinterpreting what is traditional and national food, often through the inclusion or exclusion of particular ingredients and influences. The case study also illustrates the dynamic nature of national food cultures and the ways in which they are constantly shifting and changing in response to, for example, globalisation, and changing demographics and diets.

The Scotch Whisky Industry: Lure of Banal Nationalism and the Autonomy of the Private Sector

Just as in the more generalised theme of food and identity, anthropology has been looking into the role of consumption of alcohol in the form of drinking culture in forming and maintaining group identity. Having reviewed a number of ethnographical works on the role of alcohol consumption in a variety of communities, Thomas Wilson (2005: 3) has stated:

> … drinking alcohol is an extremely important feature in the production and reproduction of ethnic, national, class, gender and local community identities, not only today but also historically, with little prospect for this importance and the situation to change.

There are a number of insights from anthropology into the relationship between alcohol and identity; that alcohol is 'a commodity and element in differential regimes of value in the history our ethnic and national groups' (Wilson 2005: 5); that 'drinking is the stuff of everyday life, quotidian culture which at the end of the day may be as important to the lifeblood of the nation as are its origin myths, heroes and grand narratives' (Wilson 2005: 12). The case study presented here is focused on Scotch whisky, but it also investigates the ways in which the private sector becomes unwittingly entangled with nationalism in its banal pursuit of profit, not in a clearly intentional endeavour to establish Scotch whisky drinking culture.[5]

---

[5] One example of this line of inquiry is Ian Russell's ethnographic investigation into North-East Scottish identity (Russell 2007).

From this perspective, Scotch whisky is interesting not as a representation of a notion of the national drink of Scotland, however defined, but as a nationally defined brand because the promotion of the brand necessarily becomes the promotion of the nation regardless of the participants' intention. This involves attributing certain meaning to as well as upholding and maintaining, the idea of 'Scotland' in the banal efforts to sell more Scotch whisky. In this regard, Scotch whisky falls in the category of place brand, in particular, a kind of 'strong territorial brands' which are studied intensively in the field of marketing in terms of brand building (Charters and Spielmann 2014 and also Jones 2003; Moss and Hume 2000; Smith 2008, 2010).

In general, when an industry becomes conscious of the need to add value through building brands, one of the ways of pursuing this aim is to integrate the 'product, price, promotion and place in new and far more effective ways' (Jones 2003: 72). The advantage of place branding for the industry is to offer 'a group of competing organizations a collective, overarching brand identity' (Charters and Spielmann 2014: 1416), and this is clearly demonstrated in the case of Scotch whisky. One of the issues that the industry has faced in its efforts to establish the 'Scotch whisky' brand is the definition of Scotch whisky. The predecessor of the Scotch Whisky Association (SWA), the present-day industry body whose declared mission is to 'protect and promote Scotch Whisky', was formed in 1912 under the name of the Wine & Spirit Brand Association in order to protect the sector against the potential fallout of the threat of tax hike proposed by the then Chancellor Lloyd George. The Association changed its name to the Whisky Association in 1917 and finally settled with the SWA in 1942.[6] By its own reckoning, the major achievements of the SWA, in its more than a hundred years of history, are being able to influence legislation either on taxation on alcohol or on definition of the product; the latter was first secured in the UK law by 1933. In the following years, a dedicated piece of legislation called Scotch Whisky Act was passed in 1988 and the SWA was very active in the run-up to the passing of Scotch Whisky Regulations in 2009. The SWA is proud of its

---

[6] Details of the Scotch Whisky Association are found on the SWA's website: http://www.scotchwhisky.org.uk/.

involvement in defining legally Scotch whisky has to come from Scotland and promoting this definition at the UK, European and global levels (SWA 2012a). The evolution of the SWA appears to fulfil the criteria for the emergence of a strong territorial brand identified by Charters and Spielmann (2014) that the brand is created by cooperation of disparate actors, not by deliberate attempts by a single actor in that the SWA is a representative of individual distilleries, who are sometimes competing against each other.

From the perspective of brand building, a clearer delineation of the place's identity which is intricately linked to a particular product is simply a necessary step for the industry's success, which has no necessary connection to any kind of nationalist project. The private sector engages with what appears to be a nationalist project of defining national identity and maintaining its integrity in order to promote the product, not to promote a particular vision of the nation in a political sense. As expected in this line of reasoning, the promotional publication of Scotch whisky published by the SWA states: 'Few products are so closely linked with the environment, culture and people of their country of origin as Scotch Whisky' (2013a: 2). The close association of the product with a certain image of Scotland is repeatedly asserted. For instance, 'Scotch Whisky is an important part of Scottish culture and identity' (SWA 2011a: 4); 'The history of Scotch Whisky is strongly linked to Scotland's culture and communities' (SWA 2012b: 5). What is obvious—the link between Scotch whisky and Scotland in that Scotch whisky can only be made in Scotland—is repeatedly cited making this connection as something to be taken for granted. While the content of Scottish identity which is associated with Scotch whisky is not usually clearly spelt out, the promotional literature places an emphasis on the importance of natural elements such as water and peat and the climate, which are often accompanied by photographs of scenes from the Highlands, rural scenes and distilleries which are typically located in a remote, rural location suggesting that association is made with purity (being natural and uncontaminated) represented by the 'rural' as opposed to the 'urban' (Hinchliffe 2009).

The industry's efforts to establish a clear identity for the product (Scotch whisky) which is inevitably tangled with various projects to establish identity of the place (Scotland) has been noted in various places.

For instance, an industry publication singles out Diago's 'Scotch initiative' as an attempt to attribute meaning to 'Scotland' on par with efforts made by the tourism industry: Diago is promoting Scotland not only as a home of Scotch whisky but also a source of knowledge and heritage apparently drawing some inspiration from the tourism industry to place more emphasis on culture and heritage (Gray 2012: 97). In this case, Diago, a multinational alcoholic beverage company headquartered in London, the UK, is no longer passively co-opted in nationalist endeavours of defining and maintaining national identity; it is now actively engaged in shaping the meaning associated with Scotland which is deemed to bring about a positive influence to its products. This is an example of different dynamics between an ostensibly commercial activity—brand building—and banal nationalism. Diago is sometimes an unwitting participant of banal nationalism in Scotland in that it is unintentionally lending support for efforts to define and maintain certain identity profiles for Scotland but at times, it is a more conscious and focused participant in the business of national identity construction and maintenance shifting the focus of our analysis away from routinised, taken-for-granted behaviour which characterises banal nationalism.

As with many other 'territorial brands', Scotch whisky is strongly associated with tourism promotion (SWA 2011a; Gray 2012). The SWA's 2011 report on Scotch whisky and tourism has a wealth of data to highlight Scotch whisky's contribution to the promotion of tourism to Scotland in particular and Britain in general: visitor centres and distilleries providing 640 jobs and contributing to the economy in tune of £14 million; against the background of culture and heritage being responsible for more than a quarter of spending in the UK by overseas tourists, Scotch whisky stands out as an ambassador of Scotland in a crowded international market; it is particularly important to attract tourist to rural area and so on (SWA 2011a). These points are highlighted by the SWA in its efforts to impress the industry's contribution to society in the form of economic benefits. The noticeable point here is that the industry, unwittingly or otherwise, projects itself according to the nationalist logic; the industry is a good citizen because it contributes to the welfare of society which is, more often than not, equated with the nation. Because of the multinational nature of the UK, in the case of Scotch whisky, the designation of the nation sometimes shifts from Scotland to the UK (or more likely, Britain), which somewhat obscures the overall picture of the ways in which the industry is co-opted in a nationalist project which is deemed to have all-pervasive influence.

Still, it is fair to say these efforts made by the Scotch whisky industry to promote Scotland are of a derivative nature, a by-product of their efforts to define Scotch whisky and to secure its legal status as a means of promoting and protecting the product. The SWA itself acknowledges the Association's greatest achievement is found in this regard. The predecessor of the SWA was founded in part in response to the 1908–1909 Royal Commission which examined the question of what is whisky; the first piece of UK law on the definition of whisky was passed in 1933; a dedicated Scotch Whisky Act was passed at Westminster in 1988 and in the same year, the Scotch Whisky geographical indication (GI) was secured; during the 1990s against tax decimation placed by countries such as Japan, Korea and Chile, the SWA secured strong regulations on the definition of Scotch whisky, protected Scotch as a drink coming only from Scotland through intensive lobbying activities; in 2009 Scotch Whisky Regulations were adopted by the UK government further tightening the definition of Scotch whisky (Moss and Hume 2000: 229; SWA 2009, 2011c, 2012a). In its efforts to secure more preferable conditions for the product, the Scotch whisky industry has been working closely with various legislative bodies including the Scottish Parliament, the UK Parliament and the European Parliament as well as indirectly with the World Trade Organization (WTO). This is yet another point where the industry's pursuit of profit sometimes overlaps with the political institution's promotion of the nation. The dynamics in this regard are complex due to current devolutionary measures which have brought about the establishment of the Scottish Parliament and Government (initially known as Executive) with devolved powers. The SWA's initial attitudes towards the Scottish Government were cautious. As the Scottish Parliament and Government started to exercise devolved powers, however, the communication between the industry and the Scottish polity became dense and close to the extent that some in the industry started to express preference of designating legal authority in relation to the definition of Scotch whisky to the Scottish level by saying 'the Scottish

Parliament is a natural home for this' (Smith 2010: 440), arguably an expression of the industry's being co-opted in the Scottish polity's efforts to promote the Scottish framework.

What is interesting here is the SWA's reaction to the establishment of a new Scottish National Party (SNP) majority government in May 2011. The SNP's credential in putting Scotland first was firmly established and if the Scotch whisky industry was fully integrated in banal and rather passive nationalist endeavours focusing on defining the nation's identity and on promoting it, an SNP-majority government would be seen as largely positive. The SWA's reaction was cautious. It prepared a briefing sheet for the Members of Scottish Parliament (MSPs) emphasising the industry's contribution to Scottish society and economy, which was widely known and acknowledged by political parties in Scotland, and extolled them to work even harder to protect and promote Scotch whisky (SWA 2011b). In particular, the SWA was opposed to the SNP's manifesto commitment of the introduction of minimum unit pricing for alcohol (MUP) arguing that it was ineffective and most likely illegal in many jurisdictions while publicly stating its continued support for the Scottish Government Alcohol Industry Partnership to tackle alcohol-related problems such as alcohol misuse (SWA 2011c). The SWA's unease with the SNP government was mostly spelt out in its opposition to MUP, not in reference to any aspect of a nationalist project. Their concern over the prospect of referendum was framed in a language of business referring to stability and predictability that were deemed to be essential for the industry's success.

Despite the emergence of an ethno-cultural attachment to the Scottish polity within it, and that of being co-opted into a nationalist project to promote Scotland in some ways, the Scotch whisky industry demonstrated a degree of autonomy as a private sector actor in regard to the 2014 independence referendum. While acknowledging the firm and inseparable link between Scotch whisky and Scotland, the SWA prioritised its concern for ensuring stability and predictability as a business over its support for the possible advantage of defining Scotland more clearly with independence (SWA 2013b, 2014a). Utmost care appeared to have been paid to be seen as a neutral participant rather than an 'anti-Scottish' one in the debate. For instance, its 2013 annual review clearly

Chapter Three: Consuming Nations—The Construction... 99

acknowledges the importance of the forthcoming referendum in 2014 as articulated in the words of David Frost, the Chief Executive:

> The people of Scotland face a historic choice in September's independence referendum. The implications are huge and the basis for the eventual decision needs to be fully discussed. So I make no apology for dealing with it at length. (SWA 2013b: 4)

Frost then goes on to emphasise the Scottishness of Scotch whisky and Scotch whisky industry:

> This industry is in a special position in this debate. We can make Scotch Whisky only in Scotland and our brands are indissolubly linked with it. 35,000 jobs depend on the industry. Our operations are at the heart of many communities around Scotland and we sustain economic activity in rural and remote areas that might otherwise have difficulty in attracting it. (SWA 2013b: 4)

Still, he brings the reader's attention to the factors that have supported the success of the industry rather than to possible advantage the industry may acquire should independence results in the referendum:

> In short, as we consider the potential impact of constitutional change, we look for reassurance on how an independent Scotland could deliver a business, regulatory, and export environment at least as supportive as that which the industry currently enjoys.
>
> Whatever the result on 18 September, we are committed to working with government in the future to deliver sustainable economic growth—either helping to shape the policy regime for an independent Scotland or engaging in the debate about further devolution. That is what the people of Scotland would expect and it is what I am determined to deliver. (SWA 2013b: 5)

In these pronouncements, the SWA is acting as an autonomous agent rather than a co-opted one putting its business interest first against a nationalist framework, thus resisting the conforming pressure of banal nationalism. At the same time, the SWA is careful not to undermine its image of a good Scottish citizen by clearly stating its intention to work with whatever Scottish people choose.

As soon as the referendum was over, the SWA published a statement welcoming the stability the referendum result brought in and resumed its efforts to emphasise the inseparable link between Scotland and Scotch whisky: 'The Scotch Whisky industry is determined to play a leading role in shaping discussions that are fundamental to the future success of our industry and our nation' (SWA 2014b). The SWA also uttered what may be seen as its willingness to be part of the Scottish nationalist project. In its submission to the Smith Commission on Devolution, the SWA not only reiterated the importance of the Scotch whisky industry to Scotland but also indicated its support for further empowerment of the Scottish Parliament in regard to tax-raising, spending and policy-making (SWA 2014c). When it made the case for more power to the Scottish Parliament, the SWA used a kind of language which would be more readily associated with the SNP than the SWA, an industry body: 'Any new powers should help to deliver the fairer and more prosperous Scotland to which so many people—on both sides of the referendum debate—aspired during the campaign' (SWA 2014c).

The brief case study of the Scotch whisky industry has shown that the private sector can be co-opted into a nationalist project through banal nationalism which is part and parcel of everyday life of contemporary society. However, the case study has also shown that the private sector is not completely taken over by the supposedly hegemonic power of nationalism. The Scotch whisky industry works within the framework of banal nationalism in establishing and promoting the brand, but when it comes to the constitutional question, the industry acted as an autonomous agent prioritising its business interest over and against nationalist interest. It is worth noting that in the post-referendum period, the SWA appeared to have assumed again its more overtly pro-Scottish stance supporting devolution of more powers that are related to Scotch whisky to the Scottish Parliament, which in turn appears to suggest the SWA is seeing Scotland as an increasingly pertinent territorial entity for the industry. This goes some way to question Andy Smith's conclusion that the UK remains to be the most significant territorial entity for the Scotch whisky industry in post-devolution Scotland (Smith 2010). It may be simply the case that the observation presented in this chapter is better at capturing the evolution of Scotland as a space for politics due to the chapter's focus on nationalism.

Conclusion

The two case studies have shown different ways in which the food industry, a private sector actor, engages with nationalism in contemporary society. The first case study illustrates the ways in which the private sector can, often unwittingly, contribute to the updating, redefining, maintaining and promoting of national identity through food items. While the traditional pie shops are in a terminal decline in the UK, pies as a category of food that represents Britishness are thriving on the supermarket shelves as well as high street chains. This has been brought about, not because the pie manufacturers and restaurants set out to promote a certain vision of Britishness/Englishness but because for them nationality sells. The demise of pie shops in contrast to the burgeoning pie industry simply points to the dynamic way food reflects what society is experiencing, and nationalism/national identity can be a useful and effective tool for the manufacturers and caterers to maximise their profit. In contrast, in the second case study, the Scotch whisky industry can clearly be seen as being involved in endeavours to define and promote the identity of Scotland, and in this sense, it is more ostensibly behaving as a nationalist. This is due to the nature of the product to be promoted—Scotch whisky; it is a territorially built brand, and in the case of Scotland, the territory in question roughly coincided with a nation. It appears at times that the Scotch whisky industry is fully immersed in the nationalist framework in its efforts to promote its product. However, as the SWA's behaviour during and after the independence referendum of 2014 shows, the industry is not completely co-opted in a nationalist project but is able to exercise its agency to be an independent actor, suggesting yet another aspect of the idea of banal nationalism that needs to be examined further. The idea of banal nationalism sometimes uncritically assigns hegemonic power to a nationalist project and assumes a high degree of homogeneity among a variety of actors as Skey has pointed out (Skey 2009). The brief analysis of the SWA's behaviour suggests more attention should be given to the autonomy of actors in their seemingly conformist actions.

Beyond showing the different ways in which the food industry relates to nationalism in its pursuit of profits, the two case studies also point to the significance of the general phenomenon of globalisation. The fact that the pie industry is thriving in the contemporary UK is partly attributed to the efforts made by the manufacturers to cater for ever diversifying tastes. Pies are still British but could be with Jamaican or Indian flavours reflecting the migrant population's experience. They could be vegetarian, vegan or gluten-free—they are still British. This strategy is adopted, it seems, in order to tie people to a specific geographical location through taste so as to provide them with a degree of security and comfort (and in some cases, excitement) in a globalising world characterised by fast-paced changes. The strategy makes the most of ethno-cultural attachment people have in the course of action. Food being such a primary material is well-suited to be used in this strategy. The history of the SWA's activity is also a history of an industry responding to various phases of globalisation. The SWA is determined to protect the Scotch whisky brand because it can be only made in Scotland, not anywhere else—a powerful selling point in the globalised market. In fact, the SWA's concern is focused on protecting the Scotch whisky brand abroad, hence its focus on GI and the EU and WTO regulations which have direct impact on their trade.[7] The SWA's seemingly nationalist behaviour is largely played out in response to globalisation in the form of expanding market. The two case studies appear to suggest therefore the main culprit in shoring up the nationalist framework is in fact globalisation, an idea which will be continuously addressed throughout the book.

---

[7] The role of GIs in food and nationalism is investigated in "Chapter Eight: International Organisations, Food and Nationalism".

Part II

Official/Top-Down: The Nation-State, Food and Nationalism

Chapter Four: Food and Diet in 'Official' Nationalism

As the current volume has demonstrated, the issue of food in nationalism/national identity is more often than not approached from banal or everyday nationalism angles. To repeat some of our arguments in the book, this is because the quotidian nature of food and eating lends itself well to the investigation of nationalism in the private sphere, the kind of investigation which has become more mainstream recently in the study of nationalism. However, an investigation of food and nationalism is not complete if it ignores the relatively well-studied, official or public side since nationalism works both in the public and private spheres.

From its historical evolution as a political ideology, to its impact on political movements and the structure of the global political system and to its current manifestation and resurgence, nationalism has been and is largely discussed and examined in relation to the nation-state, which is where we now turn our attention to. The current and the following chapters will focus on 'food and nationalism' in the more conventional setting in which the investigative focus is on the nation-state and what it does. "Chapter Four: Food and Diet in 'Official' Nationalism", "Chapter Five: National Food in the International Context I—Gastrodiplomacy" and "Chapter Six: National Food in the International Context II—Gastronationalism and Populism" examine 'food and nationalism' in the context in which the nation-state is seen as the major actor of nationalism, often as the main nation-builder; subsequent chapters will examine the nation-state and its relationship with and to the international system. The current chapter concentrates on the internal aspect of the nation-state's involvement with the construction, maintenance and transformation of the nation, while "Chapter Five: National Food in the International Context I—Gastrodiplomacy" and "Chapter Six: National Food in the International Context II—Gastronationalism and Populism" consider the external dimensions.

The shift of focus away from the bottom-up views to the perspective of the nation-state as the main nation-builder can indicate several approaches. The shift could facilitate the investigation of 'food and nationalism' in the increasingly contested context of the public-private distinction in modern society, taking into account the implications of the advent of welfare state, the increasing penetration of neoliberalism and the lightning pace of technological development. As Díaz-Méndez and Gómez-Benito (2010) have shown in their investigation of the emergence and propagation of the 'Mediterranean diet' in Spain, an investigation into this area can produce useful insights into the role of the nation-state in contemporary society highlighting the impact of increasingly technocratic aspects of the modern state on nationalism.

It also suggests a more conventional approach to nationalism, a modernist approach in which the rise of nationalism is tied to the notion of modernisation in the broadest sense.[1] This is the territory which has been examined and argued by the eminent scholars of nationalism including Ernest Gellner, Benedict Anderson, Eric Hobsbawm, Michael Hechter, Tom Nairn, John Breuilly, Anthony Giddens and Michael Mann, to name but a few (Gellner 1983; Anderson 1992; Hobsbawm 1990; Nairn 1977; Hechter 1975; Breuilly 1982; Giddens 1985; Mann 1993). The basic tenet here is that the nation is created by nationalism which works through the apparatus of the modern state in response to industrialisation, capitalist expansion, competition amongst the states and so on. The predominant focus on the structural aspect of the development of

---

[1] For an insightful discussion of the differentiation of modernisation and westernisation in the non-western societies (Ottoman Turkey and Meiji Japan in particular) in the nineteenth century, see Esenbel (1994).

nationalism has been problematised in response to the rise of the everyday nationhood approach which argues for attributing more importance to the individual's agency rather than treating individuals as something to be formed and moulded by institutions (Fox and Miller-Idriss 2008a; Ichijo 2013).

These leading scholars of nationalism have not paid much attention to the 'food and nationalism' theme. Food and diet are often subsumed in the discussion of manipulation of symbols by the state or the elite in society, in this line of investigation, as explored in the celebrated work by Hobsbawm and Ranger (1983), *The Invention of Tradition*. Reflecting this situation, until relatively recently, there were not many studies on the role of the nation-state in nationalism that focused on the ways in which food is used. A handful of studies including Arjun Appadurai (1988), Igor Cusack's work on African states (2000, 2003, 2004) and Pilcher on Mexico (1996, 1998) have applied the conventional, top-down approach to nationalism to the evolution of national cuisine and illustrated the different social forces at work as discussed in the introduction to this volume. More recently, there has been a noticeable shift towards focusing on the role of the nation-state, for example, Cwiertka with regard to Japan and Korea (2006, 2015); Ichijo, Johannes and Ranta (2019) on the emergence, or non-emergence, of national food; Raviv on Israel (2015); and Simpson-Miller on Ghana (2022).

The lack of sufficient attention to the apparent mundane issues of food and diet in the conventional theories of nationalism is therefore a lacuna this chapter and the following ones attempt to address. Food and diet are given particular meaning by the state and state-backed organisations in pursuit of the nation-state's objectives, most commonly to sustain the nation-state's independence, which at times is articulated as food self-sufficiency. Therefore in this line of inquiry, the focus tends to be placed on the idea of 'official' nationalism of a modernising state (e.g., Germany, Japan and Turkey) and the nationalist forces in the colonial context.

While the 'top-down' aspect of nationalism in these cases is on the whole well-surveyed, what the chapter shows is that the particular quality the 'food and nationalism' angle can assume, when investigating these cases for modernisation, is not only about structures and institutions but also about values and meanings. As it has been pointed out mainly by anthropologists, food is not only material to sustain life but also imbued with symbolism and meanings, and food and diet easily turn into an ideological battleground. This is particularly relevant, as we will demonstrate below and in subsequent chapters, for attempts by the state to mobilise food in order to defend, reshape and/or transform the nation.

The chapter highlights what the 'food and nationalism' angle can bring to the study of 'top-down' nationalism. It investigates the reasons why food and diet can be powerful tools for the state and the state-sponsored organisations to pursue a nationalist programme by examining several examples including Japan, Italy, Germany and Israel/Palestine in a comparative context.

Food, Diet and Nationalism in a Comparative Historical Perspective: Japan, Germany and Italy

Meiji Japan

Meiji Japan, which came into being in 1868 as a result of a coup d'état by disgruntled, middle- and lower-ranking samurais from peripheral domains with the emperor as the figurehead, is often associated with a top-down form of nationalism which is led by the state in contrast to a more voluntaristic version found in, for example, eighteenth-century England (Greenfeld 1992; Kohn 1944). Because Japan was a latecomer to industrial and capitalist development as well as imperialism, it is often argued that the 1868 coup led to the establishment of an overtly strong and centralised state which pursued a series of reformist programmes to modernise Japanese society. One of the major objectives of the early Meiji Japanese government was to 'enrich the country, strengthen the military' which framed a number of policy areas including diet (Ichijo 2013; Takeda 2008; Cwiertka 2006). In discussing the establishment of the tripartite structure of Japanese, Chinese and western cuisine in modern Japan, Cwiertka (2006) focuses on the role of conscription in introducing meat, a food item which had not been widely consumed since the mid-Edo period, to the diet of ordinary Japanese. Conscription was part and parcel of Japanese modernisation to 'strengthen the military'. While Tokugawa Japan was never militarily defeated by the western nations, the ruling class of the time was made aware of the inferiority of the Japanese military system both in terms of equipment and organisation through several armed clashes between some domains and western powers in the 1860s. They were also aware of the defeat of Qing China in the First Opium War (1839–1842). Before the Meiji government engaged with modernisation/westernisation of the Japanese military system, Tokugawa shogunate had started to introduce western equipment and ideas. Since it did not have the modern, centralised structure of governing, Tokugawa shogunate never got round to make specific policies related to education, health, diet and so on with a view to 'strengthen the military', but with a newly instituted, modern and centralised system of governance such as compulsory primary education (introduced in 1872) and conscription (1873), the Meiji government's involvement with 'food and nationalism' is recorded and easier to trace.

The role of conscription in nation-building is well-documented (see, for the classical study, Weber 1976). Cwiertka (2006: Ch. 3) points out two relevant effects of conscription to our concern in 'food and nationalism'. First, conscription contributed to the homogenisation of the food ordinary people of various parts of Japan ate, because the conscripts were subjected to a unified routine for a period of time—the very essence of homogenising effects of conscription. When they went home upon completing their service, they brought back their new knowledge of what was eaten elsewhere in Japan, thus contributing to the establishment of the idea of 'Japanese cuisine'. Second, it introduced meat into the diet of ordinary Japanese from which meat had been largely absent for the preceding 200 years or so. While the establishment of the Japanese cuisine through homogenisation of diet of ordinary Japanese was probably one of the unintended consequences of the Meiji government's drive to modernise Japanese society, the introduction of meat to the diet was a deliberate act by the Meiji government to achieve the objective of strengthening the military. The military introduced meat into the diet of their conscripts in order to combat the problem of vitamin B deficiency that comes with heavy reliance on polished white rice (Ohnuki-Tierney 1999).

The (re)introduction of meat into Japanese diet in the Meiji era was a top-down affair, part and parcel of the project of 'civilisation and improvement'. Adopting a western style of diet including menus and manners was one aspect of the national mission to modernise/westernise Japanese society in order to catch up with the West. The underlying assumption was the inferiority of Japanese society and people in many aspects of life including physique. In order to compete with westerners, the Japanese needed to eat like westerners, many Meiji elites reasoned. And the Meiji Emperor led the way. In 1871, he eliminated the prohibition of eating meat in the imperial household and issued an order that the imperial kitchen should serve meat on a regular basis (Harada 2005; Ohnuki-Tierney 1999; Cwiertka 2006). The military in this regard was merely following the lead from the top.

This top-down gesture did not go unopposed despite an extremely large amount of authority attributed to the Emperor. The idea of being defiled from eating meat persisted among the general population till about the 1920s (Ohnuki-Tierney 1999). It is also suggested that because of the combination of the custom of meat avoidance and the scarce supply of meat, it was not until the 1960s when Japan experienced a rapid economic growth that meat became an everyday item on the table for the majority of Japanese people (Ehara 2014). More starkly, in response to the Emperor's order to the imperial kitchen to serve meat on a regular basis, a group of nativist cult priests attempted to enter the Imperial Palace in 1872 to censure the Emperor of his decision and to ask him to reinstate the prohibition of meat eating (Ohnuki-Tierney 1999). The incident ended with a number of deaths but the momentum of 'civilisation and improvement' through meat eating continued unabated, perhaps testifying to the power of the modern, centralised nation-state.

The promotion of meat eating led by the Emperor, the very top of the new Japanese polity, however, did not dislodge rice from its position at the heart of Japanese diet. Meat eating was promoted *as well as*, not *instead of*, the idea of rice as the staple even in the army (Cwiertka 2006, Ohnuki-Tierney 1993). The representation of rice as the Japanese collective self was established in the post-Meiji era, and the association of purity of white rice with Japanese spiritual superiority was overtly enhanced during World War II; 'white rice—symbolically the most powerful but nutritionally the most deficient—was saved for the most precious sector of the population—the soldiers' (Ohnuki-Tierney 1993: 106). The situation during World War II could be easily explained by the dwindling supply of food including meat and white rice, but the top-down promotion of meat eating as well as the preservation of the cult of white rice continued in the postwar era. The defeat in World War II was often attributed to poor Japanese physique and the inclusion of protein items in diet was therefore encouraged by the postwar government.[2] At the same time, the white rice has kept its place as the essence of Japanese collective self, and the postwar, 'symbolic' and constitutional emperors' chief duty is to pray for abundant harvest of rice every autumn.

And in Germany and Italy

It is easily expected that a top-down approach to food as a tool of pursuing a nationalist project would be prominent under an authoritarian or totalitarian regime, or under a wartime regime. The Nazis, which met both conditions, were not an exception. As they took power in Germany and started to plan for war to ensure the German society's survival in the 1930s, Nazi leaders were paying a lot of attention to food and diet (Treitel 2009). By the means of their formidable propaganda machine which loudly propagated the idea of harmonious and homogeneous national community (Welch 2004), the message that eating more naturally was good for the country: it 'would promote racial health, boost physical performance, and maximize the efficient use of resources, all qualities needed to fight and win the coming war' (Treitel 2009). In this case, eating more naturally meant less meat and more plant food which could be produced in German lands. Corinna Treitel (2009) analyses the Nazi promotion of 'natural diet' and points out a number of factors behind it. With the memory of hunger and starvation during and in the immediate aftermath of World War I still fresh, the Nazis made achieving nutritional self-sufficiency a priority, and nudging the population away from eating

---

[2] The consumption of whale meat in Japan needs to be seen in this context. In the aftermath of World War II, whales were seen as a cheap and accessible source of protein to nurture Japanese population.

meat, which was reliant on imports, was one of the ways to approach nutritional self-sufficiency. In addition, there was a long-standing call for promoting vegetarianism in order to improve the health of the nation as well as the nation's economy in Germany. The Nazis did not embrace vegetarianism as such; rather the Nazi state recommended and promoted what it called 'a mixed diet' from which 'the artificial' was removed. Instead of industrially produced bread with chemically treated wheat flour, the Germans were encouraged to eat whole-grain loaves in order to increase health, fitness and fertility. To encourage the Germans to take up a natural diet, the Nazi leaders turned their attention to agricultural policies which had economic and ideological objectives. The economic objective was to achieve nutritional self-sufficiency with the introduction of a type of organic farming called biodynamics to replenish the soil which had been depleted of nitrates due to war efforts during World War I. The ideological objective was to nurture a healthy nation firmly linked to its land reflecting the romantic view of nationhood emphasising the organic nature of the nation.

In the minds of the Nazi leaders, the natural diet was the foundation for their war efforts, to promote racial and national health with efficient management of resources available. It was defined by down-to-earth economic considerations as well as an organic vision of the race and nation which emphasised the importance of being firmly rooted in one's environment to achieve health. The Nazi example illustrates the multifaceted utility of the 'food and nationalism' in investigating politics; because food is essential to life, it is about political economy which any state thrives to manage. Because it has an immense capacity to carry symbolism, it can carry a variety of ideologies, some of which may be mutually contradictory but are held in one item.

The importance the Nazi regime placed on food extended beyond the nation's diet. Food was one of the central motivations behind its decision to invade Poland in 1939 and in its thinking regarding the nature of the nation-state. Influenced by the experience of starvation during World War I, which was blamed as a key factor for the loss, Nazi leaders sought to ensure sufficient food production to satisfy the future needs of the nation and the army, taking into account future expansion through military conquest. This would be accomplished not only by changing the national diet but also through the expansion of agricultural lands open to farmers and cultivation in the east, known as *Lebensraum* (lit. 'living space'), which resembled a highly racialised and genocidal version of settler colonialism. In addition, Nazi leaders envisioned a reduction in the food allocated to those deemed as either not belonging to the nation or unworthy, which would further ensure adequate supplies (Collingham 2012). In short, food and achieving self-sufficiency were central to the Nazi nation-state.

Interestingly, the Nazi ideas of 'autarky' or self-sufficiency might have been copied from its close ideological and strategic ally Italy. Under Benito Mussolini, fascist Italy promoted, what it termed, an 'ideal Italian diet' based on locally produced grains, legumes, fruit and vegetables, and restricted the use of meat products. The diet was promoted through direct government intervention in the economy and the agricultural sector and restricted food imports (Helstosky 2004). The government's intervention in the nation's diet was based on a number of elements which linked together what people ate, the requirements of the state, the Italian food markets and global supplies. In particular, the fascist government sought to reduce imports of cheap grains and the promotion of local products, at times to the detriment of the Italian public. This can be seen in the regime's promotion of humble and simple Italian food items, such as pig's ears, lettuce soup, meat balls and polenta, at the expense of, what it saw as an unhealthy national obsession with pasta (Helstosky 2003: 127). The focus on reducing pasta consumption, to combat growing food and grain imports, and the promotion of bread, rice and polenta as substitutes went against traditional Italian foodways, particularly in southern Italy (Garvin 2014).

Domestic cookbooks implored upon housewives the importance of buying only Italian products and to be proud of cooking traditional and humble food, such as polenta. Basing their arguments on modernisation, nutrition and national success, national cookbooks, such as *La Cucina Futurista*, and popular magazines rallied against the expenses of the middle class and promoted the ideas of self-sufficiency (Helstosky 2003). The propaganda campaign also included the dissemination of 'appropriate' regional cooking ideas and recipes nationally, in what can be seen as an attempt to homogenise the national cuisine. The government's intervention was also not limited to food items. Through its various publications, the state called for the reorganisation of the domestic kitchen, in terms of space, equipment and workload. The fascist state was linking together the structure and function of the domestic sphere (kitchen) with that of the national one, providing and promoting the performance of the nation at the centre of the house and domestic life (Garvin 2014). However, while the 'fascist association between nation and food has mostly a negative impact on health and consumer expectations', it did have a direct effect on what is now seen as 'a characteristically Italian form of cuisine' (Helstosky 2004: 19).

'Food and Nationalism' in a Modernised State: The Japanese Government's Rice Policy Since 1945

The direct intervention of the government in food policies to pursue nation-building and national aims is also evident in the example of Japan's rice policies. The symbolic importance of rice, in particular white rice, in Japanese society has been noted widely (Ohnuki-Tierney 1993, 1999; Cwiertka 2006; Francks 1998, 2007; Knecht 2007). As a latecomer to modernisation, the Japanese state is often seen as a strong state taking the lead in various spheres of life. Putting the two together suggests the government-led, top-down programme to protect and promote rice as the stable food for Japanese should be a feature of modern Japanese society. As reviewed briefly earlier, in Meiji Japan, the government was promoting and encouraging rice cultivation as part of its 'enrich the country, strengthen the military' strategy while advocating meat eating as a way of improving the health and fitness of the nation. As seen in the Nazi and fascist Italy examples, the importance of securing enough food, rice in the Japanese case, to feed the population was emphasised under war conditions. The idea of rice as the staple food for the Japanese had long been established by the end of World War II (Ohnuki-Tierney 1993). In postwar Japan, rice farmers came to be seen as the most powerful interest group which kept the Liberal Democratic Party in power for a long time,

Chapter Four: Food and Diet in 'Official' Nationalism

and the rice market became the symbol of the closed nature of Japanese society in successive trade negotiations, in particular since the 1980s (Francks 1998; Horiuchi and Saito 2010).

The Food Control System which was in place as late as 1994 arguably embodies the assumption that the government-led promotion of rice cultivation and consumption was a prominent feature of postwar Japanese nationalism. The system was based on the 1942 Staple Food Control Act, a wartime legislation which aimed to 'guarantee a sufficient supply of rice for its fighting soldiers and to provide for an equal distribution of rice to non-combatant citizens to keep them healthy' (Knecht 2007: 16–17). The law attributed the central role to the state in planning and distributing the entire supply of the staple food, thus rendering the control of the country to the state (Francks 1998; Knecht 2007). The 1942 act was supersede by the revision in 1952, and under the 1952 act the government retained the exclusive right only to rice; salt and other items were freed from the state monopoly. The rice producers were obligated to sell rice at an officially set price to the government, which alone was authorised to sell it to third parties. The system, made up of the Food Agency of the Ministry of Agriculture, Forestry and Fisheries, Zenno, the nationwide agricultural cooperative, wholesalers and retailers of rice, worked for the farmers because it acted as a guarantee of a minimum income and for the government because it had in principle the control of the whole country, but did not benefit the consumers who had to pay 'an extraordinary high price for rice relative to the world price' (Fell and MacLarren 2013: 617). The Food Control System afforded a high level of protection to the rice market in Japan.

The puzzle here was that the consumers did not revolt against the government's control of rice. When the closed nature of the Japanese rice market became a regular item in international negotiations in the 1980s, the majority of the consumers was against the liberalisation of rice import because Japanese rice tasted better and because in any case it was not too expensive even compared to imported rice (Ohnuki-Tierney 1993: 25). This attitude contrasted their generally relaxed attitudes towards imported food; by 1988 35.9 per cent of fish and shellfish were imported, 14.6 per cent of grains, 14.8 per cent of meat and 12.7 per cent of fruits (Ohnuki-Tierney 1993: 27). Clearly Japanese consumers treated rice as a different kind of agricultural produce from others suggesting that they had internalised the idea of rice as a representation of Japaneseness and that they were willingly colluding with the government, rice farmers and retailers to maintain rice sacred.

Still the statistics show that rice consumption steadily declined over the years while the idea of 'rice as the Japanese self' did not wither. Per capita consumption of rice peaked in 1962 and almost halved by the end of the 1990s (Chern et al. 2003). This could mean that the reason why the Japanese consumers acquiesced with the extortionate price for rice for a long while was because they were eating less and less of it, so they did not feel the pinch. However, what is sometimes referred to as Heisei Rice Riots of 1993–1994 suggests otherwise. Due to exceptionally cold summer, rice crop in autumn 1993 failed and the government was forced to resort to emergency import of rice in order to make up for the shortfall. This led to a series of events including criticisms towards the government's failure to secure the rice crop, the rumours about imported rice and panic buying of domestically produced rice (Francks 1998; Horie 2004; Knecht 2007). Any panic is irrational but this one was particularly so given that while the supply of Japanese-produced rice fell short of the demand, there was more than enough supply from abroad. There was in a way no shortage of rice as such; it was shortage of domestically produced rice that led to a series of panics, which may indicate the degree to which the idea of rice as the embodiment of Japaneseness had been internalised (Ishikawa 1994). In particular the hysteria about the imported rice was suggestive: rumours circulated to strengthen the belief that eating foreign, imported rice would be hazardous to one's health because of heavy use of chemicals in growing and during the shipping of rice (Knecht 2007). Concern that rice importation would undermine the fundamental aspect of Japanese society of being built on rice cultivation was expressed by a variety of people (Knecht 2007). Clearly rice was 'not simply food to fill the stomach. Japanese attitudes and behaviours towards rice are not governed by economic rationale' (Ohnuki-Tierney 1993: 28).

What was ironic was that the Heisei Rice Riots took place while the negotiations for the Uruguay Round of GATT were taking place. In December 1993, the Japanese government agreed to a partial liberalisation of the rice market as part of conditions to the accession to the World

Trade Organization (Francks 1998). The opening up of the Japanese market did not come because of the pressure from the consumer but because of the 'external' pressure of the general trend of globalisation of trade. A year later, in December 1994, New Food Act was passed by the Diet which signalled the demise of the Food Control System. Under the new regime, the farmers were allowed to sell their crops freely without being subjected to the government's control. The regime was further reformed in 2004 and anyone could now engage with selling and distributing rice as long as they were registered with the government. All these reforms are seen as the government's efforts to prepare the rice farmers to face up global competition.

The evolution of postwar Japanese government's rice policy suggests a weakening of officially sponsored nationalism due to the pressure of globalisation. However, the discourse around rice has not changed much. It is still the case that 'a bowl of steaming, pure white, home-grown rice remains a convenient symbol of the essential and enduring qualities of "traditional" Japanese life' (Francks 2007: 148). This may indicate the triumph of top-down nationalism; the idea of rice as the essence of Japaneseness has successfully been internalised by the population after years of works by the successive government. The idea that because rice embodies the Japanese national self, domestically produced rice is the best for the Japanese, which came to the surface during the Heisei Rice Riots, arguably constitutes part of the anti-globalisation movement in Japan as seen in the current opposition to the Trans-Pacific Partnership scheme.

The above brief survey points to the utility of food for the nation-state in pursuit of a variety of objectives. The utility stems from the life-sustaining quality of food, its fundamental role and food's symbolic capacity. The above also shows that with the advent of the modern, centralised nation-state, the use of food, diet, nutrition and health by the state in order to define and enhance the nation and that fills the nation-state frame has become much more evident. Furthermore, food provides a link between humans and the environment through agriculture—working on the land—and therefore ties humans to a particular geological and geographical location which can also be imbued with symbolism. The latter point poses a particular challenge to a settler society such as Israel, which is explored in detail in the rest of the chapter.

Zionism and the Creation of Jewish State in Palestine

Nationalist ideologies do not appear on the surface to be overly concerned with ideas relating to food and diet, and in this respect, Zionism is no exception. However, and as will be demonstrated below, nationalist ideas and ideals regarding, among other things, the economy, national security and immigration, require at times direct engagement and intervention in and with food production and the public's diet.

Zionism is an ideology that arose in the late nineteenth century in Europe and that had as its main aim the creation of a separate state for Jews in Palestine. Zionism as an ideology, and the political movement that it spawned, were born in response to the growing European failure to integrate Jews socially and politically—a process known also as emancipation—and to the rise of modern racial anti-Semitism, in particular in Central and Eastern Europe. The failure of Jewish emancipation also hindered attempts to reform, modernise and secularise Jewish life in Europe. As such, Zionism sought to provide the answer for the problems faced by Jews in Europe. Zionism was based on the creation of a Jewish homeland in Palestine, known by Jews as *Eretz Yisrael* ('the Land of Israel') and, through the process of settling the land, creating a new Jewish cultural and national identity that would be premised on the negation of diaspora Jewish identity and culture. The creation of a new Jewish identity and state would be achieved through the revival and monopolisation of the Hebrew language and the radical transformation and modernisation of Jewish political, cultural, social and economic life (Laqueur 2003). Specifically with regard to food, we argue that Zionism sought to utilise food, including its production, commodification and consumption, to accomplish three main tasks: create a new Jewish identity; establish a Jewish separate economy and polity in Palestine; and support the integration of new immigrants based on a melting pot approach. The period this case study deals with is roughly from the beginning of Zionist immigration to Palestine at the end of the nineteenth century, through the establishment of a British Mandate over Palestine (1919–1948) and up to the early state period in the 1950s.

The 'New' Jew

Though Zionism as a national movement is associated with the establishment of a settler-colonial Jewish state in Israel/Palestine, it had as one of its main aims the construction of a new Jewish identity.

The 'new' Jew was to be an 'antithesis' to the 'old' Jew of the diaspora (Laqueur 2003). In a similar manner to other cultural nationalist movements (see, e.g., Hutchinson 1987), the new national movement and identity were based on the romantic notion of an ethnic group returning to the land and the soil, to nature and to agriculture. At the heart of the construction of the 'new' Jew therefore was a strong emphasis on agricultural work and rural life. This included the establishment of communal agricultural settlements as the centre pieces of the Zionist movement. Agricultural work and life were expected to spiritually and physically liberate Jews on route to becoming 'new' Jews. The 'new' Jew was to be strong in body and spirit, live in the rural environment, have an 'active lifestyle' and be 'physically uninhibited' (Almog 2000: 78–80). The historical emphasis on working the land and on communal agricultural settlements is still very evident in Israel today. The image of the early settlers is held up as a model for modern Jewish-Israelis, and most of Israel's cities and towns still pay homage to the historic importance of agriculture in their coat-of-arms, which depict idealised images of rural life and agricultural tools and produce, even if today this idealised lifestyle is only practised by a very small minority (Ranta and Mendel 2016; see also coat of arms of three Israeli cities, Photos 1, 2 and 3).

In terms of food consumption, the construction of the 'new' Jew also necessitated the creation of a new Jewish diet. The new diet would, on the one hand, highlight the rejection of diaspora values and norms, while on the other hand connect the settlers to their 'new-old' land and physically transform them. The new diet, in a similar way to some of the examples given above, was to be rich in fruits, fresh vegetables and dairy products rather than the Jewish Eastern European diet of meat, fish and boiled vegetables (Almog 2000). Though the process of changing the nation's diet was directed mostly from above, according to Claudia Roden, many of the early settlers were 'happy to abandon the "Yiddish" foods of Russia

Photo 1 Coat of arms Petah Tikva

Photo 2 Coat of arms of Hadera

and Poland as a revolt against a past identity and an old life … and foods that represented exile and martyrdom' (1999: 175). The inspiration for many of the new dishes and food ingredients came from imitating and

Chapter Four: Food and Diet in 'Official' Nationalism

Photo 3 Coat of arms of Afula

adapting elements from the regional and local Arab-Palestinian food culture. However, as time passed and relations between the two national communities deteriorated, imitation of Arab-Palestinian food gave way to appropriation and nationalisation. In Zionist discourse the role and importance of Arab-Palestinian food was marginalised and 'forgotten' (Ranta and Mendel 2014, 2016).

It is important to mention that the desire to change the settlers' diet was not only motivated by issues concerning identity. Indeed, there are a few additional motivations, among them the Zionist emphasis on self-sufficiency and the creation of a Jewish only economy, which will be discussed below, and the importance attached to modernisation, progress and science. Some of the reasons put forward for emphasising the new diet were based on the growing importance attached to issues concerning public health and nutrition (Raviv 2015). From the 1930s onwards a number of important food surveys were conducted in the pre-state period by leading Zionist health and academic institutions. The surveys examined and compared food consumption patterns in Palestine among various communities and made specific recommendations regarding calorie consumption and vitamin and mineral uptakes, based on the then prevailing concepts of nutrition (on food surveys in Palestine, see Guggenheim, et al.: 1991).

In order to change the eating habits and diets of the new and arriving settlers, the Zionist movement employed a number of mechanisms, including health initiatives, publications of journals and books and public campaigns; most of the cookbooks and cooking pamphlets circulated in the period were published by Zionist organisations. What is interesting for us is not the nutrition and health-based reasons employed but the attempts through these changes to shape the nation's identity. This shaping is clear with regard to the ideas of orientalism, ethnicity, behaviour, gender and habits that the Zionist movements espoused to and emphasised. At the heart of this change was the presumption of European cultural superiority. In a way, even though Zionism was based on the negation of Jewish diaspora life in Europe, it still perceived itself as a European movement. The new diet and eating habits promoted were mostly based on a European understanding of the meal structure—three courses rather than presenting all of the food at once, which was common in the region. Local and Mizrahi (a term denoting Jews from North Arica and the Middle East) food items and ingredients were included only if they fitted in with the prevailing concepts of nutrition and were found to be useful and appropriate. These decisions were taken by mostly Ashkenazi (name given to European Jews) Zionist professionals with regard to mostly non-European foods; some items were not included in the nation's diet and simply categorised as 'oriental'. The foods and habits promoted were also directly linked to ideas of patriarchy and the creation of a strong and resilient nation that would be able to withstand the challenges it faced (Segev 1998; Tene 2002). As a result, the Israeli melting pot became a painful process, in which Mizrahi Jewish identities were questioned and silenced, while their food traditions were only enjoyed in the privacy of their homes or as street foods (Prieto-Piastro 2021).

The points made above can be clearly seen in the introduction to the first and also popular Zionist cookbook *How to Cook in Palestine* (Meyer 1937), which was published by Women's International Zionist Organisation (WIZO) and which was continually in print well into the

1950s; important to note that many of the early cookbooks were written and published by women's Zionist associations and were targeted at women (Prieto-Piastro 2021). The book openly called upon 'the woman who arrives from Europe' to change her lifestyle and her cooking and eating habits. The book asked women and house wives to (1937: 8)

> …try with greater vigour than before to free our kitchen from the diaspora tradition that has clung to it… and consciously replace the European cuisine with a healthy Israeli one…. This is one of the most important mechanisms for growing roots in our old-new homeland.

Interestingly, the changes promoted by the Zionist movement were not always fully accepted. Despite the strong emphasis on changing eating habits, it is clear that many were not convinced to change theirs. There are a number of examples of official cookbooks in the decades that continued to try and convince their readers to make use of local ingredients such as mint, aubergines and cumin (Ranta and Prieto-Piastro 2019). Failure to successfully change the nation's diet can be attributed to the high levels of immigration experienced by the Jewish community before and after the creation of the state of Israel in 1948. Nevertheless, the changes promoted did substantially and fundamentally alter the nation's diet and approach to food. Several of the most widely consumed and symbolic dishes in Israel can trace their beginning to these food policies.

Establishing a Jewish Economy in Palestine

The emphasis on a particular diet and specific food products was not only related to issues of public health and identity but also related to the establishment of a separate Jewish economic and political entity in Palestine. In other words, the Zionist movement and its main institutions sought to advance the nationalist aim of establishing a Jewish state in Palestine through specific food policies. These policies were based on a number of important elements including self-sufficiency, austerity and control over agricultural labour as well as the main sources of food production. The issue of agricultural labour, as well as labour in general, was part of a wider Zionist aim, known as the conquest of labour, to ensure that only Jewish workers were employed in the Jewish economy. This meant the active and conscious separation of the Jewish economy and growing community from the Arab-Palestinian one (Shafir 1996).

Beyond the issue of promoting and controlling Jewish labour, the Zionist leadership during the British Mandate period (1919–1948) used food to further demarcate communal and national boundaries between Jews and Arab-Palestinians. One of the main food Policies used was the promotion of and emphasis on Jewish only products. This was epitomised in the Zionist campaign of 'Tozteret Ha'aretz' (lit. produce of the land). Writing for the Hadassah newsletter in 1940,[3] Sulamith Schwartz explains (quoted in Raviv 2002b: 77):

> The more we use the products of Jewish fields and factories, the more we encourage the development of Palestinian Jewish industry and agriculture, thus creating room and work for tens of thousands of new immigrants, strengthening the Palestinian Jewish economy, making it sounder and more self-reliant.

The promotion of Jewish only products was officially marketed and publicised and several Zionist organisations, for example, the 'organisation for Tozteret Ha'aretz', were tasked with ensuring compliance. Jewish approved products were labelled as 'Hebrew' to differentiate them from non-Jewish ones. Campaigns highlighted the 'Hebrew' produce and called upon Jewish consumers to buy only 'Hebrew' bananas or watermelons. Zionist food enterprises, such as the dairy monopoly Tnuva (lit. produce), produced posters informing Jewish consumers that 'our produce' is 100 per cent Jewish (Raviv 2015). 'The organisation for Tozteret Ha'aretz also produced weekly and monthly specific poster and pamphlet campaigns.[4] For example, a poster depicting two young children with an orange tree background stating that 'the future of your children is in your hands and the future is in Tozteret Ha'aretz: buy only Tozteret Ha'aretz'.

---

[3] Hadassah is the Women's Zionist Organisation of America. During the Mandate period it was active in providing health and welfare support to the Jewish population.

[4] The poster and pamphlets discussed are available online through the Zionist archive: http://www.zionistarchives.org.il/en/Pages/TozeretHaaretz.aspx#!prettyPhoto (accessed 9.2.2022).

Another approach was through direct appeal pamphlets and posters. For example, an appeal to the 'Jewish public of Haifa' (a mixed Jewish-Arab city) stating that:

> In the difficult struggle for our survival and the future of our endeavour, it is our duty to inform the Hebrew public of the internal danger we all face from the lack of loyalty to Tozteret Ha'aretz ... the public committee calls upon every man and woman to strengthen the Yishuv's [the term referring to the Jewish community in Palestine] economy! To stop the firing of Hebrew workers and the destruction of families! To give a hand to the creation of work places for the survivors of the diaspora! And to defend against all conspiracies from within and from abroad!

The campaign was also featured in the leading Zionist newspapers, publications and cookbooks. For example, the *How to Cook in Palestine* mentioned above cookbook directly related the recipes it provided with the Zionist campaign to promote only Jewish products. The cookbook informs its readers that the recipes are based on the available 'Tozteret Ha'arezt' agricultural and preserved produce. Moreover, among the recipe pages are advertisements targeting Jewish housewives in English and Hebrew: 'To the Jewish housewife: Serve Tozereth-Haaretz food only. In this way you will help strengthen the economic foundation of Erez-Israel. Take active part in promoting Tozereth-Haaretz' (Meyer 1937: 26).

The campaign, which began in the 1920s, and which was taken on by all leading Zionist organisations in Palestine, tied together the food produced, purchased and consumed by Jews, the land of Israel, and the national aim of establishing a separate Jewish state. The campaign promoted the ideas of asceticism and austerity, calling for communal sacrifice over the individual good. Preaching the ideals of self-sufficiency—making use of what was available and produced by the Jewish community—reduction of imports and communal resilience, the same ideals that formed the bedrock of communal agricultural settlements (Raviv 2002b).

The campaign was taken on and promoted through Zionist institutions and organisations, for example, through the provisions of Tozteret Ha'arezt lunch programmes in hospitals, workplaces, health clinics, nurseries and schools, and in the communal mess halls in collective agricultural settlements. It was not only the consumption of specific local 'Hebrew' products that was highlighted but also the links made between individual eating habits and choices and the historic bonds between Jews and Israel. This placed the success or failure of the Zionist endeavour and project at the door of consumers.

Integrating New Immigrants

The relationship between food policies and Zionist aims was also evident in the application of the 'tsena' (lit. Austerity) measures. In the aftermath of the 1948 war, and the establishment of the state of Israel, and leading up to the early 1950s, the Israeli state and society experienced rapid change. From 1948 to 1951 Israeli population doubled as a consequence of mass migration of Jews from Europe, North Africa and the Middle East. The impact of mass migration and the fragile economic situation in the aftermath of the 1948 war—unemployment rate was over 14 per cent—meant that the state struggled to cope. Many of the new immigrants were housed in temporary camps and were completely reliant on government support. In order to address these problems, that state initiated an austerity programme referred to in Hebrew as 'tsena' (Segev 1998). Many of the austerity measures applied directly to the production, sale and consumption of food. Additionally, and despite the fact that they were mostly necessary to tackle the economic, but also food security situation, austerity measure also provided an opportunity for the state and its apparatuses to promote national unity and homogeneity as well as integrate the new migrants. In other words, and as argued by Rozin (2006), the austerity measures were used as a way of nation-building and the public compliance with the measures was seen as a way of performing the nation in their daily lives.

With regard to food the austerity measures were based on two important elements. First, they included direct government intervention in the economy to regulate staple food prices and the standardisation of certain staple food (e.g., bread). Second, it also included the rationing of available food according to a point system. The system was calculated based on age, occupation, family situation, number of dependent and so on.

Chapter Four: Food and Diet in 'Official' Nationalism

What the system did not try to achieve was the provision of food based on the immigrants' cultural tastes and preferences. It is now well known that the rations provided did not meet the cultural needs of many of the new immigrants; at times the provision did not meet their physically needs as well (Segev 1998). The rationing system was based on the food the state already produced and the nutritional requirements of a modern diet and not on providing culturally acceptable food. As a result, many accused the state of trying to force immigrants, particularly Mizrahi Jews, to become European by eating Ashkenazi food (Rozin 2006).

Unlike some of the previous examples provided, in particular the case of Japan, the Israeli state was attempting to bring together a diverse group of people who came from a large number of different regions and cultures and whose only unifying element was an imagination of being part of a Jewish nation. As a result, there is no doubt that the state used the austerity measures in its attempts 'to forge a united and unified community from a diverse population of immigrants in a short period of time' (Raviv 2002b: 85). The measures helped establish standardised food provisions in a number of different areas. For example, the state used the army, also known as the Israeli defence forces (IDF), which was based on conscription, as one of its most important tools for integrating new immigrants. With regard to food this meant that the diet offered by the IDF became the closest thing to an 'authentic Israeli kitchen'. New migrants were presented with a top-down constructed diet that was supposed to address their physical needs but also introduce them to Israeli food, manners and culture. As a result, some of the food items provided by the IDF during the austerity period became national icons, probably none more so than the 'infamous' tinned army meat loaf ('luf' in Hebrew) (Raviv 2002a).

In order to help facilitate the integration of immigrants, the state also sought to help them learn how to use the rations provided properly. At times, it was clear that decision-makers in charge of the measures took a very critical approach towards the new immigrants. They viewed them, especially Mizrahi Jews, as well as their eating habits as backwards and as an impediment on progress (Raviv 2002b; Rozin 2006). This meant having to teach immigrants how and what to cook, which included the emphasis on the European meal structure and the provision of particular food items and dishes, for example, the consumption of European-style tea and butter and jam. It also included the publication of cookbooks that demonstrated how to use the austerity rations (see, e.g., Cornfled 1949).[5]

According to Raviv (2002b), the austerity period also included some efforts to address and incorporate immigrant concerns and tastes. This brought about the first inclusion of Mizrahi, and at times local Arab-Palestinian food into Israeli cookbooks. In other words, while the state's policies were trying to impose a more homogenous diet on the Israeli public, it is also clear that there were some compromises along the way. These compromises helped establish what is today considered by many as Israeli food. Nevertheless, and despite some of these compromises, the cultural dominance of Ashkenazi-Jews on the process was very evident, with the overall aim of constructing a European-western nation in Israel/Palestine. Through including a number of Mizrahi and Arab-Palestinian food items, which were mostly provided in book chapters titles 'oriental food', European concepts of meal structure, nutrition, hygiene and health were imposed.

Conclusion

The chapter, and specifically the case studies provided, highlights the unique nature of food as political resource connected to security, economic concerns and health but also to issue of identity, integration and nation-building. In a way, the chapter illustrates the dichotomous nature of food, which comprises the entire range of the spiritual-material spectrum. It also demonstrates how the study of food is useful in bridging the gap between politics (political economy, security, propaganda, resistance of colonisation, public health, etc.) and anthropology (symbolism, values, culture, etc.).

The case study of diet in Japan has shown that the conventional, 'top-down' approach to nationalism retains a degree of explanatory power. When the Meiji government embarked on the project of modernisation,

---

[5] For more on the role of cookbooks in the construction of Israeli national identity, see Ranta and Prieto-Piastro (2019).

Chapter Four: Food and Diet in 'Official' Nationalism   129

the traditional Japanese diet which was considered to be nutritiously inferior was included in the government's reform plans: the Japanese were to encourage to eat meat and the production of rice was to be promoted so as to strengthen the Japanese nation. The government used conscription, a quintessentially modernising and centralising method of nation-building, to propagate meat eating and it also mobilised the emperor's symbolic power. Not all were happy with this development and there were struggles over the admission of meat eating on the symbolic ground, and for the majority of the population, meat was simply too expensive to put on the table. The successive wars the new Japanese state fought helped to modernise Japanese diet while establishing the idea of rice as the Japanese self. The system of rice control, instituted during World War II, crumbled due to the pressure of the globalising market but the idea lingers: domestically produced rice is the best because it is safe and nourishing.

The case study of Zionism has showcased how food, including its production and consumption, can be mobilised for national aims and drawn into the national framework. Through their control and manipulation of food, Zionist leaders engaged directly in nation-building and promotion of certain food-related images and values. In particular the ideas of creating a 'new' Jew through changing the nation's diet and the ideal of 'autarky', or self-sufficiency, appear to have played an important and integral part in Zionist propaganda. The nation's diet was seen as one that has a direct impact on the nation's health, which affected productivity and security, but also on its psyche and character. The promotion of self-sufficiency drew a clear link between individual food choices and the success or failure of the nation. It is clear from some of the other examples we provided that this was also the case in other 'modernising' states. In other words, the state's actions required and necessitated the performance of the nation in the everyday.

What is clear from our two case studies and from the other examples provided is that what is often referred to and considered as national cuisine is more often than not a top-down construction based on the needs of the state. Through its apparatuses and institutions, such as the army and the education system, but also through the important mediums of cookbooks and magazines directed at housewives, the state, masking its aims through the language of modernity, economic needs and science, propagates and disseminates its ideas regarding the nation's diet. The state's needs tie in together the symbolic nature of food, the requirements of nation-building and the state's economic and social considerations. This means that the state has vested interests in what is considered and imagined as the national cuisine and in its symbolic ownership over and use of particular food items. This gives rise, as we will discuss in the next two chapters, to competing national claims over symbolic food ownership, the linking between national food and sovereignty, and also to the use of national cuisine as a tool for diplomacy and for promoting the nation internationally.

Chapter Five: National Food in the International Context I—Gastrodiplomacy

The previous chapter examined the importance food plays at the nation-state level and the ways in which the state uses food in its attempts to control, modernise and homogenise the nation. It also showcased the close relationship between the state's domestic political, social and economic policies and its intervention in its citizens' diet. However, the relationship between food and nationalism and its importance to the nation-state extends far beyond the borders of the state. Food is not only used for domestic purposes and as an internal and banal symbol of the nation but also internationally by the state in its diplomatic engagements and as a form of soft power, often referred to as gastrodiplomacy. In this regard, national food can be seen as exhibiting a duality; on the one hand, it can be used to indicate the attractiveness of the nation and increase its appeal, while, on the other hand, it can also be seen as a 'contested medium of cultural politics that demarcates national boundaries and identities' (DeSoucey 2010: 433). This means that what is viewed as national food items or traditions can be used in branding and marketing the nation internationally but might also require state intervention and protection from foreign claims.

The concept of food as a resource that can be utilised by the state in international relations will be explored in this and the following chapter through a number of examples that will highlight several such initiatives.

This chapter focuses on gastrodiplomacy and the ways in which food is branded, promoted and articulated as national in the international arena. It will be complemented by the following chapter which will focus on the securitisation of national food and its contestation internationally. This chapter will examine the case studies of Thailand's 'Global Thai' campaign and the promotion of Taiwanese food. In addition, and to provide a broader sense of the phenomenon and some of the complexities that arise from attempts to promote the nation globally, the chapter will also discuss the promotion of the New Nordic Cuisine (NNC) and the failed case of the Japanese Sushi police.

Gastrodiplomacy

The term gastrodiplomacy first appeared in a short article in *The Economist* magazine in 2002 discussing efforts by the Thai government to promote Thai food through an ambitious 'Global Thai' plan, which we will discuss below. *The Economist* claimed that as a result of the Thai government's 'discovery' that foreigners 'like Thai food', it decided to promote and introduce Thai food globally in order to 'persuade more people to visit Thailand' but also to 'subtly help to deepen relations with other countries' (*Economist* 2002).

Gastrodiplomacy can be understood to encompass three elements: cultural diplomacy, soft power and nation branding. Sam Chapple-Sokol explains that the use of food and national cuisine as part of cultural diplomacy is meant to 'create a cross-cultural understanding in hopes of improving interactions and cooperation' between people, cultures and states (2013: 162). A number of authors, including Paul Rockower (2014), propose a slightly different take and use the term to refer only to track three diplomacy and interactions that occur between actors below state level.

Beyond the issue of diplomacy, the promotion of national food can also be seen as a form of 'soft power', a term coined by Joseph Nye (1990) that refers to the state's ability to attract, influence and accommodate other actors through its culture and values rather than coerce them through the use of military and economic 'hard' power. Unlike traditional banal symbols of the nation-state, such as flags, coins and anthems, food has the power to attract and be desired by others, thus enhancing the appeal and prestige of the state. Gastrodiplomacy allows states to use their national food as a 'soft power' resource to increase the appeal and desirability of its culture, people, values, ideals and landscape. The fact that it familiarises people with a particular country and associates that country with particular tastes, textures, smells and images can be seen as useful for states that do not have a good reputation or that are not particularly well known (Rockower 2011). Additionally, national food, because of its symbolic but also vital nature, has the ability to not only bring people together and enhance cultural diplomacy but also promote economic growth, trade and tourism. The promotion and marketing of the nation's food as a brand helps link together banal and everyday aspects of nationalism with the private sector, the state and international relations. It is also useful for the state as a means of exploiting its appeal for economic growth and trade and supporting its tourism industry.

The importance of food and gastronomy, whether the provision of food, as an attraction, the role of local producers and/or culinary heritage, in tourism has been well known for some time now (see, e.g., Hjalager and Richards 2002). It has also been highlighted by the World Tourism Organization, which claimed that 'the cuisine of the destination is an aspect of utmost importance in the quality of the holiday experience' (UNWTO 2012: 6). Several recent studies have discussed and demonstrated how gastrodiplomatic efforts, for example, the use of food ambassadors, food festivals and culinary schools, could help states in developing and strengthening their tourism industry (see, e.g., Suntikul 2019; White et al. 2019). The case studies below provide further details on how gastrodiplomacy relates to and supports tourism.

According to Chapple-Sokol (2013: 171), 'foreign publics eating national cuisines are not only contributing to the cooks and farmers, but to their own understanding of nationhood and, along with that, their attitudes towards the other'. This is because through gastrodiplomacy the state is promoting a specific and particular image of itself and its national cuisine. Through branding and marketing its food, it is defining and refining what is considered national food as well as constructing and reproducing national boundaries. This issue of redefining, in some cases homogenising, the nation through branding and marketing its food, will be discussed in greater depth below.

The idea of using national food as an element in diplomacy and international relations has a very long history. For centuries, food and specific food items such as spices, and particularly salt, were used for important economic and diplomatic missions, either as currency or as gifts to build and/or strengthen relations (Nirwandy and Awang 2014). However, what is interesting in the case of gastrodiplomacy is how different it is from the historical examples of using food as a diplomatic tool, or indeed from some of the more modern uses of food in international relations, for example, the provision of food aid. This is because these types of initiatives, such as food aid, are not directly related to food as a national element. Nevertheless, it should be noted that the provision of food aid can be seen and used as a political tool and a form of soft power. Food aid can be a way of affecting international relations and increasing national prestige and power (see, e.g., Clapp 2012).

The first major example of national food used as an integral element in cultural diplomacy comes from France in the nineteenth century. In order to increase the appeal of the state, ease relations and strengthen its diplomatic initiatives, the French state made use of its cuisine and chefs. This was done through a number of different initiatives. French ambassadors were asked to frequently entertain in order to befriend and familiarise themselves with local dignitaries. One of the highlights of such events was the provision of French food and wine. Such was the appeal of these types of initiatives that in Britain, for example, elites became enamoured by all things French, and in particular French food, and many as a result employed French chefs (Rogers 2003). Even more importantly, French food was used in direct support of French diplomatic efforts. Chapple-Sokol (2013) provides the example of the French diplomat, and later Prime Minister, Charles Maurice de Talleyrand-Périgord, who asked the famous French chef Anton Careme, often regarded as the 'King of cooks and the cook of kings', to accompany the French delegation to the Congress of Vienna in 1814 after the abdication of Napoleon. Careme was expected to 'provide culinary support to the French delegation' through cooking but also to impress the European leaders who gathered at Vienna. Talleyrand-Périgord and Careme are rumoured to have won over the European leaders who gathered at Vienna, and who all expressed their love of cheese, by winning an impromptu European cheese competition with the presentation of *Brie de Meaux*, which was proclaimed 'king of cheeses'.

The degree of success of the French state in this regard is evident in the fact that just as French was the language of diplomacy for a long time, French cuisine became the *de facto* official cuisine of diplomacy. There are many examples of states serving mostly French food during diplomatic engagements, for example, Meiji Japan entering the Westphalian system of states in the latter half of the nineteenth century adopted French cuisine as its cuisine of choice when entertaining foreign diplomats (Harada 2005).

Global Thai

Thailand is often presented as the prime example of a country utilising gastrodiplomacy. What is clear is that it was the first state to actively use its food in pursuit of its cultural diplomatic effort and as a way of increasing its soft power: it has also been one of the most successful promotions of national food to date, with Thai food becoming one of the most recognised and loved cuisines globally (Ranta 2015). The idea of using food as part of its cultural diplomacy was a by-product of Thailand's unique situation in the 1960s and 1970s. During this period, and in response to war in neighbouring Vietnam, Thailand became a rest and recuperation base for US soldiers; in addition, the US established a number of air force bases in Thailand. The presence of large numbers of US personnel resulted in the modernisation and to some extent westernisation of Thai hospitality and food industry, which profited from catering to the US troops. This in turn helped stir and promote Thai food globally as well as establish Thailand as a tourist destination. The popularity of Thai food brought with it the growth and expansion of Thai agriculture and food industry (Murray 2007).

Thailand's official engagement with gastrodiplomacy began in 2002 with the launching of its 'Global Thai' programme under former Prime Minister Thaksin Shinawatra. The project aimed to significantly increase the number of Thai restaurants globally from around 5000 to 20,000 by 2008. In order to facilitate this rapid growth in Thai restaurants, the Thai government provided a substantial amount of loans, supervised and oversaw the establishment of restaurants, created business links between the global Thai restaurants and the Thai food industry, and helped to establish Thai cooking school to train and supply Thai chefs (Sunanta 2005).

Additionally, the Thai government also sought to use these restaurants to promote a particular image of Thailand. This was accomplished through awards given to 'successful' restaurants as well as the provision of the 'Thai Select' label. The label indicated a Thai official recognition of the restaurants' standard and the quality and authenticity of the food provided. In order to be awarded the label, Thai restaurants had to adhere to not only hygiene, safety and quality standards but also those dealing with the Thai national image. The restaurants were required to provide and promote specific Thai dishes in their menus—Sunanta (2005) gives the example of a number of particular dishes, such as Tom Yam and Tom Kha soups, Green curry and Padthai (the Thai Select programme, which will be discussed below, includes 29 specific Thai dishes: http://www.thaiselect.com/main.php?filename=index). Moreover, the restaurants were expected to emphasise a particular image of Thai culture through staff dress ('traditional' Thai dress and colours were encouraged) and the décor and atmosphere provided, including paintings, sculptures and music. The idea was to create an appealing image of Thai people, culture and geography (Murray 2007). This encouraged the promotion of a particular top-down idea of Thai identity and to some extent forced Thai people to engage with the image sold to non-Thais as Thai identity. One could argue that through the promotion of Thai food globally, the Thai government engaged in the homogenisation of Thai culture and identity.

The idea behind promoting Thai restaurants through the 'Global Thai' initiative was part of a wider Thai food policy that aimed to link the promotion of Thailand and its culture and geography with spurring innovation and expansion in Thai agriculture and food industry. Thailand today is one of the largest food processing countries in the world as well as the world's largest exporter of rice (Ranta 2015).

The 'Global Thai' initiative was followed up by the launching of the 'Thailand the Kitchen of the World' e-book and campaign. The e-book and campaign were designed to educate and promote Thai food and culture. According to Chapple-Sokol (2013), the 'Thailand the Kitchen of the World' e-book and campaign were run by the Thai Public Relations Department. The introduction of the e-book explains that:

> Thai food and Thai cuisine from the past to the present are distinctive in their charms and characters. The cuisine is a proud heritage of the Thai people that they believe is second to none, and it has been handed down through generations. Apart from the delicate blend of tastes and the rich nutritional value, the elaborate arrangement of Thai food and the decorations with fruit and vegetable carvings make it all the more inviting. At the same time, Thai food and Thai cooking reflect the wisdom and culture of the Thai nation. Today, Thai food and Thai cuisine stand ready to make Thailand a proud Kitchen of the World. (http://thailand.prd.go.th/ebook2/kitchen/intro.html)

The Thai gastrodiplomatic effort can be seen as a way of linking together and framing the Thai state's economic, agricultural and diplomatic policies as part of the national discourse. Through the promotion of Thai restaurants, an initiative that has been extremely successful—from around 5000 restaurants in 2002 to around 13,000 by 2009 (Chapple-Sokol 2013)—the Thai government has shown how gastrodiplomacy can achieve far more than simply support a state's diplomatic effort. While it is true that each new 'Thai Select' restaurant opened also acts as 'an unofficial embassy', supports diaspora Thai population and provides the possibility for cultural interaction (Chapple-Sokol 2013), it also homogenises the Thai national food and image, enhances the particular national brand the Thai government seeks to promote and helps support the Thai economy. The success of the 'Thai Select' brand can also be seen in the global growth of restaurants that exhibit the label. According to the Thai Department of International Trade Promotion, which runs the 'Thai Select' programme, there were 1135 'Thai Select' restaurants outside of Thailand in 2015. As of 2022 in the US alone, there were 322 Thai Select restaurants (www.thaiselect.com/en). In 2015 there were 67 'Thai Select' restaurants in Thailand; as of 2022 there were 213 certified restaurants (www.thaiselect.com/en).

Taiwan

Since the launch of the 'Global Thai' initiative, many countries have tried to emulate it, both with regard to national branding and marketing, for example, Malaysia's 'Malaysian Kitchen for the World' initiative and Peru's 'Cocina Peruana Para el Mundo' ('Peruvian Cuisine for the World'), and cultural diplomacy, for example, the launching of South Korea's 'Kimchi Diplomacy'. The potential implications of a successful gastrodiplomatic initiative have also convinced many in the UK of the need to pay closer attention to the role of food post-Brexit. The House of Commons Environment and Rural Affairs Committee, for example, published a report titled 'Brand Britain: Promoting British Food and Drink' (2019). In the report they acknowledged that outside a small number of niche food items, such as whiskey, cheese and salmon, awareness and knowledge of British food internationally was low. They recommend raising awareness of British food internationally in order to support British businesses but also to help support the rebranding of the country in the aftermath of Brexit.

One of the more recent gastrodiplomatic campaigns has been the one launched by the Taiwanese government. Taiwan's campaign is often used as an example for the reasons for and merits of gastrodiplomacy. What is interesting about the Taiwanese example is that it is a national campaign undertaken by a unique international actor that is not widely recognised as an independent state—in fact its nature, territory and sovereignty are a source of international tension and are in dispute. The dispute goes back to the Chinese civil war in the aftermath of World War II. The Chinese civil war ended in a victory for the Communist party headed by Mao Zedong and the establishment of the People's Republic of China. The losing side, the nationalist party headed by Chiang Kai Shek, established themselves in Taiwan, which they proclaimed the Republic of China, in preparation for continuing their struggle for China. The island, which had been under Chinese rule for several centuries and under Japanese rule for several decades (1895–1945) preceding World War II, was 'returned' to China after it was liberated from the Japanese. To this day no official cease fire or end to the conflict between the two sides has been achieved, though Taiwan no longer holds any aspirations for the takeover of China.

Taiwan's complex diplomatic situation, especially its fraught relationship with China, which views it as a 'renegade province', creates great difficulty for its diplomatic efforts and its ability to project its national image. It is not a member of the UN, and because of its tense relations with China, it does not have diplomatic relations and is not recognised by a number of states. 'Taiwan is a unique case of a nation that must conduct public diplomacy not only as a means of promotion, but also as a means for ensuring its diplomatic survival and access to the international arena' (Rockower 2011: 109). As a consequence, one of the few avenues open to Taiwan is through cultural diplomacy and specifically through the use of gastrodiplomacy. Taiwanese gastrodiplomacy is predicated on the idea 'that the easiest way to win hearts and minds is through the stomach' (Rockower 2011: 125) to further promote Taiwan and its reputation and appeal. By promoting and supporting the spread of its food through various means, which will be discussed below, the Taiwanese government is trying to engage with the international community and achieve a number of aims. First, it seeks to be better recognised and be seen as separate from China; this is done through promotion of specific Taiwanese indigenous food culture in addition to highlighting the Taiwanese characteristics of the traditional Chinese culture that has been preserved on the island for several centuries. This also entails the promotion and celebration of indigenous culture (the more than a dozen non-Chinese indigenous groups) in support of the Taiwanese national identity and image (see, for example, Chen [2022] on the complexity of indigeneity and the promotion of indigenous food). Second is to promote Taiwan as an appealing and interesting country, a country with strong democratic values, distinctive culture and good food—in other words enhance Taiwanese soft power or power of influence. Lastly, through the promotion of its food Taiwan hopes to market itself as a desirable destination for tourists and promote its food as attractive to global consumers. This helps promote economic growth, Taiwanese economic diversification and private sector, and also supports and strengthens domestic tourist industry.

The Taiwanese gastrodiplomacy campaign includes a number of specific elements including government investment in the international promotion of Taiwanese food—in 2013, for example, Taiwan invested $34.2

million in promoting its cuisine; hosting international food festivals and cooking competitions as well as launching Taiwanese food festivals abroad; support for Taiwanese restaurants and the training of Taiwanese chefs; establishing a 'culinary think tank' (Chapple-Sokol 2013: 176); support for Taiwanese culinary tours, for example, the 'traveling night markets'; and creating networks of support to bring together the food and tourism industries (Chapple-Sokol 2013; Rockower 2011).

Many of the elements mentioned above are utilised in combination with other cultural diplomacy initiatives. For example, in the UK a number of Taiwanese organisations and groups—including the 'Taiwanese Association in the UK', the Taiwanese chamber of commerce in the UK, UK Taiwanese students' groups and the Taiwanese ministry of culture—have set up annual Taiwanese festivals. These festivals promote and celebrate Taiwanese culture and business, including music, dance, film, tourism and even medical tourism. However, looking at the range of festivals and events promoted, it is clear that food has been at the forefront of this cultural diplomacy initiative.

The Taiwanese government's gastrodiplomacy initiative in the UK was launched by President Ma Ying-Jeou in 2010 with a £20 million investment to promote Taiwanese food and brands and to highlight and differentiate 'the country from its giant and sometimes antagonistic neighbour, China, and to end the perception that Taiwan is little more than the mass-production workshop of the world' (Booth 2010). The initiative came to support and add to the already existing attempts to promote Taiwanese food, mostly by the Taiwanese community in the UK and the Taiwanese food and beverage industry. The gastrodiplomacy initiative in the UK sits along aside many similar ones undertaken by the Taiwanese government across the world. For example, in September 2014 the Taiwanese Ministry of Culture held a nine-day celebration of Taiwanese food in Paris, which included films, theatre plays and music performances.

While it is hard to assess the success of the Taiwanese gastrodiplomacy initiative, taking the UK as an example, it is clear that there is far more recognition of Taiwanese food and food culture than before; for example, there are dozens of Taiwanese food business and restaurants in the country. A mere example of this has been the rapid spread of the

Taiwanese-based 'bubble tea' craze. The popularity of the drink is such that there are now dozens of companies selling it across the UK.[1]

If, as Chapple-Sokol (2013) notes, gastrodiplomacy is used to reach not only policy-maker elites, who remain mostly behind closed doors, but also the wider international public and engage with them, then the mere acknowledgement of Taiwan as a culinary hotspot and destination, and of the quality of its food as well as food trends and fashions, from the bubble tea to night markets, would imply its success. Additionally, it has been noted that over the past decade Taiwan's image as a tourist destination and specifically as a culinary tourist destination has increased dramatically. The rapid increase in culinary tourism demonstrates how an international campaign to promote national food has a direct impact in the domestic sphere. In a similar way to the Thai case, the promotion of a specific idea and image of Taiwanese food, and the importance attached to culinary tourism, has led to a redefinition of Taiwanese food and as a consequence Taiwanese national identity. This has also meant the growing differentiation between Taiwanese and Chinese identities and an increasing emphasis on the local and indigenous Taiwanese identity (Chuang 2009). According to Chapple-Sokol (2013), Taiwan's gastrodiplomacy initiative is not only done to differentiate it from China but also to improve its relationship with its giant neighbour. By bringing and promoting Taiwanese cuisine to and in mainland China, Taiwan is hoping to influence the Chinese public's view of the country and the relationship between the two states.

The New Nordic Cuisine

The state is not the only actor active in constructing and engaging with national food. As discussed in the previous four chapters, and as will be demonstrated in subsequent chapters, individuals, groups, the private sector and a variety of international non-state actors are also active

---

[1] According to Allied Market Research, as of 2019, the global bubble tea market is worth more than $2 billion and is projected to double over the next decade (https://www.alliedmarketresearch.com/bubble-tea-market)

participants in this endeavour. In this sense, gastrodiplomacy is simply another 'zone of conflict' in which engagement with and contestation of what and where the nation is occurs. The emergence of the New Nordic Cuisine (NNC) is a useful case study to illustrate the complexity of gastrodiplomacy, where actors have different ideas of what the nation and national food are, and how to promote them globally. For the purpose of clarity, the direct contestation and securitisation of national food between states will be discussed in the next chapter on gastronationalism.

The NNC emerged in the early 2000s as the brainchild of Chef Rene Redzepi and restaurateur Claus Meyer of Noma restaurant in Copenhagen, Denmark, which has been considered one of the best in the world for the past two decades. The initial idea of the NNC, influenced by the concept of the Mediterranean diet, was presented by Redzepi and Meyer in a manifesto and signed by several prominent chefs in Sweden, Finland, Denmark, Iceland, Greenland and Norway. The manifesto states that the time has come for Nordic chefs to 'create a New Nordic Kitchen, which in virtue of its good taste and special character compares favourably with the standard of the greatest kitchens of the world' (The Nordic Council n.d.). The manifesto's stated aims are to showcase the Nordic *terroir* and the freshness, simplicity and seasonality of its food; to promote and emphasise the ethical and sustainable side of Nordic food production; and to support and promote local and regional stakeholders 'for the benefit and advantage of everyone in the Nordic countries' (The Nordic Council n.d.). The Nordic region in discussion consists of Denmark, Norway, Sweden, Finland and Iceland, the self-governing Danish territories of Greenland and the Faeroe Islands, and the self-governing Finish isles of Aland.

The main questions that emerge out of this manifesto, with regard to nationalism, are what is Nordic food and *terroir* and where and who is the Nordic nation. The pan-nationalist idea espoused by the manifesto has historic precedents in the region, which is often referred to as the Nordic region and/or Scandinavia, though the idea has become more prominent since the nineteenth century. Pan-nationalist ideas have been part of the political and social relations between the people and governments of Norway, Denmark and Sweden for several centuries; Finland, which was part of Sweden until 1809, and Iceland and Greenland, which have been at various times ruled by Denmark and Norway, were rarely part of this conversation. The top-down promotion of a pan-national identity was part of a desire to foster closer cooperation between these three like-minded countries against common security threats, such as those emanating from Russia and Prussia. The idea of being like-minded derives from a sense of common history, culture and language that has partly evolved out of a number of political unions that have existed between the three countries; it is important to note that these unions were normally formed and dissolved through wars. These unions, however, never culminated in a unified or federal Nordic or Scandinavian state. It is the nationalist projects in Norway, Denmark and Sweden that put an end to the idea of a unified or federal Nordic state. The paradox, as stated by Hemstad, is that 'while [Nordic countries] supported nation building programmes, they also sought a trans-nationalist arrangement' (2010: 183).

The idea that the Nordic region shares much in common is popular and widely accepted. In terms of food culture, there is a shared sense of landscape and environment, outdoor activities such as fishing and hunting and viewing food as associated with scarcity, nutrition and health. 'There is nevertheless a question whether we can speak of a Nordic Food Culture or instead should refer to Nordic Food Cultures?' (Bergflodt et al. 2012). This is particularly relevant given that, unlike in other examples provided in this book, food did not play a prominent role in the construction of regional and/or national identities. As explained by Simonsen (2019), the idea of a unified regional cuisine and a common sense of *terroir* is a recent one. In this sense, NNC attempts to redefine Nordic food culture/s and identity/ies. It bases its concept of Nordic *terroir* not only on food production, the land and the environment, but also on, what it views as, shared ideas around taste, history, memory and landscape. The NNC focuses on and emphasises several perceived and shared culinary ideas, such as the importance of eating together; observing seasonality; cooking at home; eating regional and local food; and ethical and sustainable food production and consumption (Simonsen 2019). Whether these ideas form a coherent transnational cuisine is not clear.

In the sense of creating a new Nordic cuisine, redefining regional food culture/s and promoting regional food products and producers, the NNC has been successful. The region, its restaurants and its approach to food, focusing on ethics and sustainability, are now seen as an alternative to the dominant French and Mediterranean food cultures that have previously defined what good food is in the Global North (Leer 2016). As a result, the NNC endeavour has been strongly supported by Nordic national and regional stakeholders, from local artisanal food producers to regional international organisations, one of the most important of which has been the Nordic Council.

The Nordic Council, an international organisation representing the five states and three territories of region, and focused on promoting and strengthening cooperation and understanding in the region, was one of the early advocates for and promoters of the NNC. In its 2015 report on its programme of new 'Nordic food II 2010–2014', it stated that the NNC had helped promote the Nordic region as a gastronomic region by supporting and promoting regional food products and producers, and regional restaurants and hospitality, as well as helping to connect people and stakeholders in the region (Nodic Council of Ministers 2015).

The Nordic Council's stated gastrodiplomatic aim is to use the NNC as part of Nordic diplomacy to build and strengthen the Nordic and regional national brands, using food as a symbol of regional and national pride. This it argues will increase Nordic food exports and support local and regional food producers as well as the regional hospitality and tourism sectors (2015). In order to support the NNC, the Nordic Council has invested in promoting it in the region and globally. The report and the Nordic Council's website list several gastrodiplomatic events and activities carried out, among other places, in the US, China and Japan and across Europe and the Nordic region. Examples of these gastrodiplomatic events include the provision of a Nordic signature on all foods provided at the 2013 Eurovision song contest hosted by Malmo, Sweden, and promoting NNC at the Nordic Design and Fashion week in Shanghai, China, in 2014.

The Nordic Council states in its report that the NNC has been a great success. The report, however, does not provide in-depth details. Instead, it claims that the NNC has created new jobs in the food and hospitality sectors, increased food exports and trade in food, particularly for local and artisanal producers, and has increased tourism, particularly food tourism to the region. The report also claims the NNC has become a symbol of regional pride helping to spread Nordic ideas regarding sustainability, food ethics and cooperation (Nordic Council 2015). It is particularly noticeable, given the general aims of the organisation, that the Nordic Council views the NNC as a way of promoting the region as a whole and less about promoting the region's national states. However, as Neuman and Leer explain (2018), this post- or transnational approach is somewhat at odds with the gastrodiplomatic policies pursued by the regional states.

Examining the way in which the states in the region present their food culture to the world, it is particularly interesting to note how little they mention the NNC, with the exception of Denmark. Iceland's official 'Visit Iceland' website starts by stating how Icelandic cuisine has been 'influenced by the philosophy of the New Nordic Cuisine', but then goes on to discuss Icelandic cuisine—with examples of traditional Icelandic fares, dishes and ingredients—and the importance of fishing to Icelandic history, culture and traditions (https://visiticeland.com/article/enjoy-icelandic-food). On the official 'Visit Sweden' website, there is no mention of NNC. Instead, the site explains the importance of Swedish history (going back to Viking times), culture, geography and climate to modern Swedish cuisine. The site provides examples of Swedish national dishes, such as Swedish meatballs, cinnamon rolls and rotten herring, and explains the importance of spices, such as cinnamon, ginger, cardamom and saffron to Swedish baking (https://visitsweden.com/what-to-do/food-drink/swedish-food-culture/). There is also no mention of the NNC, other than lists of restaurants associated with the movement, on Norway's and Finland's official websites. These sites provide lists of national dishes and ingredients and the importance of their own history, environment, traditions and culinary roots (https://www.visitnorway.com/things-to-do/food-and-drink/cuisine/; https://www.visitfinland.com/food/).

From its inception, the NNC and its potential in terms of gastrodiplomacy were viewed differently by the region's states (Leer 2016; Neuman and Leer 2018). As explained by Neuman and Leer (2018) Danish culinary excellence was promoted as and through NNC, whereas for other regional states the movement was an opportunity to promote their own national and political agendas. This divergence in approach is clear when we examine how the NNC has been used by Denmark. On the official 'Visit Denmark' website, it is stated that 'Denmark has led the way in Scandinavian gourmet cuisine for over a decade so what better place than here to dive in face-first and experience delicious and elegant New Nordic Cuisine?'; in the official Denmark webpage, it is explained that 'over the past 30 years, traditional Danish food has been re-invented as New Nordic Cuisine' (https://denmark.dk/people-and-culture/cuisine; https://www.visitdenmark.com/denmark/things-do/danish-food). In other words, and as previously mentioned by Leer (2016), there is a clear top-down articulation of Danish and Nordic food as being representative of Denmark. This might to an extent also feed into Danish perceptions of their own political geography, which includes Greenland and the Faroe Islands, and political history, which includes periods of regional dominance.

The use of Danish and Nordic food labels is also present in Denmark's gastrodiplomatic efforts and plans. On the one hand in the government's 'Gastro 2025 Plan' to promote and strengthen Danish gastronomy, including its use for culinary diplomacy, there is no mention of the NNC. On the other hand, in its gastrodiplomatic events, Denmark has blended the two together. For example, Danish embassies around the world have organised food events that celebrated Danish and Nordic food and gastronomy as a way of promoting Denmark.

The NNC emerged out of a particular culinary movement connected to the Noma restaurant in Copenhagen. It is clear that Denmark prides itself on this fact. It presents itself as the home of the NNC and movement and as the region's gastronomic powerhouse. Nevertheless, the case study also illustrates the fluidity and complexity of trying to define and promote national food internationally and the tensions that arise, as part of globalisation, between the aims and objectives of different local, regional, national and international political actors.

Japan's Sushi Police

Like any other thing in life, gastrodiplomacy does not always succeed. Or rather, it is usually very difficult to ascertain whether it has been successful or not. In this context, the case of the Japanese 'sushi police' is exceptional in that it is a clear-cut example of a failed attempt at pursuing government-led gastrodiplomacy.

In 2006, *The Washington Post* carried an article by Anthony Faiola (2006) entitled 'Putting the Bite on Pseudo Sushi and Other Insults: Japan Plans to Scrutinize Restaurant Offerings Abroad', which reported on the Japanese government's plan for quality control of restaurants abroad that served Japanese food. 'So beware, America, home of the California roll. The Sushi Police are on their way', so warned Faiola, and a new term, 'sushi police', entered popular vocabulary. This was quickly picked up by wide western readership and fans of Japanese food both in Japan and abroad attracting expressions of incredulity and scepticism (Daliot-Bul 2009; Sakamoto and Allen 2011).

What was then dubbed as the 'sushi police' referred to the government's plan to put in place a system of authenticating Japanese restaurants abroad in a similar manner that the Thai and Italian governments were attempting in order to control the quality of Thai or Italian restraints across the world. The Ministry of Agriculture, Forestry and Fishery (MAFF) took the lead in this initiative, and the idea was officially discussed for the first time at a meeting of the advisory council made up of experts in Japanese food/cuisine and cultural exchange (chefs, food manufactures, a restaurant information provider, representatives of tourism industry and the Japan Foundation) and MAFF officials on 27 November 2006 with a view to designing a system of authenticating Japanese restaurants abroad (MAFF 2006). The government's intention was clearly about ensuring the authenticity of Japanese food served at Japanese restaurants abroad as Minister Matsuoka, the then Minister of Agriculture, made it clear at this inaugural meeting: 'Above all, the fundamental aim is to provide authentic and proper Japanese cuisine. Not the type of thing which looks Japanese on the surface but which is not at all Japanese in its content, but I would like to provide what we can proudly call authentic

Japanese cuisine'.[2] The minister's wish was to set up a system to judge which restaurants served the 'correct/appropriate' Japanese cuisine in order to protect the integrity of Japanese cuisine as Faiola and others surmised. The idea was clearly built on the belief that only the Japanese knew the truth about Japanese cuisine. Notwithstanding the minister's passion for serving something authentic ostensibly as a way of promoting exports of Japanese foodstuff as well as of attracting more tourists to Japan, other members of the meeting were more cautious about the idea of 'authentication'. 'Authentic to whom?' was one of the points made by a number of experts and attention was drawn to the fuzzy boundary of Japanese cuisine as well as the importance of fusion in the development of Japanese food culture.

The intention to 'authenticate' was again interrogated in the second meeting on 1 February 2007 with contributions from those who were involved in a variety of activities to promote Japanese cuisine abroad, and the minutes clearly conveyed a change in direction away from 'authentication by the government' to 'recommendation by the private sector' (MAFF 2007a). What was seen as problematic by many of the council members was the impression that the Japanese government was telling the world what was right and correct about things Japanese. The shift in the direction was confirmed in the third meeting on 16 March 2007. It was agreed that the implementation of the 'Japanese Restaurant Recommendation Program' would be proposed to the government (MAFF 2007b). The aim of the programme was defined as enabling people living outside Japan to enjoy tasty and safe Japanese cuisine in Japanese restaurants, and it was noted that the programme should be pursued by the private sector with the government assuming a supporting role. The programme also emphasised the widely spread hybrid nature of Japanese cuisine offered outside Japan and declared to be non-exclusionary and non-discriminatory in any sense (ibid.).

Upon this recommendation, the Organization to Promote Japanese Restaurants Abroad (JRO) was set up as the implementation body of the programme in July 2007 (JRO 2007). JRO's stated objectives are 'to

---

[2] This is not official translation by MAFF. This is translated from the Japanese original by Atsuko Ichijo.

promote the reliability of restaurants serving Japanese food overseas while providing vital information on Japanese food and food culture, and to contribute to the further development of Japanese food culture as well as the enhancement of the global dining experience' (JRO, http://jronet.org/ accessed on 17 February 2022), and in the first year of its existence, it developed the 'recommendation guidelines' (which appears to have been quietly dropped since then) for the purpose of the implementation of the programme and adopted an official logo. In the subsequent years, JRO's activities have been focused on hosting training sessions and seminars for cooking professionals, developing a network of Japanese restaurant owners and food importers in various places in the world, holding symposia to discuss issues related to spread Japanese cuisine abroad and so on, and their activities do not include anything akin to inspection, evaluation or authentication of Japanese restaurants outside Japan. Clearly JRO is not the 'sushi police' as envisaged by Minister Matsuoka and in this sense the gastrodiplomacy initiative of the Japanese government has clearly failed.

The 'sushi police' idea, although it was quickly shot down by the body set up by the government, was certainly an aspect of a wider programme of official nationalism pursued by the Japanese government, and it needs to be examined in the context of the 'Cool Japan' initiative (Daliot-Bul 2009; Sakamoto and Allen 2011; Valaskivi 2013). The 'Cool Japan' initiative emerged in 2002 when the Japanese government started to assess the value of Japanese popular culture, probably for the first time, within the newly emerging framework of intellectual property. The Council for Intellectual Property Strategy was set up in 2002 by the order of then Prime Minister Koizumi. The move was christened as 'Cool Japan' in an influential article entitled 'Japan's Gross National Cool' by Douglas McGray published in *Foreign Policy* in May 2002. The surge of interest in intellectual property was due to the increased awareness on the part of Japanese policy-makers of the importance of creative industry in shoring up the stagnating economy and McGray's depiction of Japan as an emerging 'Empire of Cool' found a captive audience among Japanese policy-makers who were looking into Tony Blair's UK government's 'Cool Britannia' initiative in the late 1990s. The 'Cool Japan' initiative refers to a range of government policies to promote Japanese, mainly creative, industry and export by focusing on what is deemed to be 'cool', usually popular culture such as *manga* and *anime*, but as the initiative developed it started to include a wider range of objects such as food, martial arts and traditional culture. There is a consensus that the 'sushi police' scheme emerged within a wider framework of the 'Cool Japan' initiative as an expression of the Japanese government's desire to be in full control of cultural products as the rightful owner of those (Daliot-Bul 2009; Sakamoto and Allen 2011; Valaskivi 2013). While the 'sushi police' idea never materialised in the form it was originally envisaged, the 'Cool Japan' initiative has been steadily pursued by the successive Japanese government as seen in the setting up of the 'Cool Japan' unit in the Ministry of Economy, Trade and Industry (METI) in 2010, and in the aftermath of the Great East Japan Earthquake of 2011, the initiative was repositioned to be the driving force of the regeneration of the areas hit by the disaster as well as Japan as a whole (Valaskivi 2013). The Japanese government's application to UNESCO for the inscription of washoku, Japanese traditional cuisine, in the intangible cultural heritage list was also seen by the METI as an integral part of the 'Cool Japan' strategy (MAFF 2011a, b, c, d).

The 'Cool Japan' initiative has been variably seen as a form of soft power, in the game of which McGray argued that Japan had surpassed the US because its popular culture was not seen as threatening by others (McGray 2022); it is also seen as a clear case of nation branding drawing from cultural nationalism (Daliot-Bul 2009; Sakamoto and Allen 2011). It is often understood as the government's efforts to project a favourable image of itself abroad in order to secure an increase in its influence in the world and to stimulate the economy by expanding export and by attracting more tourists based on culture. The 'sushi police' initiative was also conceived in this context: the aim of authenticating Japanese restaurants abroad was to promote export of Japanese agricultural products, services and skills associated with Japanese cuisine as well as to entice more tourists to Japan to expiring 'the real stuff' after being introduced to authentic Japanese culture at an authenticated Japanese restaurant. However, as Daliot-Bul (2009) points out, the true target of the 'Cool Japan' initiative including the 'sushi police' is in fact the domestic population; it is a means of national mobilisation because if national culture was to be promoted abroad, the promoter is required to have enough knowledge of the very culture he/she is promoting. Culture is notoriously difficult to pin down, and its proprietorship is always contested. Sakamoto and Allen (2011) point out that the majority of the Japanese population are not very sure of the 'correct' way of having sushi as the vast number of books and other information available as to what is the correct way of ordering, eating and paying for sushi at a traditional sushi bar, for instance. When the Japanese government promotes the 'Cool Japan' initiative, the Japanese people are prompted to learn about what is 'cool' about Japanese culture, to define it, to create it and then to contribute to turning it into commercial goods in order to help project a particular image of Japan. In other words, it is a national mobilisation scheme at the time of economic stagnation and other crises.

The 'sushi police' initiative failed due to the appreciation of the fuzziness and hybridity of Japanese cuisine shared by the majority of the members of the advisory council. To them, to have a government-run system to certify which restaurant serves correct Japanese cuisine was simply not a done thing. Still the minutes of the advisory council's meetings show there was clear desire to affirm the ownership of Japanese food drawing from the assumption that they knew what authentic Japanese cuisine was because they were Japanese. While this particular initiative failed before it was put in place, the case of 'sushi police' demonstrates gastrodiplomacy draws from the un-reflected, essentialist assumption about the relationship between the nation, culture and food which persists in modern society.

Conclusion

The chapter has demonstrated the apparent usefulness of the food and nationalism axis in examining interaction among states, and the relationship between the everyday level, the state and the private sector in a globalised world. It has made clear the appeal food holds as a means of winning hearts and minds and in creating an appealing national brand. As the case studies of Taiwan and Thailand indicate, gastrodiplomacy is one of the more useful, though underused, tools states have in their cultural diplomacy arsenal. Though, and as we have shown regarding the NNC and Japan's sushi police, there are often competing ideas of how to promote the nation, and gastrodiplomacy is not always an easy tool to wield.

The importance of national food as a marker of national identity and its use internationally also reveals an interesting dichotomy inherent in the spread of globalisation. On the one hand, the spread of globalisation is expected to limit the scope for nationalism and the promotion of the nation by bringing about homogenisation at the global scale, or in the NNC case study more regional integration. On the other hand, the desire by states to use food in the global setting requires its identification with the nation, a strengthening of the particularistic framework. This brings about a process of both globalisation and localisation in the states' efforts to use food as a tool of diplomacy to maximise their national interest. Hence the chapter has highlighted an inherently contradictory effect of globalisation on nationalism. Globalisation is not, after all, a process of flattening out the global cultural landscape but of adding more and more layers to it.

The globalisation and localisation of food and its use by states raise a number of important issues, in particular with regard to competing national claims over food authenticity and origin, but also with regard to food security. In the next chapter we will focus on these contestations and the ways in which food and nationalism became securitised.

Chapter Six: National Food in the International Context II—Gastronationalism and Populism

As we have demonstrated in the previous two chapters, food is inherently political and decision-making around food is heavily influenced by the state, which often uses food as a resource in the pursuit of its aims. For example, and as we have shown, the production and consumption of food can be mobilised by the state in support of nation-building, and food exports and food culture can be used for supporting domestic food producers, and the promotion and branding of the state, domestically and internationally. Politics at the national level, however, is not only about maintaining and promoting the state; it is also about the pursuit and accumulation of power and the defence of national resources and what is perceived to be the national interest. In terms of food this means asserting national claims to food as a resource and as part of the nation's culture and heritage, which requires, at times, the state's protection from competing claims. The assertion of national claims, and the view of food as a national resource that requires the protection by the state, leads us to consider food, at the national and international level, as an area open to contestation and conflict between states, which is what this chapter will focus on.

It is interesting to note, as we have done in previous chapters, the general lack of engagement with and acknowledgement of food as an important element in top-down studies of nationalism. This lacuna is particularly interesting given the recent resurgence of nationalism and populist-nationalist leaders, political movements and governments, and given the explicit mentioning and mobilisation of food by these actors. The recent resurgence of nationalism has been characterised by several aspects, among them a growing importance attached to national territory, sovereignty and the control and protection of resources. These aspects include romantic notions of attachment to the state's territory and its *terroir*, giving food, food symbols and food production, whether agriculture, animal husbandry, fishing and food processing, meaning beyond dietary needs and/or economic benefits. It has also put food at the centre of political and national debates and as one of the main resources that requires state intervention and protection.

The use and mobilisation of food in recent years can be seen in many examples that span the cultural and political-economic realms. Examples include the trade wars pursued by the US, under former President Donald Trump, against the EU and China, in which symbolic food items were specifically targeted (Lane 2019). The US, for example, applied higher import tariffs on Scottish and Irish Whisky and a range of wines and cheeses that are closely associated with European countries, such as Roquefort and Parmesan; many of the items targeted are part of the European Geographic Indicator (GI) scheme. In return, the EU and China retaliated by applying tariffs on, among other things, iconic US food exports, such as Maine lobsters and US Whisky. As noted by Vadi (2016), the dispute between the US and EU over cultural heritage and GIs is not new. Indeed, this dispute has raged for over two decades and has even been termed 'the war on terroir', with each side taking different approaches regarding the protection of GIs and towards the meaning and importance of *terroir* (Josling 2006). European countries require free trade agreements to include an explicit recognition of European cultural heritage and *terroir*, which are embedded in the EU's GIs (the subject of GIs will be discussed in "Chapter Eight: International Organisations, Food and Nationalism"). The blending of food as part of the cultural heritage of the nation and its use as a political and economic resource can also be seen in requests made by governments worldwide for consumers to engage in patriotic food consumption and favour local food producers at the expense of, what are seen as, foreign imports in response to the

Covid-19 pandemic: 'I am calling for food patriotism, for agricultural patriotism' declared French Agriculture Minister Didier Guillaume in May 2020 during the first round of national lockdowns (Wanat and Wax 2020).

The above examples point towards viewing food as a national resource as well as part of the national heritage and culture. As such it is easy to see why food might require protection from challenges and competing claims, particularly if they emanate from other states. The trend of asserting national rights over food has been described as 'Culinary Nationalism' (Ferguson 2010: 102) and 'Gastronationalism' (DeSoucey 2010: 446); even though the terms can be used interchangeably, we prefer gastronationalism as it is more widely used in the literature. Food in this context includes not only particular ingredients and dishes but also methods of production, preparation and consumption, and related symbols, norms and values. DeSoucey defines gastronationalism as 'a form of claims making and a project of collective identity, [it] is responsive to and reflective of the political ramifications of connecting nationalist projects with food culture at local levels. It presumes that attacks (symbolic or otherwise) against a nation's food practices are assaults on heritage and culture, not just on the food item itself' (DeSoucey 2010: 433).

Our discussion and analysis of gastronationalism and the assertation of national rights over food will start by first looking at role and place of food in the recent resurgence of nationalism, which includes a discussion of the relationship between nationalism, populism and food. The case study of the UK's referendum on leaving the EU (from here on referred to as Brexit) will then be used to further explore some of the issues mentioned and their implication at the international level. The chapter will then move to discuss the concept of 'food wars', when food items are contested between several countries, with a particular focus on hummus and kimchi.

Nationalism, Populism and Food

Over the past decade, and arguably since Brexit and the election of US President Donald Trump, there has been a rise in gastronationalism, which can be seen through the increasing securitisation of and assertion of national rights to food. Food, whether seen as a political and economic resource or as part of the nation's culture and heritage, has been mobilised in defence of the state, from the assertion of national rights over *terroir*, agriculture and fishing rights, food products and food supply chains to the imposition of, often retaliatory, tariffs and non-tariff barriers on food imports. The impression given in the popular press is that this is a new phenomenon and that it is linked to the rise of populism. However, and as discussed in "Chapter Four: Food and Diet in 'Official' Nationalism" regarding several modernising states, the importance of utilising food and the assertion of national rights over food is not a new phenomenon. Indeed, the linking of food as a cultural and symbolic product that is intertwined with the nation and as an important national resource has been part and parcel of many nationalist and populist-nationalist movements for well over a century.

In order to delve deeper into the food, populism and nationalism nexus, we first need to define what populism is and how it relates to food and nationalism. Despite the claim that we now live in the 'Age of Populism', the term itself is not new. Indeed, the term has been discussed and debated since the late nineteenth century, for example, in the post-World War II period with reference to South America and postcolonial states (see, e.g., the edited volume by Ionescu and Gellner from 1969). It is clear though that current debates over populism and nationalism are more widespread and for the first time are discussed in reference to many developed countries and mature democracies, particularly in Europe.

Populism, like many other social science terms, is hard to define, primarily because it emerges and manifests differently in each country, and has several forms, for example, left- and right-wing populism, agrarian, authoritarian and economic populism. There are, however, a number of key characteristics that are shared by most populist movements and governments. First, the claim of speaking on behalf of and representing the people. Second, the presentation of populism, and populist leaders and movements, as standing in support of the people and in opposition to the ruling elite, which are characterised as corrupt and acting against the will of the people, and often as part of an international capitalist class. Lastly, the view of the people/the nation as homogenous, which is often associated with a rejection of pluralism and international norms (Muller 2017).

What is particularly interesting, in relation to food and nationalism, is the centrality of food to the rhetoric and policies of populist leaders, movements and governments. This can be seen in the way populist leaders and movements defend and assert what they see as the nation's cuisine and culinary heritage, which are often viewed as static, while also defining who they are, demarcating the nation and constructing the *Other* (Porciani 2019). Let us provide a few examples to illustrate this point. During their annual convention in 2013, members of the right-wing French Front National Party called for 'neither kebab nor burger, long live the ham and butter sandwich'. The call signified the members' opposition to, what they saw as, non-native food and the Islamisation and Americanisation of French cuisine and society (O'Sullivan 2017). Another indicative example has been the campaign spearheaded by Matteo Salvini, the leader of the Italian Northern League Party and former deputy Prime Minister, for the rejection of Turkish hazelnuts and other non-native ingredients in Nutella (a popular chocolate and hazelnut spread).[1] Salvini's campaign was part of his broader push for an Italian first food policy that would, in his words, protect and promote Italian farmers and fishermen (Garcia-Santamaria 2020). Perhaps one of the most publicised expressions of populist food nationalism and of demarcating the nation was the 2019 White House celebratory meal, hosted by the then President Trump, for the Clemson Tigers, the College football national champions. The meal, which included popular fast foods, such as burgers, fries and pizza, was described by Trump as 'great American food' produced by 'American companies'. Trump's assertion of Americanness to these fast foods could also be seen as a rejection of, what he saw as, international and cosmopolitan food items favoured by liberal elites (Bock 2021).

---

[1] The campaign was overall unsuccessful. Part of the reason lies in the fact that Italy does not produce enough hazelnuts to satisfy the demands for the production of Nutella, which consumes around quarter of the world's supply. The other part is that Turkey is the largest producer and exporter of hazelnuts, and the industry has been heavily supported and protected by the Turkish government, itself led by a nationalist-populist leader and political party. In an interesting demonstration of the impacts of globalisation and the way it complicates national aims and ideals, Ferrero, the Italian multinational company that manufactures Nutella, has been directly involved in the Turkish hazelnut industry (Gurel et al. 2021).

Populism and nationalism are not only about signalling what the nation is and indicating what its food culture or cuisine is. They also include support for a number of food-related initiatives and policies. These often focus on supporting and protecting food producers and growers, in particular small-scale farmers and fishermen; support for rural communities; a belief in the importance of food self-sufficiency; and an emphasis on the people's right to cheap and accessible food. These policies are widely shared among populist movements and governments, whether right- or left-wing, though the particular way they manifest often differs. Right-wing populists tend to focus more on self-sufficiency, support for rural communities and farmers and opposition to urban cosmopolitan liberal elites, while left-wing populists often focus on indigenous communities, land reform, food sovereignty and opposition to large agri-food businesses (see, e.g., the discussion on agrarian populism in Borras 2020; Lubarda's 2019 account of discursive overlapping between populist and green parties in Hungary).

As we stated above, the association between populist movements and food and nationalism is not new, it has been a feature of many countries' political systems since the mid- to late nineteenth century. Examples for this span the globe, from the Narodnik movement in Tsarist Russia to the People's Party in the late nineteenth- to early twentieth-century US (Borras 2020; Hajdu and Mamonova 2020). What these movements had in common is a shared antagonism to the prevailing economic structures that, in their view, favoured the establishment at the expense of small-scale farmers, and the urban elite at the expense of the rural population (Borras 2020). These movements did not always adhere to the traditional right-left division in politics and exhibited many overlaps. The overlap between them and the close association between populism and rural communities is still a prominent feature (see, e.g., the special issue edited by Mamonova and Franquesa on right-wing populism and rural Europe, 2020, and the edited volume on authoritarian populism and the rural world by Scoones et al. 2021).

One of the classic examples of populism and its relationship with food and nationalism is that of Argentina, in the period immediately after World War II, under the Presidency of Juan Peron. Peron sought to use food as a way of reshaping the nation, the state, its economy and its relationship with voters (Milanesio 2010). At the heart of Peron's populist food policy was the argument that Argentinian food industry had been dominated by foreign interest and had not served the interest of its people. For Peron rectifying this problem took place across two levels. First, he countered the previous government's fixation with exporting high-quality food, particularly beef, stating that foreigners were eating Argentina's food. He claimed the exports largely benefited foreign interests and countries, particularly Britain and the US, to which Argentina had subjugated itself. However, reneging and attempting to renegotiate food export quotas and prices with Argentina's main exporting partners invariably led to trade disputes. It appears that Peron believed that Argentina's position as a food exporter, in a starving world that was just recovering from war, gave it a strong voice in the new world order as well as additional leverage in trade negotiations. The second level Peron focused on was the domestic, favouring domestic consumption, and 'inexpensive and abundant food', over international markets. One of the main ways this manifested is through emphasising the consumption of more beef, which was casted as a symbol of Argentina's *terroir* and its masculinity, and presented as an Argentinian 'right'. Peron's 'beef nationalism' signalled the ascendance of a new voting bloc, comprising the working-class, urban poor and rural communities.[2] It also demonstrated the intervention of the state to protect its food resources and ensure the 'right' of its population, or segments of the population, to access desirable, cheap and abundant food (Milanesio 2010)

Brexit

There are many factors behind the British government's decision to set up the referendum and for why a plurality of British voters supported leaving the European Union; as a result, the question of whether Brexit was

---

[2] The relationship between meat eating (often in connection to grilling or barbecuing, and mostly beef) and nationalism has been extensively written about, particularly in relation to settler colonial states, such as Argentina, Chile, Uruguay, the US, Australia, South Africa and Israel. See, for example, Avieli's 'grilled nationalism' (2013), Orlove on Chile (1997) and Tal on white South African nationalism (2022). See also Edwards (2019) and Rogers (2003) on beef and British nationalism.

at heart a populist endeavour is hard to answer (Edwards 2019). What is clear is that Brexit, including the run-up to the referendum and the ensuing post-referendum negotiations between the UK and the EU, encapsulates many of the issues discussed above and demonstrates the merging of populism, nationalism and food, and the ensuing complications these bring about at the international level. The case study also illustrates the ways in which food can be and is mobilised by political movements and governments in support of national, at times populist, aims. The starting point for Brexit is an interesting one, as food issues, unlike immigration and sovereignty, did not feature heavily in the run-up to the referendum (Ranta 2019). As we will demonstrate below, however, food was used as a prism through which leading Brexit supporters (from here on referred to as Brexiteers) in the UK tabloid press and within the British government defined UK-EU relations and as a tool to mobilise public opinion and assert British sovereignty as well as independence vis-à-vis the EU.

Looking at the two decades preceding the referendum, it is hard not to be struck by the centrality of food images and stories to the arguments in favour of leaving the EU, particularly in the Eurosceptic tabloid press in the UK, and among key government ministers. In the run-up to the referendum, food was (mis)used by leading Brexiteers as a way of highlighting EU idiosyncrasies, the perceived lack of British sovereignty and/or control over its own food supplies and policies. The main argument made through food was that unelected, mostly non-British, bureaucrats sitting in Brussels were undermining British food producers and consumers while also wasting British taxpayers' money (Ranta 2019). To make this argument, Brexiteers put forward a long list of claims regarding the EU, many of which concerned food. These claims, mostly made through the tabloid press, included the assertions that the EU will force the UK to rename popular food items, such as Bombay mix as Mumbai mix, and brandy butter as brandy spreadable fat; will inform British farmers as to what they are allowed to grow; was trying to control British fishing, including a claim that the EU was plotting to seize British seabed (Ingham 2013); was planning on banning popular British food items, such as prawn cocktail-flavoured crisps, Caerphilly cheese and mushy peas; wanted to regulate British alcohol consumption, including regulating pubs and the production of Scotch Whisky; planned to ban the use of the

Union Jack on British food packages, in particular meat exports; and will enforce a ban on curved fruit and vegetables, including cucumbers, rhubarbs and most famously bananas.[3]

Whether the above claims are accurate or not is not important for the purposes of this chapter: they are often misleading and mostly inaccurate. What is important is the way in which these and many other examples were used to define the EU and UK-EU relations, particularly on issues such as democracy, independence and sovereignty (Rawlinson 2019). The use of food stereotypes and myths was not only done in the period before the referendum, but it was also pervasive after the referendum. In his campaign to become the Conservative party leader and Prime Minister, Boris Johnson used a number of food examples to point out the 'pointless, pointless, expensive, environmentally damaging health and safety' regulations used by the EU and champion the need to take back control over British food policies.[4]

Food was also used by leading Brexiteers, including key government ministers, to explain how the EU was undermining the British food sector; these arguments were then reused by the British government after the referendum and in their negotiations with the EU. In particular, Brexiteers highlighted two EU governing frameworks—the Common Agricultural Policy (CAP) and the Common Fisheries Policy (CFP)—as wasteful, bureaucratic and ruinous to British farmers and fishermen. For Brexiteers, and later the British government, the CAP and CFP exemplified the lack of British control over its own food policies and territorial waters. They claimed that, among other things, leaving CAP and CFP would open new opportunities for British food producers, provide the framework for a more environmentally friendly farming sector and lower food prices for consumers (Ranta 2019). The claim that Brexit would bring about lower

---

[3] The European Commission has maintained a database of these claims, which it refers to as myths. Euromyths, A–Z index: www.blogs.ec.europa.eu/ECintheUK/euromyths-a-z-index (accessed 15 October 2020).

[4] The quote is taken from what is now referred to as the 'kipper speech'. In the speech Johnson erroneously blamed the EU for the health and safety regulations that govern the sale of kippers (smoked butterfly filleted herring). In fact, these regulations were mandated by the British government and not by the EU (Quinn 2019).

food prices was very much in line with food populist arguments and policies.

The issue of control became a key element in the run-up to the referendum, with 'take back control' emerging as a key slogan; the slogan was also used repeatedly by the UK government in the period after the referendum and in UK-EU Brexit negotiations. For example, the UK government insisted in post-Brexit negotiations that all key food policy decisions must be taken by the UK and that the UK will not be part of any EU regulatory framework, even if the UK was de facto following that framework; the UK government's reasoning was that being part of EU regulatory frameworks inhibited its ability to pursue free trade agreements with other countries. A clear example of this conundrum has been the UK's refusal to follow the EU's framework and regulations governing sanitary and phytosanitary products, even though it was de facto doing so, and even though this would have helped its dispute with the EU over the trade rules governing Northern Ireland, in what later became known as the 'sausage wars' (Boscia 2021); see below for more on the concept of 'food wars'.

One particular area that was used as a rallying call for Brexit and for pursuing an antagonistic and maximalist post-Brexit negotiating approach towards the EU was fishing. The fact that fishing was used as a key example in the run-up to the referendum and assumed an important role in UK-EU Brexit negotiations, despite the fact it accounted for less than 0.1 per cent of UK GDP (Billiet 2019), demonstrated the symbolic power of this industry. Fishing and particularly British territorial waters and exclusive economic zone (EEZ) were used as exemplars of the lack of British sovereignty, independence and control.

One of the most enduring and iconic images of the Brexit referendum campaign has been the pro-Brexit fishing flotilla of the 'fishing for leave' (a pro-Brexit organisation of fishermen) travelling down the river Thames and being confronted by a smaller anti-Brexit flotilla (Tapsfield 2016). Fishing in many ways encapsulated the nationalist and populist arguments for Brexit. In the run-up to the referendum and during the ensuing UK-EU negotiations, the 'take back control' slogan was used in many instances, but it was arguably clearest in British demands to control its own territorial waters and EEZ and allow its own fishermen the lion share of, what it saw as, its fish. The way Brexit was explained by the government to the British public was that European fishing vessels were literally taking 'our' fish and the UK had little control over the process. Brexit, the government claimed, would mean 'reclaiming our waters' and 'saving our fish', through British fishing policies governing 'British' fish and fishermen. These policies, it was argued, would see an increase in the catch for British fishermen and more resources to the mostly deprived coastal communities (Billiet 2019).

The Brexit case study also illustrates the difficulties and limitations of pursuing a nationalist and populist food policy in a global world. Fish stocks are not static resources and asserting national claims to them are, therefore, not straight forward. Even the seemingly simple action of catching more fish in British waters is complicated by the fact that European fishermen have been using these waters for decades and restricting them would incur a political and diplomatic cost. This is further complicated by the very nature of British territorial waters, in that the UK and the EU (as well as the UK and Norway) are required to manage many shared fisheries. Additionally, a substantial amount of fish caught by British fishermen in the UK's EEZ is destined to be sold to the EU, which is the world's largest seafood market. Even if the UK increases its catch of fish in its EEZ, it will still need to negotiate for access to the EU's market. Lastly, there is some degree of dissonance between the fish caught in British waters and the fish eaten by British consumers, many of which are either imported or caught in European waters (Phillipson and Symes 2018). What all of the above points towards are the difficulties of reconciling the gastronationalist rhetoric and aims of Brexit with the need to negotiate internationally binding treaties with other countries and organisations, in this case the EU. It also points towards the need for arbitration between countries when assertion of food resources is contested, which points towards the importance of international law, in the case of fishing the UN Convention on the Law of the Sea (UNCLOS) (for more on the complexity of fishing and Brexit, see Billiet 2019; Phillipson and Symes 2018).

Food Wars: Contesting National Food

Over the past few decades there have been numerous articles regarding food wars or food as an area of conflict and contestation. Food wars, other than being the title of a popular Japanese manga series, have been used to define and explain a number of food-related issues, such as arguments over adequate nutrition and the place of processed food; competing narratives over food norms and values; to describe supermarket price wars; and in reference to national and international policies and legal disputes over the introduction and impacts of new technologies, such as GMO (e.g., Lang and Heasman 2015), which will be discussed in the next chapter.

In the literature regarding food and nationalism, the term food wars has mostly been used in reference to disputes over cultural heritage and authenticity. In the previous chapter we discussed gastrodiplomacy and the use of food in national branding and as a form of soft power and a tool in cultural diplomacy. Above we provided examples of food as an important economic and political resource. What happens when more than one state asserts claim to the same food? Particularly as a consequence of globalisation, national foods are constantly challenged at the international level in terms of ownership and authenticity.[5] This brings to the fore the need to arbitrate and define to whom certain food items belong as well as to agree on what should be the accepted standards and methods of production. This contest over ownership and authenticity, brought about by globalisation, produces international food clashes as well as competition between national and international private sector food manufacturers and producers. This issue will be briefly explored through two case studies focusing on food wars concerning two iconic food items, hummus and kimchi.

As discussed in earlier chapters, hummus is seen in Israel as one of its national dishes and hummus and the hummus industry in Israel are serious businesses. In Israel, almost any conversation, be it among

---

[5] A related area of food contestation occurs when borders and *terroir* intersect, for example, when states claim ownership over a disputed area or when states share a *terroir*. See, for example, Monterescu with regard to border wine regions between Hungary and Slovakia, Bulgaria and Greece, and Israel and the Occupied Palestinian Territories (2017).

Jewish-Israelis or Arab-Palestinian citizens of Israel regarding food, invariably triggers a lively debate over where and how to eat hummus. Hummus has been described by a prominent Jewish-Israeli food blogger as the embodiment of the nation (Galili 2007). Beyond its importance as a food item that is consumed regularly by all segments of the population and viewed as belonging to the nation, Israel and Israeli-owned companies have been among the leading producers and exporters of hummus globally.

The 'hummus wars' started with a marketing stunt by the US-based food company Sabra (the name given to a Jew born in Israel), which is jointly owned by PepsiCo and one of Israel's largest food companies Strauss, to produce the world's largest hummus plate, in order to increase the sales of its salads and dips in the US, in particular the sale of hummus. This was followed up by the setting in Israel of a Guinness record for the biggest hummus plate by Osem, an Israeli food company and a competitor of Strauss. Osem produced a 400 kg hummus plate that was eaten in the main Jewish food market in Jerusalem, Mahaneh Yehuda. The two marketing stunts were reported by the Israeli business newspaper *Calcalist* (2008) as being the opening shots in the 'hummus war' between the two over the lucrative US market. The 'hummus wars' helped both companies increase their share of the US hummus market and by 2016 Sabra controlled over half of it.

The 'hummus wars' became truly international when a year later, in response to the Israeli companies setting of hummus Guinness records, a group of Lebanese chefs broke the record and produced a hummus plate of over 2 tons. The Lebanese hummus plate came as a result of a campaign by the Association of Lebanese Industrialists (ALI) 'dubbed "Hands off Our Dishes"' which 'intended to stop Israel from marketing hummus and other dishes as Israeli' (Ariel 2012: 37). Fadi Abboud, the then head of ALI and later Lebanon's tourism minister, claimed that Lebanon was ready to take legal action against Israel over the marketing of Lebanese food products as Israeli. Abboud stated that even though Hummus is not internationally and officially recognised as a Lebanese dish, its claim of ownership was based on its long historical association with the product. ALI based its claim on the precedent created by Greece's successful litigation over the use of feta cheese—in 2002 the EU ruled that only Greece is allowed to market the cheese as feta because of the long history of the production of the cheese under the name feta in Greece (we will discuss the protection of geographical indicators within the EU in "Chapter Eight: International Organisations, Food and Nationalism").

After the Lebanese Guinness record, a tit-for-tat breaking of the hummus Guinness record took place. First, in 2009 Arab-Palestinian chefs in the village of Abu Ghosh, a town in Israel known for its culinary prowess, broke the record in an event that was framed in patriotic terms (Israeli flags decorated the event) and which claimed to bring back the record to Israel. An Arab-Palestinian businessman and restaurant owner claimed that 'the Lebanese can claim whatever they want, but the hummus is ours, Israelis. We, in any case, prepare it better' (quoted in, Hirsch and Tene 2013: 40). The Israeli record did not hold for long and was broken the following year by Lebanese chefs who claimed to 'stand together against this industrial and cultural violation and defend our economy, civilization and Lebanese heritage' (quoted in Knafo 2013).

Whether hummus is indeed Israeli or Lebanese, or Middle Eastern for that matter, is open to debate. What is clear, however, is that marketing and promoting of food as national in a globalised world can lead to tensions and conflict and be further linked to other political issues, in this case the Israeli occupation of the Palestinian Territories and its previous invasion of Lebanon. Abboud explained that the 'hummus wars' were not only about hummus but also about 'the organized theft carried out by Israel, not just of land, but history, traditions, architecture, poetry, singing, music, and everything that is Arab in this region. In the Imagination of the world everything bad that originates from the Arab countries is Arab, and everything that is pleasant and good in this region originated from Israel' (quoted in Ariel 2012: 37). What is apparent in Abboud's words is the importance of attractive and popular food items, such as hummus, to the image projected by nation-state. Nevertheless, and as noted by Avieli (2018) and Hirsch and Tene (2013), the 'hummus wars' also exposed the close relationship between the everyday and banal manifestation of nationalism through food, the global use and marketing of national food, and the important role played by private companies in the representation of food as national. For example, the Israeli hummus plate produced at Abu Ghosh was part of an event sponsored by the village restaurants and an Israeli food company (Miki Salads) trying to make a name for itself in a very competitive sector, and which provided the facilities and equipment. The company's logo was also present on the hummus plate (Avieli 2018).[6] The 'hummus wars' also indicated the growing prominence of international organisations in mediating competing claims: the Lebanese claim was based on the Greek feta precedent and ALI threatened to use international organisations to stake the Lebanese ownership of hummus. As of 2022, Lebanon has not taken any legal action with regard to trademarking or asserting its claim to hummus.

The example of the 'hummus wars' is not unique, as mentioned previously with regard to the case of feta cheese, there have been a number of trade disputes and challenges to the authenticity and origin of food items. Though it is also clear that the hummus war was not so much a contestation between states as between private companies and individuals with some state support. A clearer example of the contestation of food between states in the international arena is the ongoing dispute over the rights to produce and export a dish of fermented spicy cabbage known as kimchi; in the literature and the media this dispute has come to be known as the 'kimchi wars'. The term 'kimchi wars' was first popularised by *The Economist* in 2005 in an article discussing the complexity of South Korean-Chinese trade relations and a decision by the South Korean Food and Drug Administration to reject Chinese kimchi imports on food safety grounds (it was claimed that parasitic eggs were found in the Chinese imported kimchi) (The Economist 2005).

There have been several debates regarding the history of kimchi production and consumption in Korea, with arguments that the tradition extends as far back as the sixteenth century, while others point towards a

---

[6] Avieli provides additional commentary to this complex local, national and international story regarding the setting of the hummus word record at Abu Ghosh: 'Driving home, I couldn't help but reflect on the irony of the event: A Palestinian of Israeli citizenship set out, in his own words: "to save the nation's honor" by preparing the largest plate ever of hummus, a dish of his own ethnic culinary heritage but one that is also a contested marker of identity and a desired economic asset claimed by the Lebanese, Palestinians, and Israeli Jews. He did it in a village whose Palestinian-Muslim identity is purposely blurred for political and commercial reasons, and he achieved this feat with industrial hummus produced by his Jewish business partners, beating Lebanese contestants, whose culinary heritage is similar, if not identical, to his own, and who used industrial hummus for their feat' (2018: 6).

more recent period of the late nineteenth century, with mass production and industrialisation starting in the mid-twentieth century. What is clear, however, is that there is little debate over the current status of kimchi as Korea's national dish and the deep involvement of the state in its production, promotion and protection. Since the late twentieth century kimchi has been seen and accepted in South Korea as the national dish, and the government, at regional and national levels, has set up specialised units to support and promote the kimchi industry (Cho 2006).[7] The South Korean government has presented kimchi as the 'soul of Korean cuisine'. It has followed this with support and protection for the industry through, for example, the application of import tariffs, and the provision of subsidies for key kimchi ingredients, such as locally grown Chinese cabbage and onions. The support for kimchi as the national dish is also seen at the everyday level, with an overwhelming majority of Koreans reported to eat kimchi at home regularly and many also prepare it (Broude 2017).

The kimchi wars arose out of two separate but related issues. First has been the expansion of kimchi imports from Japan and in particular China, which *The Economist* article referred to, and the threats these have posed to South Korea's kimchi industry and its national brand image, domestically and internationally; this explains why the claim of parasitic eggs found in Chinese kimchi imports was taken so seriously. The second issue relates to the use of the term kimchi by these two countries, which South Korea has contested. As a result, the South Korean government has claimed, on the one hand, that the marketing of fermented spicy cabbage as kimchi by China and Japan are acts of appropriation and should be seen as illegal under international law; while, on the other hand, South Korea has accused both countries of producing products that are not of the same standard and quality as the Korean Kimchi. It has argued that the kimchi made in Japan (Kimuchi) is not fermented in the same 'traditional' way and that Chinese Kimchi is an inferior and industrialised product (Broude 2017).

South Korea's response to the kimchi wars has been multifaceted. Unlike the above-mentioned case of hummus and Lebanon's claim to it, South Korea has appealed to several international organisations in its

---

[7] On an aside, Cho's article was one of the first to directly address the issue of food and nationalism from a top-down perspective.

dispute with Japan and China (Han 2011). It has lobbied the Codex Alimentarius—a body set up by the Food and Agriculture Organization and the World Health Organization to provide food recommendations, regulations and standards with regard to labelling, hygiene, health and ethics, among others—for the provision of specific kimchi standards. It has also applied to have kimchi listed by UNESCO as part of its intangible cultural heritage. The application was accepted by UNESCO, which included kimchi in its list in 2013; kimchi was subsequently also inscribed as the cultural heritage of North Korea in 2015. South Korea has also attempted to promote and protect kimchi in its international trade negotiations. It has inscribed kimchi as its trade mark, in a similar fashion to the EU's GI scheme, in its trade agreement with Chile, and has been trying to do the same with its trade deal with the EU (Broude 2017).

Unlike the hummus wars, the kimchi wars are also an ongoing and developing international story with wider geopolitical ramifications. In late 2020, the International Organization for Standardization (ISO) certified the standards for the regional (Sichuan province) Chinese dish of pao cai, which is made of pickled vegetables. Although the ISO clearly stipulated that the certification was not applicable to kimchi, the Chinese media reported it as a China-led standardisation for kimchi. This has led to a media uproar in South Korea and has increased tensions, particularly regarding trade and imports, between the two countries (BBC Travel 2020).

Another example of a battle over the national identity of a food item illustrates the entanglement of the government-led nationalism, populism, commercial interest, globalisation and international organisations in reference to food and nationalism. Halloumi to Greek Cypriots or hellim to Turkish Cypriots is a type of cheese which is widely produced and consumed in the Eastern Mediterranean. The contestation was over whether halloumi/hellim was officially Greek Cypriot or Turkish was fought between the Greek Cypriot governments on the one hand and a German food manufacturer catering for residents in Germany of Turkish ethnicity (Welz 2013). When the manufacturer registered 'hellim' as one of its Gazi brand items with the EU in 2006, the body representing the Cypriot dairy industry filed a complaint to the EU. It argued that the cheese had already been registered with the EU as halloumi in 2000 and that consumers could be easily confused by the new 'hellim' trademark for the same food item.

The EU arbitration bodies twice turned down the Greek Cypriot's claim and ruled that Gazi hellim could be sold across the EU. Not satisfied with these rulings, the Cypriot government, which had acceded to the EU in 2004, started to explore the possibility of obtaining GI for halloumi as a way of protecting its product as well as asserting its identity. The application for the Protected Designation of Origin (PDO) was made in 2009, but the Commission was not very keen on it as it was closely related to the ongoing conflict between Greek Cyprus and Turkish Cyprus. The European Commission took time to examine the application, but in 2012, the Greek Cypriot government withdrew the application in order to protect its export of halloumi. Welz (2013) reports that by then the export of industrially produced halloumi came to assume a paramount economic importance for the Republic of Cyprus, and when the involved parties became aware of strict conditions attached to the granting of PDO, which would mean a reduced amount of production of halloumi, the drive to gain PDO recognition to protect the authenticity of halloumi disappeared. This story aptly captures the complexity which is brought by globalisation in ordinary life: 'The case of a Cypriot cheese re-invented by a German entrepreneur to cater to German residents with a Turkish background is, then, a telling example of how associations with place and culture are employed by the food sector in order to "re-enchant" food products and target specific consumer groups' (Welz 2013, 41). Welz's study shows, as DeSoucey (2010) has attempted, that globalisation is not a one-dimensional, homogenising phenomenon but something that entices and entrenches nationalism in our world. It also leads, at times, to very interesting and at times thought-provoking reimaginations and reinventions of national food (see Photos 1 and 2).

It is interesting to note at this point the growing involvement of international organisations and calls for their intervention in these food wars. This creates an interesting dynamic in that the standard and authenticity of national food can only be certified with reference to the international/global, a paradox which is found in the global regime of culture and heritage protection and its tension with nationalism. We will further untangle this paradox and the role of international organisations in food and nationalism in the following chapters.

Chapter Six: National Food in the International Context... 171

Photo 1 French Tacos

Conclusion

The chapter has built on the points we made in the previous two chapters on the dominant role played by the state in the relationship between food and nationalism. Food can be used in nation-building to construct and mould the nation. It can also be used to mobilise public opinion, and as a cultural and economic-political resource in support of state aims. When food is mobilised and/or used to support the state or national aims, it opens up to competing national claims and contestation. This latter point has been particularly evident as we have shown above in the recent increase seen in nationalism and populism globally, where states and populist movements and leaders have supported and used gastronationalism and have called for state first food policies. As we have demonstrated above, gastronationalist aims and policies bring with them a particular set of difficulties and invariably lead to disputes at the international level.

Photo 2 German Doner Kebab

The importance of national food as a marker of national identity and its use internationally also reveals an interesting dichotomy inherent in the spread of globalisation. On the one hand, the spread of globalisation is expected to limit the scope for nationalism and nationally claimed produce by bringing about homogenisation at the global scale, as seen in the idea of McDonaldisation. However, on the other hand, the desire by states to use food in the global setting requires its identification with the nation, a strengthening of the particularistic framework, which is also clearly manifested in the rise of populist nationalism and their gastronationalist pushback. This brings about a process of both globalisation and localisation in the states' efforts to use food as a tool of diplomacy and as a resource to maximise their national interests. Hence the chapter has highlighted an inherently contradictory effect of globalisation on nationalism. Globalisation is not, after all, a process of flattening out the global cultural landscape but of adding more and more layers to it.

The globalisation and localisation of food and its use by states raise a number of important issues, in particular with regard to food authenticity and origin, but also with regard to mediation and arbitration. The tensions that arise from competing national claims over food necessitate an international mechanism of conflict resolution. As we will discuss in our subsequent chapters, this means that the final arbiters of issues relating to nationalism might be the same international bodies that were heralded as bringing about the end of the nation-state.

Part III

Food and Nationalism/National Identity at the Global Level

Chapter Seven: Norms, Ethics, Food and Nationalism

Whether it is ideationally poor or not, there is a scholarly consensus that nationalism can be understood as a form of ideology, not just as a form of 'national sentiment' (Freeden 1998; Malešević 2013). It is an ideology because it is not just about *what is* but also about 'what ought to be/should be' (Özkirimli 2005: 63). After all, in Ernest Gellner's celebrated definition, nationalism is 'a political principle, which holds that the political and the national unit *should be* congruent' (Gellner 1983: 1, emphasis added). In other words, there is no denying nationalism has a normative dimension; nationalism establishes boundaries, both physical but also ideational, and touches on what is right and what is wrong.

Nationalism's normative aspect in the international arena is most commonly discussed in reference to the principle of national self-determination. Given a concrete expression for the first time in President Woodrow Wilson's Fourteen Points (1914), the right of nations to self-determination is the fundamental principle of the society of the states today. It is enshrined in the Charter of the United Nations (1945), "Chapter One: Everyday Creation of the Nation", Article 1, and has been evoked by a number of groups seeking independence and securing sovereignty. This relationship between sovereignty and nationalism, by now a cornerstone of the current international system, is taken for granted in literature (Ichijo 2009). However, as Bernard Yack has observed: 'Even a brief glance at modern history suggests that there is an important connection between popular sovereignty and the rise and spread of nationalism. For wherever popular sovereignty leads, nationalism seems to follow' (Yack 2001: 517). Undoubtedly, examining this taken-for-granted relationship with renewed analytical rigour is in order. Achieving self-determination and securing sovereignty are intricately related to negative phenomena such as tightening of the citizenship criteria, persecution of minorities, ethnic cleansing and genocide, and it is often in relation to these developments that the normative aspect of nationalism is interrogated (Moor 1998; Kymlica 1995; Yack 2012).

This chapter, however, approaches the relationship between norms and nationalism from a different point of view. Making the most of the highly symbolic nature of food, as the previous chapters have all emphasised, it investigates normative and ethical concerns related to food in reference to nationalism. The chapter is not about food taboos as widely investigated in anthropology. Instead, it focuses on the question of who decides what is appropriate to eat in the international arena. The chapter illustrates the ways in which a shift in norms and ethics leads to a new form of friction between values and norms that often assumes a nationalistic hue. It aims to demonstrate the effectiveness of the 'food and nationalism' angle in investigating different levels of politics. The chapter opens with an examination of the case of whale meat eating to review how the question about resource management has developed into a contestation of values with nationalist tinge. It then places the whale problem in a comparative context in reference to the issues of dog meat and foie gras consumption as well as the rise of veganism. To finish the chapter adds a new angle to this discussion by examining the rise in use of food technology and in particular debates concerning GM food. Using these examples, the chapter highlights the dynamic relationship between changes and shifts in dominant norms and the strengthening of the demand for the particular. Additionally, the examples provided demonstrate the tension that is inherent in the national assertion of boundaries and norms and values in a globalised world. The chapter therefore demonstrates that the 'food and nationalism' angle provides another perspective on how politics at the global level is deeply embedded in people's everyday lives.

The Case of Whale Meat Eating

On 31 March 2014, the International Court of Justice delivered its judgement in the case concerning 'Whaling in the Antarctic (Australia v. Japan: New Zealand intervening)'. It found that Japan's whaling programme in the Antarctic (JARPA II) was not in accordance with three provisions of the Schedule to the International Convention for the Regulation of Whaling (ICJ 2014). Put it more simply, the Court found that what the Japanese government termed as 'scientific whaling' did not comply with the International Whaling Commission's regulations, to which the Japanese government had signed up to, and ordered the Japanese government to stop whaling in the Antarctic. When the judgement was handed down, the Chief Cabinet Secretary of the Japanese government issued a statement expressing their regret over the judgement but confirming to abide by the judgement as a state 'that places a great importance on the international legal order and the rule of law as a basis of the international community' (MOFA 2014). As presented both by the Court and the Japanese government, the ruling was about the legality of whaling, an issue of international law and not about whale meat eating. The Japanese government's response even emphasised the presentation of Japan as a 'good and conscientious' member of the international community. However, by the time the ruling was delivered, the whaling problem had become deeply entangled with the issue of culture (Bailey 2008: 292; Blok 2011; Peace 2010; Holtzman 2017); the minutes of the 186th Agriculture, Forestry and Fisheries Committee meeting of the Japanese Diet on 16 April 2014 contains a phrase 'Given that whaling is part of Japan's unique tradition and culture' revealing that the Japanese government understood the Court's judgement as pertaining to Japanese culture including whale meat eating (The House of Representatives 2014). The whaling problem, therefore, is an international dispute in which the 'food and nationalism' angle is effectively applied.

What Is the Whaling Problem? The Emergence and Evolution of the Issue

What is understood as the whaling problem now usually refers to the deeply engrained division between the so-called whaling nations such as Japan and Norway and those who are opposed to commercial whaling at the International Whaling Commission (IWC). The IWC was set up in 1948 to administer the International Convention for the Regulation of Whaling (ICRW) of 1946 which was signed amid growing concern over the over-catching of the whale (Yasuda 2006). The IWC's objectives include 'to provide proper and effective conservation and development of whale stocks' and 'thus make possible the orderly development of the whaling industry' (International Convention for the Regulation of Whaling 1946), and it was clearly set up as an international mechanism to manage the whale population and the whaling industry.

Needless to say whaling has a long history. Human beings living in coastal regions across the world have been engaged in it since time immemorial. What we now understand as commercial whaling was pioneered by western nations which started organised whaling at the end of the seventeenth century. Japanese whaling before Meiji Restoration of 1868 was of a small scale using open boats and was conducted close to the coast. What changed the whaling industry globally was the introduction of the Norwegian cannon-fired harpoons in the 1890s, which led to a rapid growth of the industry. The industry was so successful in catching whales on a large scale that concerns over the depletion of the whale resources started to emerge in the early twentieth century. In fact, in 1925 at the League of Nations, the establishment of an international conference to prevent whale extinction was proposed, which was opposed by the UK, Norway, Germany, Japan and the Netherlands (Yasuda 2006). The oil price crash of the 1930s and the break-out of World War II led to a temporary scaling down of the whaling industry worldwide; the total catch of whales dropped from 37,709 in 1940 to 8073 in 1942 and further to 5906 in 1945 (Whale Library n.d., accessed on 3 April 2015). Commercial whaling was resumed in earnest in the aftermath of World War II. The total catch jumped to 19,348 in 1946 and then grew to 45,060 in 1950 (ibid.). The concern over the whale resource management led to the drafting of the

ICRW and the establishment of the IWC, and with the advent of whale oil substitute, western nations gradually scaled down commercial whaling: the UK stopped whaling in the Antarctic in 1963 and was followed by the Netherlands in 1964. Norway stopped whaling in the Antarctic in 1968.

While it is clear the establishment of the IWC was due to a worldwide concern over the possible depletion of whale resources, from the 1970s, opponents of commercial whaling based on conservation or environmental grounds began to make its presence felt (Yasuda 2006; Bailey 2008; Blok 2008, 2011; Aron et al. 2000). The US, a former whaling powerhouse, transformed itself to a whale protector, which significantly helped the anti-whaling lobby (Bailey 2008). According to the Japanese Fisheries Agency, around that time, 'many non-whaling countries suddenly joined the IWC while advocating the anti-whaling position under the leadership of anti-whaling groups' (Japan Fisheries Agency 2012). The division between the whaling nations and their opponents emerged around that time, but the focus of the opposition was presented as a scientific issue, that is, the size of the whale population. A moratorium on commercial whaling was adopted by the IWC in 1982 (coming into effect in 1986) on the basis of concern over a possible extinction of whales. Under the moratorium, the catch limit for commercial whaling was set to zero and a limit was placed on aboriginal subsistence whaling. The IWC members were allowed to issue a limited number of permits for whaling for scientific research. Japan opposed to the moratorium but obliged to the Commission's ruling and started a series of scientific whaling programmes. Norway and Iceland, other opponents of the moratorium, have resorted to set their own quota and have continued whaling. A handful of indigenous communities across the world have retained their right to whaling under the aboriginal subsistence whaling.

The 2014 ruling of the ICJ was about the legality of Japan's scientific whaling programme. The Australian government, driven by a strong anti-whaling domestic opinion (Peace 2010; Heazel 2013), took the Japanese government to the ICJ in 2010 claiming that Japan's 'scientific' whaling programme in the Antarctic contravened the IWC's regulation. The judgement in March 2014 caught the Japanese government by surprise as it was confident of the scientific value of its 'scientific' whaling programmes (Wada 2014). Still, the Japanese government's policy to behave as a 'good and conscientious member' of the international community prevailed and the government revised its whaling programme to exclude lethal sampling but continued to send out whalers to carry out 'scientific research'.[1] In November 2014, the Japanese government submitted a new plan for whaling for research in the Antarctic (NEWREP-A) to the IWC for its approval in which the Japanese government proposed to carry out a lethal sampling of 333 minke whales per year (The Government of Japan 2014).[2]

However, on 26 December 2018, the Japanese government announced its intention to withdraw from the IWC on 30 June 2019 and to resume commercial whaling in Japan's Exclusive Economic Zone in July 2019, thus abandoning whaling activities in the South Pacific and near the Antarctic, which Australia and New Zealand were particularly opposed, as well as its scientific whaling programme (*The Japan Times*, 26 December 2018). A number of reasons for the Japanese government's decision have been speculated including the increasing cost of carrying out the scientific whaling programme (NHK 2019), the dysfunction of the IWC (Wada 2017), persistent lobbying from the constituency relying on whaling on powerful politicians (NHK 2019) or as an act of defending interest of marine resource-dependent countries (Shima 2019). The announcement was widely criticised but as Japan ceased to be a member state of the IWC, catching Bryde's whales, widely acknowledged as not facing extinction, in the Japanese coastal water cannot be regarded as a contravention of international law.

From the Whaling Problem to the Whale Meat Problem

The whaling problem as outlined so far appears to be a matter of international legal dispute: the issue is whether a member country (Japan) of an international organisation (the IWC) is compliant with the club's rule. In

---

[1] It was reported that two whaling ships returned from the Antarctic without any catch on 29 March 2015 (*The Guardian*, 19 June 2015).

[2] The Japanese government has been maintaining that the population of Antarctic minke whales has recovered and is on the increase (Japan Fisheries Agency 2012).

this case, the member was found not to be compliant by an international court (the ICJ), and initially, the member tried to adjust its behaviour to comply with the club's rules. When it judged it could not make necessary adjustment, it left the club. A model settlement of an international dispute without resorting to violence, one might say. The process through which the club's rule was drawn up should, of course, reflect various normative claims about how members of a club should behave, what aims the club should have and on what basis the decision should be made. Given that disagreement about the continuation of whaling hinges on proof of whether the whale population is in decline or it is recovering (and a vast alley of combination of different possibilities—by species, by the geographical location of the water, etc.), help from science to resolve the disagreement has been sought. However, science is incapable of providing certainty for any policy-making purpose and it is not value neutral (Heazel 2004). With science unable to solve the disagreement for once and for all, the whaling problem remains as one of the long-lasting international disputes in the postwar world.

As briefly mentioned earlier, there is a consensus, both scholarly and popular, that the current whaling problem boils down to ethical and cultural issues. For example, Morishita Joji, often regarded as the spokesperson for the Japanese government on this issue, has identified four dimensions to the whaling problem: science (whether the whale population is on the decline or on the increase), cultural/ethical collision (whether it is right to kill whales), political (western politicians appealing to anti-whaling constituencies) and economics (Morishita 2006). It appears when the whaling problem is presented vis-à-vis Japan, the cultural/ethical collision dimension as identified by Morishita comes to the fore.

This can be seen in the way Japan's whaling is portrayed in western (or anti-whaling countries) media and how anti-whaling groups in Japan are trying to project themselves (Kimura and Egege 2018; Nomura 2020). Kimura and Egege (2018) report Japanese whalers are predominantly portrayed as villains in Australian media which tends to attribute qualities such as brutality, cruelty and inhumanity to Japanese whalers. Based on Murata's study (Murata 2007a, cited in Kimura and Egege 2018: 327), they also point out that Japanese whaling is reported using words with negative connotation in British media. The predominant portrayal of Japanese whaling by media of anti-whaling countries is that it causes suffering to whales, very special animals in their eye. While there might be a split between the conservationists, who would support whale hunting as long as the whale population is properly managed including a few anti-whaling groups in Japan (Nomura 2020), and protectionists, who would oppose to whale hunting at any cost, in the anti-whaling camp (Stoett 1999), many scholars agree that 'not killing whales' became the default option by the end of the 1980s (Bailey 2008), making whaling a binary good over which compromise is very difficult to reach (Hurd 2012). Furthermore, the global anti-whaling norm thus emerged transformed 'whales into rights-bearing persons, sacred human-like creatures, whose killing is immoral and uncivilized' (Blok 2008: 39). Consequently, the taboo of killing whales became synonymous for a taboo on eating whale meat.

The 'not killing whales' default option of the anti-whaling camp has one of its roots in the different ways in which whales were used across the globe. Many of the former industrial whaling nations mainly hunted whales for whale oil and did not include whale meat in their diet; whale meat was used for animal feed or fertiliser in contrast to Japan and Norway and indigenous communities, in which whale meat was incorporated in their food cultures (Aron et al. 2000). This seems to have influenced in focusing the whaling issue onto the subject of whale meat eating.[3]

In Japan, the familiar narrative about the whale meat is that the people who inhabited the Japanese archipelago had long engaged with whaling going back to Jomon period (c. 12,000 BC to c. 300 BC) and some of those living in the coastal areas were continuously engaged with whaling on a small scale. With the opening up of the country in the nineteenth century, advanced whaling techniques were introduced from the West and Japan became a major whaling country prior to World War II. After World War II, the GHQ, which occupied defeated Japan, encouraged the resumption of whaling as a cheap source of protein for the worn-out and starving nation (Yasuda 2006, Japan Fisheries Agency

---

[3] The reverse side of the coin is that the establishment of a view in Japan that 'Japanese people have never wasted whales; they use the whole whale from the tip to toe, even blood, unlike Western nations which wasted whale meat' (Onishi and Yamamoto 2014). This helps presenting the whaling problem as a cultural clash rather than a resource management problem.

2012, Hirata 2005). The message is that the Japanese have been continuously engaged with whaling suggesting that there is a long tradition, a cultural good, of whaling, and that they have been eating them as fish: a source of sustenance for the Japanese highlighting the whale problem's relevance to Japanese food culture. The point that the Japanese see whales as fish, not as mammals, is often repeated in this official narrative; the Chinese character used to represent the whale has a component that means fish (uo-hen) (Hirata 2005; Morishita 2006). This implies that the western idea of animal rights does not easily apply to the whale in the Japanese context in which 'traditions combine reverence for animals with an acceptance of their taking in a way that makes the western preservationists' goals incomprehensible' (Nadelmann cited in Catalinac and Chan 2005: 147). This line of discourse is clearly making a claim to ethical relativism: while there are some common understandings of fundamental issues shared by different people, each national group has different understanding of what is right and what is wrong, which requires respect. This narrative has been continuously developed by the pro-whaling camp led by the Japan Fisheries Agency which sees the dispute in the 'the West' versus 'Japan' binary scheme formed out of western cultural imperialism of Japan bashing (Hirata 2005; Blok 2008; Peace 2010; Holtzman 2017) (Photo 1).

In this climate, what whale meat signifies in Japan has changed. As the population has accepted the official narrative of whale meat, many now believe that whale meat is part of their traditional diet forgetting the fact that it was only after World War II that whale meat became widely consumed (Hirata 2005). Whale meat is no longer an indispensable source of protein as in the immediate aftermath of World War II but a highly 'select' food to be consumed in special occasions or at upmarket restaurants (Blok 2008). Bowett and Hay (2009) report that among young people in Japan, approval of whaling tends to go with approval of the consumption of whale meat, which suggests that the understanding that whaling is about Japanese culture of which eating whale meat is an indispensable part is firmly established. Therefore opposition to whale hunting is easily translated into opposition to whale meat eating, thus making the whaling problem a matter of culture and tradition in the Japanese mind. Still, Ishii (2011) points out that the talk of 'whale meat eating culture' was intensified in the early

Photo 1 The menu lists 5 different items (red meat, processed sliced tail fin, bacon, skin and tendon) substantiating the claim that the Japanese do not waste any part of a whale

2000s when the supply started to outstrip the demand; rather than eating more whale meat, the Japanese population was more interested in talking about the value of whale meat in Japanese culture.[4]

The pamphlet, 'Whales and whaling' produced by the Japan Fisheries Agency in 2012, sets out its claim of the importance of whales and whaling in Japanese culture as follows:

> The long history of whaling in Japan, from prehistoric times to the present, gave rise to the worship of whales and bore fruit in the culture witnessed today in whaling songs, dances and the various traditional handicrafts that

---

[4] After the resumption of commercial whaling in the Japanese coastal water, an industry magazine, *Suisankai (Fishery Industry)*, reported on a tasting of whale meat event hosted by the Liberal Democratic Party on 9 October 2019 (*Suisankai* 2019: 16–17). The article entitled 'Bryde's whales are in fact delicious!' reports on the industry's concern about popular antipathy towards whale meat in Japan and their plan to market it as a delicious food item with help from the political party in the government.

have been handed down from generation to generation. They are historical evidence that the Japanese people have lived in close association with whales. Now is the time to acknowledge the importance of our whaling tradition and food culture. Japanese are and should be proud of this. (Japan Fisheries Agency 2012: 22)

It then lists whale bones found in the archaeological site dating back to about 5000 years ago as evidence of continuous interaction between the Japanese people and whales, explaining the Japanese dietary habit of eating whale meat in reference to Buddhism's ban on meat (whales were seen as a kind of fish) and claims whale meat consumption became widespread in Edo period. The 'special' relationship between the Japanese people and whales is then further articulated with an emphasis on the eternity of the association:

> Whales have been utilized uninterruptedly by the Japanese people since long ago, resulting in the worship of whales and many other cultural expressions such as whaling songs, dances and traditional handicrafts handed down through generations, and it is very much alive today. Whale tombs and memorial monuments for the souls of these animals can be found throughout the land of Japan. From north to south in the country, the meat of whales has been used as food in multifarious ways. In the Hakodate region south of Hokkaido, whale soup (a[n] earthy broth made with salted whale meat, edible wild plants and vegetables) is one of the traditional foods enjoyed during the New Year festivities. In Niigata prefecture, whale soup is consumed typically in full summer to help stand the heat. In the Kansai region centered in Osaka, whale skin or "koro" is an indispensable ingredient for the oden hotch-potch stew and the traditional "hari-hari nabe" whale meat pot is another famous dish from that region. Traditional recipes such as these are still alive while many new forms of original whale cuisine are being created today. (Japan Fisheries Agency 2012: 23)

While whale meat has come to represent Japanese uniqueness and its long tradition and culture in Japan, in the anti-whaling countries, the whales have become the 'totem animal' talked about in an anthropomorphic language which is to be approached with affection, respect and awe (Blok 2008). Eating whale meat has become associated with being uncivilised, barbaric and cruel, and belonging to the 'Japanese tribe'. This seems to be more pronounced in Australia where the level of popular identification of whales is high. Whales are represented as 'our visitors from the south' and 'our gentle giants'. This anthropomorphic and proprietary representation of whales goes with a degree of Japanese-bashing: only the Japanese kill our 'Australian whales' because they are barbaric and cruel as seen in the way they behaved in World War II; demonisation of the Japanese is now complete (Peace 2010).

Jo Holtzman (2017) has further pursued this point and argues that now the anti-whaling lobby (or 'eco-imperialists') would use cultural relativism to deny that Japanese people have the right to eat whale meat. According to them: 'whale eating in Japan lacks the historical depth and/or is not sufficiently shared to be considered part of "culture"', while other groups such as the Innuits have the legitimate right to hunt and eat whales because of their 'legitimate' history/tradition/culture (Holtzman 2017: 280).

This case study shows that an initially a-cultural disagreement about the sustainability of whaling has been transformed into a highly emotive clash of norms and values in which various nationalisms are mobilised. On the Japanese side, whaling has become a deeply engrained part of the unique culture of Japan which demands respect as the dispute has dragged on despite the fact that the demand for whale meat has stagnated and the whaling industry is no longer self-sustaining. Whaling in Japan is only sustained by public subsidy to 'protect' Japanese culture from, what is seen as, western cultural imperialism. Whaling, including eating of whale meat, has been made to represent something unique about Japanese culture, and the pro-whaling lobby led by the Japan Fisheries Agency has been demanding international recognition that is due to a proper developed cultural nation. On the anti-whaling side, the fact that whale meat was never incorporated in their diet has helped the emergence and spread of the anthropomorphic view of whales as rights-bearing persons. This has facilitated the branding of eating whale meat as uncivilised, barbaric and cruel, which needs to be stopped. In this case, the opposition is found between Japan and the 'West' rather than two distinct nationalisms. However, the whaling problem needs to be put in a context which has been moulded by colonialism and imperialism of the West.

Whale Meat Eating in Context: The Case of Dog Meat Eating

The case of whale meat eating demonstrates how the emergence of new global norms and values, particularly when these clash with national ones, are articulated in a nationalist language and are perceived and questioned through the prism of nationalism. The case also illustrates the prevailing perception and influence of imperialism, despite the historical period that has elapsed since European states left the region. Below we examine the case of dog meat eating, which raises many of the same issues, while at the same time illustrating some of the complexities in associating particular cultural practices with the concept of nationalism.

While there is ample archaeological evidence to suggest that early humans across the world consumed dogs, since the late twentieth century in particular, the eating of dog meat and the debates surrounding it have focused largely on East and Southeast Asia. The issue has served as another site of clashes over norms and values, clashes which are also continuously evolving (see, e.g., Dougnoille 2018; Li et al. 2017; Oh and Jackson 2011; Podberscek 2009). The focus on East and Southeast Asia has been partly the result of the presence of cultures of dog meat eating, in countries such as Cambodia, China, South Korea and Vietnam, but also the, often erroneous, association of all Asians as 'dog eaters'.

In many Asian countries dog meat is not consumed; for example, in Japan, while whale meat is now given the status of the embodiment of a unique Japanese culture and its consumption is encouraged as seen earlier, dog meat is not eaten. Nevertheless, the term has been used in a derogatory manner to describe Filipino men by white Americans (Okamura 2010), even though the practice has been banned since 1988 (Podberscek 2009). In a similar manner, Avieli writes of Thai agricultural workers in Israel being accused of stealing and eating domestic dogs (Avieli 2018), whereas, in Thailand itself, there are conflicting reports on the eating of dog meat. While Podberscek (2009) includes Thailand in the group of countries in which dog meat is eaten, Avieli suggests that dog meat is not eaten in Thailand due to the prevailing view of the dogs 'as sort of degraded human beings that lack moral restraint [incest] and indulge in forbidden practices [eating its own excrement]' (Avieli 2011: 68). In many Asian countries, dog meat eating is strongly associated with regional and local practices and cultures. Reporting on his fieldwork in a small town in Southern Vietnam, Avieli (2011) points out that dog meat eating is more prevalent in Northern Vietnam where cultural contact with China has been stronger. Given that the current power centre is located in the north of the country, he notes there is an association between dog meat eating and power, presenting a picture of a powerful, atheist, dog meat eating North versus a gentler, Buddhist South where dog meat is not readily consumed. The complexity and regionality of dog meat eating is also present in China. Poon (2014) reports that a ban on dog eating was introduced in colonial Hong Kong in 1950 and that it did not meet strong local opposition. Furthermore, the ban was not introduced on the back of the opposition to animal cruelty by the colonial government, which could be seen as imperial imposition, but as a measure to combat rabies. According to Poon (2014), there was no strong and/or emotive opposition to the eating of dog meat among the European population in twentieth-century Hong Kong and the eating of dog meat was commonplace. The British authorities introduced a law against animal cruelty (the Prevention of Cruelty to Animals Ordinance) in 1935 but did not concern themselves with the actual eating of dog meat as long as the dogs were killed humanely.

The clash of values and norms at this point of time in Hong Kong, if there was any, was about whether animals should be killed humanely and what constituted humane killing, not about which meat was ethical to consume.[5] However, the local elite who had become ambivalent towards mainland Chinese culture chose to support a new value and norm to respect animals. In the aftermath of the 1949 rabies panic, the local elite colluded with the British colonial authority to pass the 'Dogs and Cats Regulations', which prohibited the sales and consumption of dog meat, in 1950 as a rabies prevention measure. Poon (2014) identifies the local

---

[5] Poon (2014) reports on a fascinating court case in which a Chinese resident was prosecuted for killing a rat that ran havoc. The local magistrate's judgement was that killing a pest in itself was not illegal but the rat should have been killed humanely without being tortured. The resident was found guilty of animal cruelty and was fined. The incredulous resident paid the fine but confessed that he did not understand the ruling.

elites' ambivalence towards mainland Chinese society as one of the major reasons why they went against the call to respect a local custom. Although there was a view that dog meat eating was a local tradition and as such should be preserved, some sections of the local elites who were close to the colonial government and the European/western lifestyle chose to 'sacrifice' the tradition. It is also suggested that the prohibition on dog meat eating in Hong Kong was later to be mobilised to deride the backwardness of the mainland Chinese as Hong Kong was returned to the People's Republic of China.

The ban on dog meat eating in colonial Hong Kong did not lead to an outright clash of values which was articulated with nationalist vocabulary, not because of the differing levels of attachment to the custom of dog meat eating, for dog meat eating was never eradicated in Hong Kong, but because of a particular constellation of power among the colonial authorities, local elite and mainland China. It is also the case that the practice is not seen as part of Chinese national culture and attitudes towards it are largely dependent on regional and local traditions; the practice also has a complicated history in China with periods of acceptance and rejection. Having said that, like many other countries in Asia, attitudes towards eating dog meat have been shifting in recent decades, as a response to globalisation, with younger and more urban populations less likely to participate in and/or approve the practice (Li et al. 2017).

The tension that arises from the clash between shifting global and national norms and values often comes to light during international events, particularly sporting events, where the host country does its best to market itself. This is exactly what happened with dog meat eating in the case of South Korea with the 1988 Seoul Olympics and the 2002 World Cup co-hosted with Japan, and China with the 2008 Beijing Olympics. At each global sporting event, there was an international outcry against the local custom of dog meat eating. What is interesting is that responses to the international pressure varied (Oh and Jackson 2011; Podberscek 2009). The Korean government 'yielded' to the international pressure to put a stop to this 'barbaric and archaic' practice at the 1988 Olympics by trying to ban the eating of dog meat and removing it from restaurant menus; the Chinese government banned dog meat on public health grounds and the Beijing officials removed dog meat from the menu of 112 official Olympic restaurants;[6] in 2002, however, the Korean government did not respond to international pressure, now formulated as opposition against animal cruelty rather than disgust towards dog meat eating, in the same way they did in 1988 and instead tried to foster understanding and appreciation of their cultural heritage.

There are a number of factors behind these differing responses to the international oppositions to dog meat eating. The 1988 South Korean government's response is largely explained by the geopolitical and geohistorical situation in which the country found itself. Having emerged out of military dictatorship, its priority was to be a 'good and respected member of the international community', and the government was 'ashamed' of the custom of eating dogs because the western world was against it. It took measures to ban dog meat eating against domestic opposition, but it was soon known that the ban did not have much effect; dog meat eating continued and even expanded (Oh and Jackson 2011; Podberscek 2009). The Chinese government in 2008, probably more confident of its own standing in the international arena than the Korean government in 1988, chose to avoid outright confrontation over values and norms by opting for a technocratic solution of using public health as an excuse to place a ban on the sales and consumption of dog meat in public.

In 2002, the South Korean government together with elements of the South Korean civil society chose to present dog meat eating as part of their culture and tradition, and nothing to be meddled with by the foreigners. In this instance, in a similar manner to the pro-whaling lobby in Japan, the supporters of dog meat eating mobilised a universalistic notion of cultural rights, articulated in a nationalistic language in order to fend off, what was seen as, western cultural imperialism. As noted by Oh and Jackson (2011: 48) the reaction to the international opposition to dog meat eating was fiercer in 2002 than in 1988 not because dog meat eating had become more central to the Korean diet but because it was one of the arenas in which national identity could be articulated. Podberscek (2009)

---

[6] An unexpected consequence of the Covid-19 pandemic which reportedly started in the wet market in Wuhan is that the Chinese government has suggested dog meat should no longer be consumed by humans partly to prevent transmission of diseases from animals to humans. The decision is also attributed to the 'progress of civilisation' (Standarert 2020).

notes that the consumption of dog meat is much lower than that of beef, pork and chicken, though many South Koreans defend the practice regardless of whether they participate or not. This bears striking semblance to the whale meat issue in Japan in which the instance of whale meat eating is promoted despite the decline of its consumption using the universalistic notion of cultural rights in response to what is perceived as western cultural imperialism.

This is not to say that the idea of dogs as pets is absent in South Korean society in the twenty-first century; there is a growing number of people keeping dogs as pets and there is a growing debate over whether there is a clear distinction between dogs for eating and dogs to be kept as pets, which may not be conducive to western sentiment (Podberscek 2009; Dugnoille 2014, 2018). Dog meat eating was suppressed for religious reasons during the Koryo Dynasty (918–1392) in which Buddhism was dominant. In the following Choson Dynasty (1392–1910), Confucianism became the official ideology which did not prohibit dog meat eating. In fact, dog meat in Korea is often referred to as 'Confucius meat' because Confucius apparently loved it (Podberscek 2009; Oh and Jackson 2011). Confucius scholars allegedly came up with a justification for eating dog meat by classifying dogs into three categories: hunting dogs, watch dogs and food. It is also emphasised that in Korea, dog meat has always been eaten as medicine as well as food. Dog meat eating is therefore not a mere expression of one's lowly desire to fill one's stomach but a part of complex understanding of human health with philosophical underpinning. When dog meat eating is presented as part of unique Korean culture, it is the idea of 'Confucius meat' that is brought up. Against this, the outcry against eating 'our loyal friends' from the westerners is, more often than not, understood as yet another attempt to impose western-centric view reminding many Korean people of the recent colonial and imperial past of the world. However, and in a similar manner to shifting attitudes in China, the practice of dog meat eating and the debate surrounding it have been informed by changes to global norms and values. This can be seen most clearly in debates over whether it was acceptable to eat companion dogs, and shifting attitudes towards dogs as pets among younger and more urban populations (Dougnoille 2018).

It Is Not an East-West Clash: Foie Gras Production and Consumption in France

The clash between norms and values, and the tension between the national and the global, is not only a reflection of East-West and post-colonial debates regarding cultural relativism. In fact, the clash over norms and values affects many more countries as the following example of foie gras production and consumption in France, and the tension this produces between EU member states demonstrates. The foie gras example also raises another important issue that has bearing on both previous case studies discussed above, namely, the assertion of national rights over food, a concept we discussed in the previous chapter.

Perhaps no country exemplifies the close relationship between food and nationalism and national identity as well as France. Not only is French food held in high esteem the world over, and as the epitome of cooking excellence, but it has also been synonymous with French culture, traditions, history and national identity, and has been so for at least the past 200 years. Ferguson claims that 'for the West, France supplies the most striking example of a "culinary country" one where cuisine and the nation are seen to coincide' (Ferguson 2010: 102). Tebben goes even further and argues that 'the French national identity is without question bound in its culinary identification by the world. Gastronomy is seen as French and the French are seen as gastronomes' (quoted in Wright and Annes 2013: 390).

In the previous chapters we discussed gastrodiplomacy and mentioned the recognition accorded to French cuisine across Europe in the nineteenth century. In that respect, some of the most renowned chefs of the nineteenth century, such as Marie-Antoine Careme and Georges Auguste Escoffier, that have revolutionised, codified and refined many of the cooking techniques and dishes used today, contextualised their cooking style and food within the framework of French nationalism. As a result, many of the classic food terminology we use is French and many of the dishes are closely related to French cuisine and French national identity, among the very many examples are the baguette, onion soup, quiche, crème brulee, tart tatin, nicoise salad, béchamel sauce and the foie gras.

The impact of French cuisine and the esteem in which it is held were part of the reason why UNESCO included French Gastronomy in their list of intangible cultural heritage of humanity in 2010 (UNESCO 2010). The importance of food, its symbolism and relationship with national identity are also apparent in many of the globalisation-inspired debates in France; these are manifested in, for example, the symbolic 'rejection' of fast food as Americanised and un-French and the perceived threat to French secularism from the sale and spread of halal food (Wright and Annes 2013).

Among the many food items that have come to be seen as French foie gras is arguably the most controversial. According to DeSoucey, it has also become 'increasingly viewed as an endangered asset in France's cultural treasury' (2016: 5). Foie gras (lit. fatty liver) is a food product that is made from the liver of either ducks or geese that have been fattened. It has a very long history and there are recorded examples of the production and consumption of foie gras stretching back to 2500 BCE (Kolpas 2021). Nevertheless, foie gras, partly because of its rich taste and delicate texture, has increasingly been associated with French cuisine where it is served mostly as pate, mousse or parfait; it is also added to many dishes to enhance their flavour, particularly soups, sauces and stews. Foie gras holds a special place in French culinary history and tradition. This can be seen in the fact that France is both the biggest producer of foie gras and the biggest consumer. Additionally, most of the foie gras produced outside France is for the French market.

Foie gras, traditionally made from male geese, has increasingly been made from non-migratory male ducks (because it is more economical and practical to breed and raise ducks in large numbers) that have been specially fattened, a technique that is known as 'gavage' in French. 'Gavage' refers to the force feeding of the birds over several weeks before their slaughter to ensure an enlarged liver, several times its normal size. The exact size of the enlarged liver depends on the specific method of force feeding;[7] some methods, which are seen as more ethical because the

---

[7] Traditional foie gras production was based on manual force feeding of migratory birds. In recent decades this has given way to a more industrial system based on mechanical force feeding of caged and housed ducks. There are claims that mechanical force feeding is actually safer than manual (Gille 2011).

animal is allowed to overeat on its own and involves no force feeding, result in 'only' the doubling in size of the liver (Youatt 2012). Under French culinary standards, a product can be only designated as foie gras if it is produced through force feeding. The production and consumption of foie gras in France are protected by law; under French law foie gras is 'the protected cultural and gastronomical heritage of France'. French governments have also stated they would try to include foie gras production and consumption in UNESCO's intangible cultural heritage.

The debates over foie gras, and the calls to ban it, were initially framed as part of a broader campaign for animal welfare and the humane treatment of animals. The force feeding of the birds is deemed inhumane and unethical by animal rights organisations and, it is claimed, results in numerous health complication, higher mortality rates and the unnecessary suffering of the birds involved. Additionally, because foie gras is made only from male birds, the treatment and use of female ducklings is also seen as problematic (PETA 2014). The concerns raised over the treatment of birds in the production of foie gras have been discussed by the EU's 'Scientific Committee on Animal Health and Animal Welfare'. The committee's 1998 study of foie gras production concluded that 'force feeding, as currently practised, is detrimental to the welfare of the birds' (European Commission 1998). The EU has ruled that the practice should be allowed only in traditional areas of production. As a result of public campaigns and the EU's own verdict, foie gras production is banned in most European countries; only five European countries continue to produce foie gras: France, Belgium, Hungary, Bulgaria and Spain.

There are several dimensions to the French foie gras case. On the one hand, this is an issue revolving around the tension between European integration, and the requirements this carries in terms of laws and values, and French cultural heritage and national identity. As DeSoucey (2010) notes, foie gras production and consumption has been a historical part of French rural life and traditions. It is also an important element in French cuisine and adds to French claims of cultural significance. The debate over foie gras in France, and the backlash against efforts to ban it, therefore, are framed, not as part of the animal rights discourse but as attacks against French culture and national identity; in France foie gras is increasingly seen as an imperilled French rural tradition rather than a debate over animal welfare (DeSoucey 2016). As a result, the French state is expected to intervene to protect the nation's cultural heritage. In contrast to the previous examples, in this case, the former centre of civilisation considers itself being under attack by others, and this understanding is not framed in an anti-colonial framework. It is seen as an attack on the nation's importance, identity and culture.

On the other hand, the debate is further complicated by the fact the foie gras production is also an important part of French rural economy. This is similar to our first case study with regard to whale meat and its initial importance to the Japanese fishing industry. This means that the calls to ban foie gras are seen not only as attacks on French culture but also on French rural economy and food manufacturers. It is important to note that in France the two are often closely related; French rural life holds an emotive place in the French imagination of the nation (Ferguson 2006). According to DeSoucey (2010, 2016), around 100,000 jobs are directly and indirectly related to the foie gras industry. In this respect, and similar to the two previous case studies, the impact of globalisation and international efforts to regulate food, including standards and norms, have a direct effect on national industries and brands. In this context, securing and protecting national food brands is seen as part of protecting and securing the nation and its economy.

The tension that exists over foie gras has not only affected France. In her study of foie gras production in Hungary, Zsuzsa Gille (2011) has demonstrated how the industry has been affected by animal rights campaigns and European integration, which have worked against the interest of the Hungarian food industry. The solution found was to reframe foie gras production in Hungary as part of the cultural heritage of the nation-state and emphasis its importance to national identity and sovereignty. In this case, the economic importance is translated into cultural importance in order to support the industry. In other words, the universalistic value system is made use of by economic interests to protect an important industry to the national economy. Eating foie gras itself is not essential to the maintenance of Hungarian culture, but the foie gras industry is deemed to be important enough to require the state's protection. Another case in which essentially a-cultural issue is made cultural in order to protect what is deemed to be national interest.

Does Veganism Transcend 'Food and Nationalism'?

Historical examples of nationalism intertwined with the commodification of animals are manifold; above we discussed the commodification of whales, dogs and Ducks and geese. In "Chapter Four: Food and Diet in 'Official' Nationalism", we demonstrated how in several Asian countries, including Japan, at the turn of the nineteenth century, debates over diets, in particular the consumption of meat, were viewed through a nationalist prism and in relation to the West. It is also well known that traditions and cultures surrounding the commodification of animals, and in particular meat and fish eating, are part and parcel of many national food cultures, for example, roast beef in England (Rogers 2003) and salt cod in Portugal (Sobral 2019).

The association between the commodification of animals and nationalism, and the ways in which food and nationalism are entangled in normative discussions and debates of what we eat, naturally leads to the question of veganism. Or, put it differently, does veganism as a universalistic principle transcend ethical and cultural debates over food and nationalism. Veganism as a lifestyle principle,[8] that killing and exploiting any animal is wrong, goes back to the nineteenth century in the West, but its prominence has increased since the late twentieth century, in particular with the advent of social media and increasing influence of celebrity endorsement on social media platforms in the twenty-first century (Zamir 2004; Lundahl 2020; Gheihman 2021). The reasons for taking up veganism are manifold. Albeit based on a small sample of 36 participants, Chuck et al. (2016) have identified three major reasons for adopting veganism: ethics, personal well-being and disgust with food industry. While veganism tends to have 'bad press' for its rigidity and militancy, Sneijder and te Molder (2009) argue that vegans work to present their lifestyle as 'ordinary' and 'easy to follow' and to counter the criticism that vegan diet is nutritionally deficient by devising various strategies, thus

---

[8] The section does not engage with the definition of veganism as it is clearly out of its scope, and there is no space to critically examine the concept: '… there is no one working definition of *a* veganism, but rather there exists many *veganisms*' (Wrenn 2019: 190).

trying to 'normalise' veganism. In a similar vein, Sutton (2017) argues that, in fact, many vegans and vegetarians are engaged with daily negotiation of their diet identity and are not necessarily dogmatic about their dietary principles. These studies present a different picture of vegans—ordinary and peaceful—from that of those who may be engaged in campaigns against whaling, dog meat eating or foie gras: militant and dogmatic.

The above brief discussion suggests that veganism as a universalistic principle based on unconditional respect for all forms of animal life contains two very different orientations in the context of food and nationalism: it could be militantly entangled with ethical opposition to whaling and other practices associated with commodifying and eating animal meat and, in so doing, can be entrenched in nationalistic discourse as discerned the reporting of whaling by Japan in Australian media, for example. It can also be a peaceful and 'ordinary' way of promoting a certain lifestyle which transcends various ideological antagonisms to achieve a higher level of calmness and tranquillity. In the former case, the universalistic foundation of veganism does not turn it into a vehicle to exclusively aspire for cosmopolitanism; rather it is employed to reinforce certain nationalist claims by conferring a high moral ground. In the latter, veganism could be seen as an ideology capable of transcending nationalism and other ideologies, a system of belief as to what the world should be and what action should be taken to achieve that ideal: a post-ideological ideology, as it were. Veganism, examined in this manner, is not always fully realising its promised transcending quality. In many cases, it works like any other ideology—forming alliances with others to produce a more nuanced and complex programme of political action.

There are a couple of examples in which veganism, rather than transcend, is entangled in nationalist power struggles and discourses. Esther Alloun (2020) reports on the ways in which veganism is mobilised by Jewish-Israelis to negate and erase the Palestinian Other; in other words, how veganism has been co-opted by Israeli settler-colonialism. Capitalising on the presentation of Israel as 'the first vegan nation' and the 'global centre of veganism' propagated in popular media as well as public discourse, Alloun argues that Jewish-Israelis have managed to draw parallels between issues in animal welfare and Jewish history. In particular, they draw on the history of persecution and the Holocaust and use their vegan credentials to put a claim for Jewish-Israeli exceptionalism and exclusive sovereignty on and in the land of Israel, on the basis of their superior morality and modernity. The Palestinians, on the other hand, who are not perceived as lacking strong support for veganism or concern for animal welfare, are increasingly presented as not belonging to the land of Israel.

On the other end of the spectrum, as it were, challenging the conventional association of veganism with pacifism and femininity and harking back to the association between vegetarianism/environmentalism and right-wing nationalism, in particular, Nazism via the *Völkisch* movement, a group of Neo-Nazi activists called *Balaclava Küche* (Balaclava Kitchen) has been producing a vegan cookery show on YouTube to promote their cause (Forchtner and Tominc 2017). *Balaclava Küche* deploys a variety of tropes used on social media—playful display of lifestyle and so on—to convey the message that veganism is true to the spirit of national socialism because it contributes to the maintenance of a healthy body and environment, thus reinforcing the link between the people, the soil and nature.

What this brief survey of the place of veganism in food and nationalism suggests is that veganism is, although with a potential to be universalistic, an ideology that can be recruited by other ideologies to reinforce their claims. While nationalism is often seen as a weak kind of ideology (Freeden 1998), in the examples examined here, it appears nationalism has co-opted veganism, not the other way round. In fact, as Gheihman (2021) has suggested if we should grasp contemporary veganism as a lifestyle movement related to but not wholly defined by the animal rights movement, it could provide a channel for nationalism to effect social change. In particular, as a lifestyle movement, it has the potential of bringing about change through individual consumption. This chimes in with the everyday nationhood perspective in that each consumer takes part in the creation of meaning through their acts of consumption.

It Is Not Just About Animals: Technology and GM Foods

One of the areas we did not address in the first edition concerns the increased use of technological and industrial processes in our food systems in recent decades, including biotechnology and bioengineering. This area, which is heavily contested and debated, highlights the fact that clashes between local, national and international norms, values and ethics extend beyond our relationships with animals, and raises fundamental questions regarding our relationships with nature and with technology. It also brings to the fore debates over what cultural heritage, tradition and history mean in an increasingly industrialised and technologically sophisticated global world.

There are many examples that could be used to illustrate the above points. For example, the ongoing debates in the UK over future post-Brexit trade agreements with the US, but also other countries, over food safety and security, in particular the use of chlorinated washed poultry, hormone treated livestock and pesticides (see, e.g., Millstone et al. 2019; Ranta 2019). The case study we will focus on, which is also part of the UK's future trade agreements debate, is that of genetic modification. What we are particularly interested in is how a debate over a scientific issue concerning regulatory powers and the evaluation of risk, to people and crops, has evolved into one that encompasses culture and politics, including nationalism. It is important to note at this point that the debate over the impact and safety of genetically modified (GM) foods is outside the remit of this book.

There is some debate over what exactly constitutes a GM food. According to the WHO, GM foods are those that are produced using genetically modified organisms (GMOs). GMOs in turn are organisms, mostly crops, that had their genetic material 'altered in a way that does not occur naturally by mating and/or natural recombination'.[9] Even though there are a number of international conventions and protocols concerning GM foods, it is an area that divides many countries and regions. Nowhere

---

[9] World Health Organization: https://www.who.int/news-room/questions-and-answers/item/food-genetically-modified (accessed 12 January 2022).

is this clearer than in the differing approaches taken by the EU and the US over GM foods, which in some ways mirror their approaches towards other similar issues, such as the use of hormones, antibiotics and pesticides; the EU has taken a largely precautionary approach towards the use of biotechnology, including GMOs and GM foods. These differing approaches can be seen in their respective approach towards the Cartagena Protocol on Biosafety that is meant to regulate the handling and transport of GMOs (part of the Convention on Biological Diversity), which the EU has ratified and supports, and the US opposes, alongside a number of large food exporters, such as Canada, Argentina and Australia.

The differing approaches, and their wider implications, can also be seen in the way developing countries have adapted to the approach taken by their main food exporting market, the EU or the US (Clapp 2006). It can be seen in the way many Southern African countries responded to the offer of US food aid containing GM crops over the past two decades and in particular during the early 2000s. As noted by Clapp (2012) and Zerbe (2004), the US offer was not a benign or politically neutral one. It was no doubt influenced by the food needs of Southern Africa, a region beset at the time by food insecurity, but also by the needs of US food producers and the US' desire to spread its approach to GM crops. Even though some scholars argue that Southern Africa should accept or adopt GM crops (see, e.g., Muzhinji and Ntuli 2021), the region has largely rejected GM crops and has instead followed the precautionary approach of the EU.

There are many reasons why the EU has adopted and globally advocated a precautionary approach towards GM food, including concerns of food safety and the contamination of and impact on non-GM crops. Nevertheless, it is also clear that discussions over GM foods in the EU are intertwined with political and cultural debates and concerns over wider issues, such as trade liberalisation, heritage, national sovereignty and Americanisation. In the EU, France serves as an exemplar of these issues. In France over the past two decades opposition to GM food has been extensive and widely held. The French government has largely been at the forefront of European opposition to GM foods, citing environmental, health and regulatory concerns (Ranta 2015). French opposition to GM food, however, is often framed, in a similar manner to the foie gras debate, as one also concerned with defending French food traditions and national sovereignty. For French anti-GM campaigners, led in the early 2000s by farmer-turned-activist Jose Bove, GM foods are seen as part of an unholy American trinity of global corporate politics, neoliberal economic policies and unhealthy food (*malbouffe*—often translated as junk food). With the opposition to GM foods, which now encompasses large parts of the French establishment, the introduction of GM foods is seen as a threat to French health, food and way of life, as well as a direct threat to French farmers and agriculture (Heller 2013).

A similar case is that of Mexican opposition to US GM crops, in particular US corn. Since the late 1990s, and in response to the North American Free Trade Agreement (NAFTA), maize 're-emerged' as a Mexican national symbol. Its re-emergence was initially due to the importation of, what many Mexicans saw as, 'lower-quality' corn from the US, and later GM corn. However, its prominence as a symbol of Mexican identity and food sovereignty has much deeper historical roots, with the country being the birthplace of maize domestication; to illustrate this point, in 2003, an exhibition titled 'Sin Maíz no hay País' ('without maize, there is no country') opened at the National Museum of Popular Cultures in Mexico City. The opposition to US corn and GM corn was on the one hand a rejection of neoliberal trade practices, which threatened the livelihood of Mexican farmers, and the encroachment of the US on Mexican sovereignty. On the other hand, it was opposition to what many Mexican farmers, NGOs and indigenous groups saw as a direct threat, through contamination, to Mexican cultural heritage, maize varieties (among them teosinte, a wild ancestor of maize) and national cuisine (Fitting 2006; Mendez Cota 2016). In this case, however, unlike the case of Southern Africa, Mexico's proximity to the US, its membership of NAFTA and the support of successive governments and business lobbies have ensured a more welcoming approach to US trade and GMOs (Clapp 2006).

Conclusion

This chapter focused on the normative aspect of nationalism in the international arena and examined what the 'food and nationalism' angle can illuminate in our understanding of global politics. Unlike conventional studies that investigate the normative aspect of nationalism in reference to the mostly negative consequences of the right to self-determination such as ethnic cleansing and genocide, the chapter focused on a seemingly mandarin issue of food. The examination of the cases of whale meat and dog meat eating, foie gras production and consumption as well as GM foods, has shown that there is fierce contestation of values in reference to what can be grown and eaten and that there are dynamic movements in the formulating and re-articulating of nationalist worldviews in response to changing geopolitical situations. In these cases, the eating of whale meat, dog meat and foie gras is increasingly justified in reference to the universalistic notion of cultural rights which reflects the general emergence of a global normative framework. Rather than being forced into conforming to what is deemed to be universal (not eating whale/dog meat or not force-feeding ducks and geese), responses from contemporary Japanese, South Korean and French societies are nationalistic in emphasising the importance of whale/dog/foie gras eating in their respective culture. In the first two cases, the importance of whale/dog meat is symbolic rather than substantial; neither is essential to their national diets, but the eating of these meats has been made to differentiate these societies from the rest of the world. Here the nationalist forces, which are about the particular, are actively using the universalistic discursive framework of cultural rights, thus making nationalism universal in a peculiar manner. What needs to be noted in this regard is that both cases represent a response in the post-colonial area; Japan was never colonised and Korea was colonised by Japan rather than western powers, but a common undercurrent is detected: resistance to actual or perceived western cultural imperialism. In this respect, these two cases shed light on ongoing efforts made by non-western states and societies to adapt and mould the international society of states in the way which favours them. It is also interesting to note that by making whale/dog meat as important in Japanese/Korean traditional culture, people's mundane life is directly connected to the cut and thrust of international politics. In slight contrast, the foie gras example demonstrates that the global debate over norms can have an impact not only on symbolic issues but also on substantive ones. Lastly, the case of GM foods illustrates how debates over what should be global scientific standards over risks and regulations cannot be understood without reference to the importance of national norms and values. It is also clear in all cases that the changing of norms directly affects national food industries, which in these cases are expecting protection from the state and framing their struggle within a nationalist discourse.

Our brief examination of the place of veganism in these debates suggests that veganism, a fundamentally universalistic ideology or principle, can be co-opted by nationalism to strengthen a particular nationalist claim rather than transcending the nationalist opposition. Debates about veganism themselves show that food and the act of eating are fundamentally political, and our examination has shed light on the complexity of veganism as an ideology in relation to other ideologies.

It is clear from the examples provided that the spread of globalisation will continue to create tension and raise debates over norms and values. This raises a number of important questions, for example, who should be the ultimate arbitrator when it comes to international clashes over norms and how should these be negotiated/mediated? The following chapter takes up this question.

Chapter Eight: International Organisations, Food and Nationalism

The previous chapter finished with a question: when there is contestation of values over cuisine, food culture and diet, who would or should be the arbiter? When there is an international dispute, the first candidates for such a position are usually international organisations. At the one end of the scale, there is a range of international conventions and treaties such as the Convention on the Prevention and Punishment of the Crime of Genocide of 1948, widely known as the genocide convention, as rule books on how individuals, groups and states should behave, and there are mechanisms through which these rules are applied such as the International Criminal Court. In this context, international organisations assume the role of a judge in determining if any crime has been committed, and if so who the perpetrator is and what the punishment should be. Consequently, these international organisations in their efforts to deliver global justice are often seen as independent actors and a restraining factor on the nation-state and other entities; in other words, the international organisations are understood to be the suppressors of nationalism and the imposers of global/universal norms and standards. However, in the area with which the current volume is concerned, food, rather than imposing what is deemed to be global or universal standards, international organisations appear to be unwittingly used by the nation-state and other entities in the promotion of national identity or nationalism. This may well be one of the consequences of the spread and permeation of neoliberalism in reference to culture as Scher (2010) argues, but the impact of neoliberalism unfortunately falls outside the scope of this volume.

This chapter investigates this paradoxical phenomenon in relation to two fields: the preservation of culture and international trade. In particular, the chapter investigates UNESCO's intangible cultural heritage scheme and geographical indications (GIs) in international trade in relation to food. In the current edition, the latter is supplemented by a brief investigation into the impact of Brexit on the GIs scheme. By doing so, the chapter continues to highlight what the 'food and nationalism' angle can bring to the analysis of politics at the global level as well as bring to the fore a debate over the purpose and independence of international organisations and their effect on state sovereignty and power.

UNESCO's Intangible Cultural Heritage

UNESCO, the United Nations Educational, Scientific and Cultural Organization, does not need introduction. It is one of the best known UN institutions and has been subjected to wide-ranging investigations as an international organisation, in particular with regard to its description and engagement with national culture (see, e.g., Erkisen 2001; Scholze 2008). From the current volume's point of view, what is most interesting about UNESCO is its impact as an international organisation on nationalism and the idea of national heritage; since UNESCO deals with culture, the focal point of nationalism and efforts to build and maintain national identity in the form of 'cultural diversity' in an international context, it occupies a seemingly contradictory position vis-à-vis nationalism. On the one hand, UNESCO is working towards the universal, to pursue peace through 'humanity's moral and intellectual solidarity' (UNESCO, http://en.unesco.org/about-us/introducing-unesco), which could be seen as a constraining factor on the pursuit of the particular by the nation-state and other groups; on the other, UNESCO is the most authoritative guardian of a variety of cultures on the planet because diversity of culture in itself is seen as a common good, an idea which various nation-states and other groups mobilise in pursuit of their own nationalist agenda. This dichotomous position partly relates to the fact that as an international organisation UNESCO is expected to pursue and aspire to universal values, while it is, at the same time, governed by its members, most of whom are nation-states.

This interesting position of UNESCO is probably most visible in the area of world heritage. Since the adoption of the 1972 Convention Concerning the Protection of the World Cultural and Natural Heritage,[1] widely known as the World Heritage Convention, to which 190 countries adhere, UNESCO has been playing a dual role of the promoter of universal values (peace, mutual understanding and solidarity among other things) and the protector of the particular by championing the preservation of culture and cultural artefacts. UNESCO has been at the forefront of producing and shaping 'globality' or cosmopolitanism through its World Heritage Convention since the idea of world heritage 'rests on the assumption that the world's most prized natural and cultural sites belong to all of us, entailing a shared responsibility for their care' (Brumann 2014: 2177). As Brumann (2014) reports, the committees entrusted to manage and administer the World Heritage List were originally and mainly staffed by specialists in cultural conservation and heritage who were operating at an arm's length from the nation-state, which suggests a cosmopolitan orientation emanating from UNESCO, but these committees are increasingly staffed by career diplomats who tend to prioritise the nation-state's agenda.[2] From the nation-state's end, world heritage is seen mainly as an opportunity to project a positive image of itself to promote tourism and possibly trade (nation branding) and/or to increase its influence on the world stage ('soft power') rather than a route to pursue cosmopolitan values though plenty of lip service is paid to it. For instance, Sarina Wakefield (2012) traces how the United Arab Emirates (UAE) uses the idea of and tools associated with UNESCO's world heritage in order to establish falconry to represent the UAE's uniqueness and its contribution to world culture. In the similar vein,

---

[1] http://whc.unesco.org/en/conventiontext/.
[2] Brumann (2014) reports on a more nuanced and complex change in UNESCO. While career diplomats are more likely to follow their governments' instructions, they still aspire for different kinds of cosmopolitan values such as peace. His fine ethnography of diplomacy, however, falls outside the scope of this volume.

Dong Wang (2010) argues that the application for the world heritage status for Longmen Grottoes has in fact strengthened the Chinese state at various levels. UNESCO's custodianship of world heritage therefore has, wittingly or unwittingly, contributed to the strengthening of the position of those promoting nationalism in these cases, thereby making a case of UNESCO as a site of the creation of nationalist images.

Within the field of world heritage of which UNESCO is the chief custodian, what is particularly relevant to the current volume is not the World Heritage Convention as such but the idea of 'intangible cultural heritage', otherwise known as 'living heritage', which has been formalised by UNESCO's 2003 Convention for the Safeguarding of the Intangible Cultural Heritage.[3] Food culture or cuisine, which do not have tangible shape but would mark traditional rituals together with songs and dances, cannot be listed as World Heritage, but starting with the inscription of 'gastronomic meal of the French', and 'traditional Mexican cuisine' in 2010, there are at least 22 elements related to food culture and/or cuisine in the representative list of the intangible cultural heritage of humanity out of a total of 584 elements as of June 2021.[4] The idea of 'intangible cultural heritage' itself has received a lot of scholarly attention, but on the whole the experts in cultural conservation and heritage seem to have a positive view of the 2003 treaty as corrective to the World Heritage List, which tends to exclude the states from Global South because of the lack of monuments and sites deemed to be suitable (Kurin 2004; Leimgruber 2010; Romagnoli 2019).[5] Furthermore, Richard Kurin points out other positive aspects associated with the idea of intangible cultural heritage:

---

[3] https://ich.unesco.org/en/what-is-intangible-heritage-00003 (last accessed on 20 June 2021) http://www.unesco.org/culture/ich/index.php?lg=en&pg=00006.

[4] https://ich.unesco.org/en/lists (last accessed on 20 June 2021).

[5] Leimgruber (2010) provides an interesting critique of the 2003 convention from the compatibility of a few ideas underpinning the convention and the type of state. According to him, there is no equivalent of 'intangible culture' in German and what is used in order to adhere to the convention roughly translates as 'immaterial culture'. The assumption that 'intangible culture' belongs to a national/ethnic group in the convention also poses a problem for German-speaking people because of the term 'Volkskulture' which has negative connotation in respect to Nazism. He also points out that the federal state like Switzerland cannot relate to UNESCO in the same manner as more centralised states such as France.

The Convention does some very good things. It reinforces the idea that the practice of one's culture is a human right. It seeks government recognition and respect for the varied cultural traditions practised by people within its jurisdiction. It seeks to bolster the idea that all cultures give purpose and meaning to lives and thus deserve to be safeguarded. It privileges the culture bearers over the state. It suggests that forms of safeguarding be integrated with legal, educational, and economic development efforts where appropriate so that culture retains its vitality and dynamism. Now, with this Convention, a mechanism will be put into place at the international level where those efforts may be energized and improved to take on the task. While doubts persist about the institutional machinery and the ability of the Convention to attract adequate external funding appropriate to the level of need, the Convention may still provide an important opportunity. For cultural advocates around the globe, and for many communities and tradition bearers, the International Convention for the Safeguarding of the Intangible Cultural Heritage is a welcome addition to the tool-kit of resources available for accomplishing valuable cultural work. (Kurin 2004: 76)

What is suggested here is that the idea of intangible cultural heritage would enhance the universalistic aspect of UNESCO's work by establishing cultural rights as part of human rights and empowering culture bearers to the extent the World Heritage List has not managed to do. The point is emphasised by Walter Leimgruber (2010) who acknowledges in his discussion of the 2003 convention that the claim to cultural diversity is politically established and that the convention aims to the preservation of culture and the promotion of sustainable development. Nonetheless, the mechanism through which intangible cultural heritage is recognised and protected is based on the member states, which leads to a fundamental question about the nature of international organisations: are they inter-governmental or supranational in nature? This question is most urgently asked in reference to the European Union because of its stated aim of achieving 'ever closer union'. Is the EU an inter-governmental organisation built on voluntary cooperation of sovereign nation-states, or is it a supranational organisation in the making which is going to subsume various nationalisms to create a higher order of loyalty? While in the case of UNESCO, its supranational potential is not regarded as threatening state sovereignty; by contributing to the establishment of global norms such as the respect for cultural diversity, UNESCO is also shaping the ways in which nation-states and other entities in the international arena act.

Our cases show that the idea of intangible cultural heritage is not so much used by Japan and France to project their image to the world or as part of a formal gastrodiplomatic effort; rather, it is mobilised as a way of responding to what they perceive as a crisis in national culture, one aspect of which is food culture and cuisine, and in order to support their own food industries.

Since the inception of the intangible cultural heritage treaty till 2021, UNESCO has inscribed 25 elements related to food culture and cuisine to the list (Table 1).

The chapter now investigates food and nationalism in the earlier cases of *washoku* and the gastronomic meal of the French from the list.

Washoku

The inscription of *washoku* on 4 December 2013 in the representative list of the intangible cultural heritage of humanity was greeted with much enthusiasm in Japan, which has added further impetus to a variety of projects to promote food culture and 'food education (*shokuiku*)'[6] pursued by the government, private sector and civil society groups (for a nutritionist's view, see Shiratori 2014). In particular, the government intensified its efforts to promote Japanese cuisine abroad has been enhanced as a way of increasing export of Japanese agricultural produce and attracting more tourists as briefly discussed in "Chapter Five: National Food in the International Context I—Gastrodiplomacy".

---

[6] *Shokuiku* (食育) is an idea that children should be educated to be able to live a healthy diet by acquiring knowledge about food and ability to choose food items through a variety of experiences, and what is particular in Japan that the idea was legislated in 2005 in the form of Basic Law on *Shokuiku* (food and nutrition education). Perhaps conscious of the law's peculiarity, the Ministry of Agriculture, Forestry and Fishery has published a leaflet in English entitled *What Is 'Shokuiku (Food Education)'* which is available from their website (http://www.maff.go.jp/e/pdf/shokuiku.pdf).

Table 1 The list of elements related to food culture/cuisine in the Representative List of the Intangible Cultural Heritage of Humanity as of December 2021

2010
Gastronomic meal of the French
Traditional Mexican cuisine—ancestral, ongoing community culture, the Michoacán paradigm
2011
Ceremonial Keşkek tradition (Turkey)
2013
Kimjang, making and sharing *kimchi* in the Republic of Korea
Mediterranean diet
Turkish coffee culture and tradition
Washoku, traditional dietary cultures of the Japanese, notably for the celebration of New Year
2014
Lavash, the preparation meaning and appearance of traditional bread as an expression of culture in Armenia
2015
Arabic coffee, a symbol of generosity
Tradition of kimchi-making in the Democratic People's Republic of Korea
2016
Beer culture in Belgium
Flatbread making and sharing culture: Lavash, Katyrma, Jupka, Yufka
Oshi Palav, a traditional meal and its social and cultural contexts in Tajikistan
2017
Art of Neapolitan 'Pizzaiuolo'
Dolma making and sharing tradition, a marker of cultural identity
Nsima, culinary tradition of Malawi
2019
Traditional technique of making Airag in Khokhuur and its associated customs
2020
Hawker culture in Singapore, community dining and culinary practices in a multicultural urban context
Il-Ftira, culinary art and culture of flattened sourdough bread in Malta
Knowledge, know-how and practices pertaining to the production and consumption of couscous
Nar Bayrami, traditional pomegranate festivity and culture
Practices and traditional knowledge of Terere in the culture of Pohã Ñana, Guaraní ancestral drink in Paraguay
2021
Ceebu Jën, a culinary art of Senegal
Joumou soup of Haiti
Truffle hunting and extraction in Italy, traditional knowledge and practice

---

Source: Compiled by Atsuko Ichijo based on information available from https://ich.unesco.org/en/lists (last accessed on 22 December 2021)

The description of *washoku* on the list starts with the following sentences: '*Washoku* is a social practice based on a set of skills, knowledge, practice and traditions related to the production, processing, preparation and consumption of food. It is associated with an essential spirit of respect for nature that is closely related to the sustainable use of natural resources' (http://www.unesco.org/culture/ich/index.php?lg=en&pg=00011 &RL=00869). In other words, it is not a particular food item or cuisine itself but the 'traditional food culture of the Japanese' that has been officially deemed suitable for recognition as part of common human heritage (Imoo 2014: 102; Ehara 2014). As touched upon earlier, the application for the inscription in the list can only be done by the UNESCO member state, and in this case, the Japanese government, in particular, the Ministry of Agriculture, Forestry and Fishery (MAFF), was in the driving seat. The MAFF has a webpage dedicated to dietary culture (http://www.maff. go.jp/j/keikaku/syokubunka/index.html) which includes a number of documents related to the application to UNESCO, which reinforces the impression that the inscription of *washoku* in the UNESCO's intangible cultural heritage list is an outcome of yet another state-sponsored nationalist project of nation branding or exercise of 'soft power' as seen, for instance, in the case of falconry of the UAE. In other words, the case of the inscription of washoku appears to suggest that UNESCO, an international organisation, is used by the nation-state as a means of nation branding.

However, an investigation into the background of the application to UNESCO has highlighted a different aspect of the role of international organisations in the relationship between food and nationalism. Despite the state-led nature of the application (which is an inevitable consequence of the inter-governmental nature of UNESCO as an organisation), sources show that the idea to apply for the inscription of Japanese cuisine in the intangible cultural heritage list came from cooking professionals who were deeply concerned with the possibility of extinction of traditional Japanese cuisine, not from the government which was planning to use it as a means of nation branding (Hashimoto 2015). Mutsuru Suda, from the secretariat of Washoku Association of Japan (Washoku Japan),[7]

---

[7] http://washokujapan.jp/.

a private-sector-run successor (formally set up in February 2015) to the government-sponsored National Council for the Protection and Transmission of Washoku Culture which was set up in 2013 in the run-up to the application to UNESCO, identified a heightened sense of crisis over the future of Japanese traditional cuisine shared by mainly Kyoto-based chefs of Japanese traditional cuisine as the main driving force.[8] According to Suda, these chefs were concerned with the low social status of chefs ('no *washoku* chef has received the Order of Culture') and the shortage of young chefs entering the profession; the largest proportion of students in cooking schools across Japan are learning to be a *pâtissier* (pastry chef) followed by those learning Italian, French and Chinese cooking, and those who are learning Japanese traditional cooking are in a minority.[9] One of those concerned chefs, Yoshioka Murata, the owner and the chief chef of Kikunoi, a traditional Japanese restaurant (*ryotei*) in Kyoto with three Michelin stars, set up the Japanese Culinary Academy in 2004 for the purpose of 'promoting global understanding of Japanese cuisine' and 'contributing to the next generation of Japanese food chefs' (http://culinary-academy.jp/english). According to Suda, it was the Japanese Culinary Academy with strong support from Murata that contacted MAFF about the idea of applying for the inscription of *washoku*. In Murata's own words, when he learned that the South Korean government was planning to make an application for Korean court cuisine at the time of the Great East Japan Earthquake in 2011, he mobilised the Academy to petition the Kyoto Prefectural government about applying to UNESCO as a way of ensuring the future of Japanese traditional cuisine (Murata 2014). These sources show that what appeared to be a state-led initiative was originally triggered by concern held by a particular section of the private sector, and UNESCO's intangible cultural heritage list was made use of by both the government and the private sector to address their concern over the perceived decline in national identity.

The *washoku* chefs' concern was quickly taken up by the government. In July 2011, the Working Group to Prepare for the Inscription of

---

[8] Interview on 9 April 2015.
[9] This is also confirmed by Murata in the second meeting of the Working Group to Prepare for the Inscription of Japanese Food Culture in the Intangible Cultural Heritage List (MAFF 2011b).

Japanese Food Culture in the Intangible Cultural Heritage List was set up by MAFF drawing participants from other ministries (Agency for Cultural Affairs, Ministry of Foreign Affairs and Ministry for Economy, Trade and Industry), universities, cooking profession and catering industry. The government's response was quick mainly due to the Great East Japan Earthquake that took place several months earlier in March; working towards the inscription of *washoku* was probably seen as conducive to the overall efforts of the government at that time: to rebuild and rejuvenate Japan and its national image (see the minutes of the first meeting of the Working Group, MAFF 2011a). Also it appeared that the washoku chefs' concern chimed in with the government's concern about food in general. As seen in the law on food and nutrition education in 2005, the Japanese government had been concerned with the state of diet and nutrition in Japan in relation to a range of issues: general health of the Japanese population in the context of rapid ageing, food safety, the decline in food self-sufficiency and weakening of national identity (Cabinet Office 2006). From the government's perspective, therefore, the UNESCO application presented an opportunity to address these concerns in the form of promotion of washoku, which could also be accompanied by other policies such as the promotion of export of Japanese agricultural produce.[10]

The minutes of the Working Group's meetings shed light on the way UNESCO as an organisation conditioned the way the application was prepared: in other words, the influence of an international organisation on the articulation and development of a nationalist project. The definition of Japanese cuisine was right from the beginning of a contested issue among the members of the group. Given the prominent role played by the chefs of Japanese traditional cuisine mainly based in Kyoto in starting this initiative, the idea of defining Japanese cuisine in reference to *kaiseki*, the top end of Japanese cuisine which is normally served at a top-end

---

[10] Needless to say, due to the nuclear incident that followed the earthquake, export of Japanese agricultural produce came to a halt in 2011. The impact of the Earthquake and the nuclear incident in the preparation of the UNESCO application can be seen in the minutes of the second meeting of the Working Group (MAFF 2011b). The Ministry of Economy, Trade and Industry, on the other hand, clearly understood the inscription of washoku in the intangible cultural heritage list as part of its 'Cool Japan' strategy (MAFF 2011a, b, c, d).

traditional Japanese restaurant, was initially proposed. After conducting an Internet-based questionnaire to gauge the level of national support for the application and a fact-finding trip to France to learn about their experience of having the gastronomic meals of the French inscribed, in the third meeting, doubts about the suitability of representing Japanese cuisine mainly through reference to *kaiseki* were raised because it may look elitist (MAFF 2011c). Attention was drawn to UNESCO's interest to protect ethnic/national culture which was supported by the majority of the group, not what was perceived as elite culture. The strategic importance of presenting the application as a means of preserving cultural tradition which was being threatened due to the decrease in consumption of Japanese foodstuff and the number of Japanese cuisine chefs was also emphasised (ibid.). In other words, it was clearly articulated that the UNESCO application was not about projecting Japanese culture as part of a soft power strategy but a way of asking help from an international organisation in protecting, preserving and promoting an expression of national particularity. The shift from the definition of Japanese cuisine in reference to *kaiseki* to washoku as a wide concept covering many ways the Japanese engaged with food including home cooking to the top-end cuisine was completed in the fourth meeting when the Working Group members learned that the South Korean government's application to have Korean court cuisine inscribed was in the status of information reference, presumably because it was judged to be elitist (MAFF 2011d).

Other MAFF publications on washoku published following the application have also presented the inscription of *washoku* in UNESCO's intangible cultural heritage list as a way of asking help from the international community for Japanese efforts to preserve, protect and promote what is deemed to be invaluable common heritage for the future. *Washoku: Traditional Food Culture of the Japanese* (2013), a booklet drafted by MAFF is peppered with concern over the fate of washoku; that it is 'disappearing from our tables' (2013: 1) and that washoku is 'in crisis' (2013: 31–32). Another, shorter booklet compiling the findings from a project 'Research into Protection and Transmission of "Washoku"' (November 2014–March 2015) also highlights the withering of washoku in contemporary Japan and widespread concern over it (MAFF 2015). These publications clearly reflect the Working Group's attitude that the inscription of washoku has very little to do with nation branding, though some derivative effects were expected by various ministries and industries, but fundamentally it is about reviving an aspect of national culture with the help from an international authority.

What this case study shows is that UNESCO's intangible cultural heritage is used by the Japanese government and private groups to revive an aspect of national culture rather than for the purpose of nation branding. The private sector that was the driving force behind the application initiative was driven by their concern over their own survival and their agenda coincided with the governmental objectives to rebuild and rejuvenate Japan after the 2011 earthquake as well as to address various domestic concerns about food the Japanese ate and diet they followed. In the convergence of different agendas and interests, UNESCO emerged as a convenient authority to back the revivalist programme. UNESCO acts as an authority to confer legitimacy to cultural practice which these different interests were concerned with, an unwitting supporter of the nation-state and what it sees as the dominant culture, not as a restraining force on cultural nationalism.

The Gastronomic Meal of the French

'The gastronomic meal of the French' was the first amongst a variety of food cultures of the world that was inscribed in the representative list of the intangible cultural heritage of humanity in 2010. As such it was closely studied by those who were behind the Japanese bid, and the development of the French bid also reveals how the system of recognising world heritage maintained by an international organisation can shape the way a nationalist project evolves.

The gastronomic meal of the French is described as:

> … a customary social practice for celebrating important moments in the lives of individuals and groups, such as births, weddings, birthdays, anniversaries, achievements and reunions. It is a festive meal bringing people together for an occasion to enjoy the art of good eating and drinking. The

gastronomic meal emphasizes togetherness, the pleasure of taste, and the balance between human beings and the products of nature. ... (http://www.unesco.org/culture/ich/index.php?lg=en&pg=00011&RL=00437)

The emphasis on the social aspect of the practice as something widely enjoyed in all corners of France was quickly noted by those behind the Japanese bid, which eventually led to the redefinition of Japanese cuisine as *washoku* to represent a variety of food items and styles enjoyed by the Japanese on a daily basis away from a more elitist conception with strong link to *kaiseki* as seen earlier. Upon receiving the report from the fact-finding trip to France, the Working Group also took note of the fact that the name of the element changed from the originally proposed 'French cuisine' to 'French gastronomy' to settle on 'the gastronomic meal of the French' with qualification that 'in French, the term "gastronomic" refers to the popular culture of enjoying good food and drink' as in the nomination file (UNESCO 2010) as a strong indication of what UNESCO gives priority to: protection and preservation of what is widely shared in a national/ethnic group, not elitist culture (MAFF 2011c).

The above points to the curious effect UNESCO's intangible cultural heritage list has. While one of the stated aims of UNESCO is to preserve the diversity of cultures on the planet, since the application to the list has to be seen as representing the whole group on behalf of which the application is made, be it a national, ethnic or regional group, it in effect encourages the homogenisation of what is presented as cultural heritage, which in turn creates a degree of tension with respect to diversity in culture in general. This is clearly seen in the nomination file of the gastronomic meal of the French. In identifying 'the communities, groups or, if applicable, individuals concerned' (C. 1.), the nomination file states:

> The French. The community concerned by the element is the entire French nation people. The community is large, diverse and unified. Its collective experience has been built over several centuries. The product of social and cultural mixes, regional plurality and contributions by immigrants, the community is united by shared practices like the gastronomic meal. Important moments in the lives of individuals and groups are celebrated in a ritualistic way through this festive meal. (UNESCO 2010)

Here the inherent diversity of the French nation is emphasised in a political correct manner. However, a few pages on the nomination file places more emphasis on the homogenising aspect of the gastronomic meal. In response to '1. Identification and Definition of the Element (cf. Criterion R.1)', the file states the 'gastronomic meal is a homogeneous social practice in the whole community' and lists 'its meaning and social function' and 'its rites necessitating knowledge and know-how' as the source of this homogenising power. The file attempts to find a solution to the tension between diversity and homogeneity by highlighting the ritualistic aspect of the gastronomic meal: the content of the meal might vary but it always follows a strict order to bring about unifying, if not homogenising, effects on the diverse French (UNESCO 2010). The requirement to be inscribed in the list appears to have led to certain redefinition of national particularity; it has to be expressed through something common and universal, which is worthy of being shared by all humanity.

In the fact-finding trip to France the Japanese Working Group undertook, they found that there was similarity in the background to the UNESCO application in that there was a deep concern over the perceived weakening of French food culture due to various social changes including globalisation: the spread of fast food was of a particular concern (MAFF 2011c). This is a point we raised in the previous chapter with regard to the production of foie gras. The preparation of the UNESCO application had more prominent state intervention than in the Japanese case from early on. The nomination file identifies the state initiative, in the late 1980s, to carry out a census of heritage-related foodways which has resulted in the publication of the *Inventaire du patrimoine culinaire de la France* (*inventory of French culinary heritage*) as the beginning of the process. From 2000 onwards, the French government launched a number of major initiatives to promote research into the gastronomic meal of the French as well as to raise awareness among children through the organisation of 'Taste Week', for instance. In 2001, the European Institute of Food History and Culture (IEHCA)[11] was created in Tours as the centre of research into food culture, and in 2006, it assumed the leading role in preparing an application for the inscription

---

[11] http://www.iehca.eu/IEHCA_v4/iehca.html.

of French cuisine in the intangible cultural heritage list. Following President Sarkozy's public statement that the French government was to seek the inscription of French gastronomy in the intangible cultural heritage list in 2008, a new organisation, the Mission Française du Patrimoine et des Cultures Alimentaires (MFPCA),[12] with support from various sectors, was set up to lead the preparation of the nomination file (UNESCO 2010).

The contrast to the Japanese experience, in terms of the degree of the state's involvement in the application process, suggests a comparative point. Those states with a tradition of powerful centralising tendency are naturally expected to be involved with the range of initiatives as seen in the French case. And because of this tradition, states like France are better placed to mobilise different forces of society in one direction. On the other hand, UNESCO is set up as an inter-governmental organisation in which the member states act as the medium between the organisation and culture (or more precisely, the bearers of culture that UNESCO affords recognition and protection), and strong/centralising states may be better placed to fulfil their expected roles. In fact, Leimgruber (2010) points out the federal nature of Switzerland as one of the obstacles for Swiss groups to make the most of the world heritage system.

The two examples provided above indicate that often the reason behind applying to UNESCO, as well as to other international organisations, is not in order to project and promote the nation abroad but to strengthen domestic industries and stop what is seen as the decline of a particular aspect of national identity. This means that international organisations are used by the state in order to legitimise their efforts to pursue cultural nationalism in response to globalisation and maintain and strengthen their version of the nation. Though appearing to function as independent actors, international organisations perform an instrumental function for states.

What is remarkable about these examples, and this is a point we alluded to in "Chapter Five: National Food in the International Context

---

[12] While MFPCA was tasked to continue engaging with promotion of the gastronomic meal of the French after the inscription, its website suggests that its activities have been considerably slowed down of late. See http://mfpca.blogspot.fr/ accessed on 3 May 2020.

I—Gastrodiplomacy", "Chapter Six: National Food in the International Context II—Gastronationalism and Populism" and "Chapter Seven: Norms, Ethics, Food and Nationalism", is that the international organisations that are meant to limit the scope of nationalism, and in the case of UNESCO protect the culture and rights of local communities, end up enhancing and promoting the nationalist case. Our finding is collaborated by Marco Romagnoli (2019) who highlights the homogenising effect on culture and cultural practices of the application to the list and by Bahar Aykan (2016) who illustrates how UNESCO works to empower the nation-state in reference to the case study of keşkek which has been clearly marked out as Turkish heritage despite its regional character.[13] In effect, UNESCO's focus on protecting the local in the global context results in strengthening the national. It is therefore not a surprise that more and more states are applying to UNESCO to recognise their national food cultures and are using the application as part of their gastronationalist and/or gastrodiplomatic efforts (see, e.g., with regard to Singapore, Lee and Kim 2020; on Peru, Wilson 2011; and the survey of gastrodiplomatic efforts by Zhang 2015).

Geographical Indications and International Trade

The case study of UNESCO's intangible cultural heritage list in relation to food culture has shown that UNESCO, an international organisation, functions as the source of authority for the nation-state and other groups in pursuing their version of nation-rebuilding/maintenance which is primarily targeted at the domestic audience. In the case of geographical indications (GIs) and international trade, different dynamics between the international organisations and actors at the national level can be observed. These relate to some of the tensions and challenges that occur

---

[13] Bahar Ayhan (2015) provides a more nuanced analysis of the ways in which UNESCO's intangible cultural heritage scheme ends up encouraging national proprietorship of cultural practices despite the provision in the scheme to encourage multi-state applications.

from gastronationalism, gastrodiplomacy and the promotion of national food we discussed in previous chapters.

Geographical indications (GIs) are defined by the European Commission, the widely acknowledged vocal proponent of the concept (Agarwal and Barone 2005; Charlier and Ngo 2012; Tosato 2013), as follows: 'A geographical indication is a distinctive sign used to identify a product as originating in the territory of a particular country, region or locality where its quality, reputation or other characteristic is linked to its geographical origin'.[14] This is in line with the understanding of the World Trade Organization (WTO): 'A product's quality, reputation or other characteristics can be determined by where it comes from. Geographical indications are place names (in some countries also words associated with a place) used to identify products that come from these places and have these characteristics (for example, "Champagne", "Tequila" or "Roquefort")'.[15] The prime function of GIs is to facilitate free trade by providing relevant and reliable information about the product to the consumer, a tool of free trade that is regulated by international organisations such as the Court of Justice of European Communities and the WTO. GIs are therefore part of the regulatory system of international food trade such as the Codex Alimentarius International Food Standards (hereafter 'Codex standards') managed by the Codex Commission (Smythe 2014). The Codex Commission was originally founded by the World Health Organization (WHO) and Food and Agricultural Organizations of the United Nations (FAO) in 1963 and is now an inter-governmental organisation with 185 member countries and 1 member organisation (the EU). The Codex standards is the reference point in the WTO's Agreement on Sanitary and Phytosanitary measures (SPS Agreement) and as such the *de facto* highest authority in international standards for food trade. Since the primary aim of setting up the Codex standards is to realise 'safe, good food for everyone—everywhere',[16] GIs, as part of this wider system, are

---

[14] http://ec.europa.eu/trade/policy/accessing-markets/intellectual-property/geographical-indications/ accessed on 15 January 2021.

[15] https://www.wto.org/english/tratop_e/trips_e/gi_background_e.htm accessed on 15 January 2021.

[16] http://www.codexalimentarius.org/about-codex/en/ accessed on 15 January 2021.

fundamentally a means of consumer protection deployed by the international system in its pursuit of a universalistic value: free and fair trade.

There is an additional aspect to GIs in international trade: GIs are categorised as intellectual property (IP) by the EU and WTO, and as such they have another normative implication in the fast developing global IP protection scheme (Agarwal and Barone 2005; Charlier and Ngo 2012; Rippon 2014). The protection of IP is deeply embedded in the free trade regime, and as such GIs as IP is part of the structure that supports further liberalisation of trade. The nation-state and private sector actors are generally compliant with the idea of IP protection because it is part and parcel of the current dominant convention regarding free trade. In other words, the IP protection scheme makes the nation-state and private sector actors prioritise the pursuit of a universalistic value of achieving free trade. However, GIs are by their very nature particularistic, and the protection of GIs is also seen as having an empowering effect on developing countries in the free trade regime. This suggests that within a universalistic scheme of IP protection, GIs can be a disturbing factor because they are built on the particular, which suggests that GIs constitute an arena where the universal and the particular, often in the form of 'national interests' collide, and as such, provides fascinating material for the current chapter which looks into international organisations' role in the relationship between food and nationalism.

Because GIs are a form of IP justified by the linkage to a particular geographical area, they are seen as marketing tools as well as tools for rural economy development. The value of GIs as a marketing tool has been extensively explored. Among them, Agarwal and Barone (2005: 1) identify the chief strength of GIs as a marketing tool as their capacity to differentiate commodity products by associating them to 'unique quality characteristics associated with a particular location or quality images that are based on the history, tradition, and folklore in a region'. Others have described the effect of GIs as the 'terroir factor' invoking intangible but profound connection between the product and a specific locality (Huysmans and Swinnen 2019; Prescott et al. 2020). While GIs are not without some drawbacks, differentiation in general is a positive quality because it can allow the sellers to command higher premiums on the product, which explains why producers are in general favourable to defining a GI.¹⁷ It is also expected that a successful definition of a GI leads to the promotion of tourism as touched upon in "Chapter Three: Consuming Nations—The Construction of National Identities in the Food Industry" in reference to the Scotch whisky industry.

GIs as a differentiation tool can benefit private sector actors as well as regions/nation-states. Agarwal and Barone (2005: 2) quote a study into the effect of GI on speciality salts such as French Fleur De Sel and report that '… as a consequence of the success of GI strategies for these salt products, gourmet cooks pay as much as $80 a pound for such varieties versus 30¢ per pound for common table salt'. In terms of the GI's developmental potential, Jena and Grote (2010) acknowledge that there is theoretical justification for GI protection in India and conclude that two prominent GI products of India, Basmati rice and Darjeeling tea, have achieved an increased access to export market which has led to a significant increase in export earnings of the producers, which may lead to an improvement of living standards of the agricultural workers. Adopting a more comprehensive perspective to regional development, Suh and MacPherson (2007) assess that securing GI for Boseong green tea for the first time in South Korea in 2002 has had a positive impact on the revitalisation of local economy. The protection of GI as part of the trade liberalisation movement prompted the local officials to design an economic development plan with Boseong green tea cultivation and processing at the centre but also incorporating tourism. With the granting of GI for Boseong green tea, all three aspects of the local economic structure, cultivation, processing and tourism, have seen positive impact. In addition, there has been indication of ripple effects to adjacent regions. Suh and MacPherson (2007) conclude that Boseong green tea is one of the success stories facilitated by GI with Boseong green tea-related income accounting for more than 40 per cent of the regional economy. After conducting a comparative analysis of the impact of GI in two cases, tequila in Mexico and Comté cheese in France, Bowen (2010: 211) concludes that 'the GI for Comté cheese has had very positive effects on the maintenance of the

---

¹⁷ Huysmans and Swinnen (2019) caution against over-appreciating the price premium GIs would usually bring as typically the produces with GIs tend to have higher production cost. They also note the contradictory effect of GIs as a tool to 'reduce information asymmetries and improve efficiency' and as protectionist measures.

local economy and landscape' because it fits with the local conditions and is better than in the case of tequila. These cases demonstrate the attraction of GIs to the private sector as well as the nation-state as a means of economic success rather than of realising free trade.

In the field of GIs, the EU features prominently as seen in its enthusiastic lobbying for the protection of GIs for alcoholic beverages and in disputes with its trading partners about, say, cheese. In a sense, this is only natural that the EU has high visibility in trade issues since the EU is fundamentally a trading bloc and because the European Commission negotiates trade issues on behalf of all member states. There are many examples of the EU standing up for the member states' collective interests in food trade, and the most well-known cases are related to cheese. First, the EU has been involved with a dispute regarding the standardisation of parmesan cheese with the Codex Commission (Araki 2013). The currently valid 2021 Codex standards regarding cheese and other dairy products contains 16 standards regarding individual cheese: Mozzarella, Cheddar, Danbo, Edam, Gouda, Havarti, Samsoe, Emmental, Tilsiter, Saint-Paulin, Provolone, Cottage Cheese, Coulommiers, Cream Cheese, Camembert and Brie.[18] In 1996, the Milk and Dairy Products Committee, a sub-committee of the Codex Commission, opened the discussion about defining the codex standard for parmesan cheese but the EU opposed to the proposal on the basis that parmigiano reggiano had already been registered as a GI under its scheme by then and therefore it should be managed by the EU's GI protection scheme. Faced with a strong opposition from the EU, the Milk and Dairy Products Committee effectively shelved the discussion in 2005. In this instance, the EU has resisted the attempt to standardise parmesan cheese at the global level in order to protect its own GI protection regime and, by inference, the member states' interests. A similar stance is observed in the EU's ongoing dispute with the US about GI protection, especially with regard to cheese.

On 11 March 2014, *The Guardian*, quoting Associated Press in Washington, reported that 'the EU wants to ban the use of European

---

[18] http://www.fao.org/fao-who-codexalimentarius/codex-texts/list-standards/en/ accessed on 15 January 2021.

names like parmesan and gruyere on cheeses made in the US'.[19] According to the article, the EU insisted that US-based manufacturers could not use the name 'parmesan' because their product was not produced in Parma, Italy, and 'feta' cheese produced by them had to be labelled as 'feta-like' or 'feta-style' as agreed with Canada. The small- and medium-sized producers of cheese in the US were worried about possible cost of complying with this requirement and large manufacturers such as Kraft, which had been selling grated parmesan cheese for a long while, regarded this as a trade barrier. As in the case of the dispute with the Codex Commission, the EU appears to be prioritising the protection of IP of its member states over the contribution to liberalising trade. However, the protection of member states' GIs is not always by design. The EU's ability to pursue a free trade agreement with Canada was held up by Greece over, what it considered, insufficient protection for feta (Huysmans 2020).

There has been considerable academic debate over the merits and justifications for the EU's GI scheme, for example, over whether it positively contributed to trade. According to Curzi and Huysmans (2021), GIs did not have a positive effect on trade. The main argument is that GIs protect rural livelihoods and preserve traditional culture. Huysmans and Swinnen (2019) have pointed out that while the EU has the most GIs in the world, they are predominantly registered by southern member states; over 70 per cent of the GIs are held by France, Greece, Italy, Portugal and Spain. They speculated various factors are at work to explain this uneven distribution of GIs among the EU member states. One possible explanation is the role of gastronationalism. The EU appears more likely to protect GIs in its trade negotiations that are of high sales value and are of particular national importance to the five southern European countries mentioned above (Huysmans 2020).

However, the EU is also involved with disputes regarding GIs with its member states, too. The Court of Justice of the European Communities, a judicial arbiter of the EU, has ruled that the attempts by some member states to establish national quality signs such as Belgium's 'Walloon' sign and Germany's 'Markenqualität aus deutschen Landen' sign are

---

[19] http://www.theguardian.com/lifeandstyle/2014/mar/11/europe-trade-talks-cheese-back-parmesan-feta accessed on 15 January 2021.

incompliant with the principle of free movement of goods (Charlier and Ngo 2012). In other words, in the field of GIs, the EU sometimes acts primarily as the supporter of free trade and effectively works to undermine each member state's national interests and sometimes as the protector of the member states' interests, on whose behalf it engages in disputes with the WTO or the Codex Commission. This highlights the unique nature of the EU as an international organisation; it is a regional organisation which is deeply embedded in the free trade regime with contradictory effects on the power of the nation-state.

Given the EU's prominent role in promoting the GI scheme worldwide and given the importance countries across the globe afford to GIs to promote their trade and tourism, a brief examination of the impact of Brexit on the GI scheme is due. In June 2016, the UK government held a referendum on the continuation of its EU membership, and surprisingly the result was 52 per cent in favour of leaving the EU while 48 per cent in favour of remaining. The UK parliament accepted the referendum result and started a protracted negotiation with the EU to withdraw from it (see also our discussion on UK-EU negotiation and relations in "Chapter Six: National Food in the International Context II—Gastronationalism and Populism"). Prescott et al. (2020) report that as of November 2019 there were 1457 registered GIs on the European Commission's database and 73 of these were registered from the UK. Since the UK made up approximately 16 per cent of the EU economy measured in GDP, 5 per cent of all registered GIs coming from the UK could be seen as underrepresentation. Still as seen in the persistent lobbying by the Scotch Whisky Association, a trade body, ensuring to legally protect Scotch whisky, the brand, in the post-Brexit world still featured high on their list of demands (Ichijo 2019). For the producers, the protection of what the EU's GI scheme had achieved for their products was as important as 'friction-free' trade.

The UK left the EU on 31 January 2021 in accordance with the European Union (Withdrawal Agreement) Act 2020. In terms of GIs, the Department for Environment, Food and Rural Affairs (DEFRA) published guidance on 'Protected geographical food and drink names: UK GI schemes' on 31 December 2020, which in the main replicated the EU scheme of protected designation of origin (PDO), protected geographical indication (PGI) and traditional speciality guaranteed (TSG) in a way that could be applied to the post-Brexit trade scenes.[20] In terms of implementation: 'From 1 January 2021 GIs with UK origin protected under the EU scheme as at 31 December 2020 will continue to have effect in the 27 member states of the European Union. GIs with EU origin protected under the EU scheme have been granted equivalent UK protection under the new UK GI scheme' and '(P)roducts with GIs from Great Britain before 1 January 2021 must display the relevant UK GI logo by 1 January 2024 when sold in Great Britain. However, products protected under the EU GI scheme must display an EU GI logo when sold in Northern Ireland or the European Union—although this is optional when sold in the rest of the world (including the United Kingdom)' (Khwaja and Elkin 2021). While the UK GI system will be subjected to review each time a new trade agreement is negotiated, what is relevant to this chapter is the fact that the UK government has put in place a system that would uphold the established GIs/IP system to facilitate the continuation of free trade. In other words, the change in the UK's relationship with the EU does not indicate a change in the UK government's view of the importance of GIs or its willingness to continue to play part in upholding the universalistic scheme to protect its 'national interest'.

The examination of GIs in relation to food and nationalism directs our attention to an issue, which has also surfaced in the discussion of UNESCO's intangible cultural heritage list: globalisation and its relationship with neoliberalism. In the field of cultural conservation, globalisation is clearly a source of concern; it means homogenisation and flattening out of the diverse cultural landscape mainly through the penetration of market forces to every sphere of life. Intangible cultural practices such as food culture, dances and songs need to be inscribed in the list and firmly embedded in a commercial structure of tourism promotion and regional economic development in order to withstand the pressure of globalisation. Obviously culture is not static and the bearers of culture do interact with globalisation, which will lead to changes and

---

[20] https://www.gov.uk/guidance/protected-geographical-food-and-drink-names-uk-gi-schemes (last accessed on 21 June 2021).

transformations, but the motivation behind UNESCO's list is to mobilise the state structure and market forces in order to protect common human heritage. In the case of GIs, the effects of globalisation as an expression of neoliberalism are more complex. The idea of GIs as IP is the very product of neoliberalism and GIs are primarily a tool to promote free and fair trade. However, GIs are valuable because of their grounding in a particular geographical location. In other words, GIs, the product of neoliberalism, draw their strength from the particular, the antithesis of the universalism envisaged in neoliberalism. Is globalisation as neoliberalism weakening or strengthening nationalism? What are the roles of international organisations in this context in which contradictory and competing forces and interests interact? This is yet another theme to be developed further in the future.

Conclusion

One of the main debates in international relations and global politics revolves around the purpose and function of international organisations. In the context of growing interdependence and the spread of globalisation, international organisations appear to promote universal values in opposition to national ones. Particularly to our case, international organisations are seen at the forefront of attempts to promote international free trade, universal food standards, and support food culture as a common good. This emphasis on the global at the expense of the national would suggest that international organisations act in a manner that constrains nationalist forces and state power. Additionally, the need for international mediation over conflicting national food claims, in terms of standards, trade rights, cultural ownership and brands, would further indicate the enhancement of international organisations' power at the expense of states' and would suggest the gradual erosion of state sovereignty.

However, as the two case studies provided demonstrate, in the case of food, international organisations' need to protect local communities and consumers, promote free trade and secure intellectual property rights, in effect help bolster nationalist claims. In particular, UNESCO's intangible cultural heritage campaign and the EU's support for geographic indicators highlight the contradictory position international organisations occupy in the international system. In pursuit of a universal value (free trade) and the protection of the particular and the local (GI as IP), international organisations support the nation-state domestically, in its pursuit of cultural nationalism, and globally, by supporting national claims of food ownership. This last point is particularly controversial because the concept of food authenticity, as we have shown in previous chapters, is problematic and highly contested.

Conclusion: From Everyday to Global Politics

We concluded the first edition with the following paragraphs:

'The current volume has set out with two major aims: to investigate the relationship between food and nationalism, which has been largely neglected in the study of nationalism, and to demonstrate that the 'food and nationalism' axis provides a useful angle to study politics at various levels'. We have argued in our introduction that it is high time that the relationship between food and nationalism was taken seriously in the study of politics in general and in the study of nationalism more specifically. Food is essential to life and as such it is powerful in a multitude of ways; it literally sustains life; it is imbued with meanings; it is highly symbolic and emotive and therefore it is highly political as a number of anthropologists have argued. Food features prominently in politics: in defining the problems which are important for a society ('it is part of our cultural heritage to eat dog meat and therefore foreigners should not meddle with it'); in the contest over power and values in public as seen in the Zionist attempt to create new Jews through diet and the sometimes hostile responses to it; and in 'the authoritative allocation of values, rights and duties for the community as a whole' as seen in the EU's granting of a GI (Huysmans 2005: 75). On the other hand, politics today is permeated by the ideology of nationalism as a nation-centric worldview. Notwithstanding the all-too-often conflation of the nation and the state, today's politics is fundamentally shaped by nationalism from the everyday to global levels. Given all these, the relationship between food and nationalism, a largely neglected topic in the study of nationalism, deserves serious attention, and that is what the current volume has set out to do and it has, in our view, provided an outline for this important research area.

Has the volume shown that the 'food and nationalism' axis is a useful tool in the study of politics? We think it has. Both food and nationalism are ubiquitous in modern life, and the variety of cases examined in the volume suggests that the axis provides a number of entry points to investigate politics in many, if not all, aspects of life. The fact that a range of whale meat products is itemised in a wine bar's menu leads to a realisation of the formation of a particular discourse about the food culture of a group in response to certain normative pressure from the outside, which is then legitimised in reference to globally shared norms. The collision of *the universal* and *the particular* or *the global* and *the national* then enters into people's lives in a mundane manner, connecting the everyday reality of people to 'high' politics. Behind the increased exposure to foreign food and cuisine, the 'food and nationalism' angle reveals there are gastrodiplomacy initiatives, nation branding, the emergence of global norms about consumer protection, the idea of corporate social responsibility and the promotion of free trade. The reason why we are served Costa Rican coffee, not anonymous one, is a complex interaction among all these movements, initiatives and strategies, not just profit motives. The 'food and nationalism' axis can therefore be made into a useful pedagogical tool in the study of nationalism by allowing students to link their everyday life experiences to more abstract ideas in politics. This is because 'the "food and nationlaism" axis has an almost unique potential for illuminating the ways in which these various levels of politics and analysis overlap, connect and influence one another'.

We very much stand by these claims in this current edition. As acknowledged in the introduction, the first edition insufficiently explored a number of topics and there were several notable gaps. Since the first edition came out in 2016, we have come to realise there is and has been more scholarly work on food and nationalism, scattered across many disciplines. What we have set out do in this edition is to address the gaps that we noted; provide additional and up-to-date case studies; include some of the scholarly work that has come out since; deepen the analyses provided; and suggest additional directions for further research.

Looking at what we set out to accomplish, we think we have by and large achieved our aims for this edition. The selection of case studies is still eclectic and largely draws from the authors' own work as well as a wide range of literature from across the social sciences and humanities. We maintain, as we did in the first edition, the utility and usefulness of the 'food and nationalism' in investigating the world we live. Recent events, including the rise of nationalist-populism, Brexit and the pandemic, have further illustrated the importance of nationalism as a political ideology and a feature of the world we live in. We also reiterate that 'the fact that the volume has drawn from a range of sources shows the attractiveness of the "food and nationalism" axis: it is necessarily interdisciplinary and as such has the potential to offer a more holistic understanding of the world we live in, which is inherently complex and nuanced'.

We have continued to maintain focus on everyday nationhood and banal nationalism as our starting points, due to the quotidian nature of food, and these ideas have proven to be useful in examining the ways in which individuals and groups relate to the idea of the nation as expected. The volume's particular contribution with respect to everyday nationhood and banal nationalism is "Chapter Three: Consuming Nations— The Construction of National Identities in the Food Industry" which shows how the activities of private sector actors (profit-making entities— supermarkets, restauranteurs and food producers) are shaped and conditioned by the framework of nationalism. For example, chocolate in UK supermarkets is no longer generic chocolate but chocolate with a nationality, which is linked to a distinctive idea about what that nation represents. By doing so, the UK supermarkets are, most likely unwittingly, reifying the fundamental understanding in the ideology of nationalism: the world is divided into nations and each nation has its own unique personality. This is, as far as we can see, a new insight into everyday and banal nationalism.

In regard to our contribution to the ideas of everyday nationhood and banal nationalism, we have highlighted a utility of netnography, an emerging methodological approach to conduct qualitative studies in the cyberspace. The development of the Internet, in particular, social media, is widely credited to have enhanced ordinary people's participation in a wide range of societal activities and for qualitative researchers, review sites where users post their views and evaluations can be a treasure trove. Netnography is already widely used in tourism studies and marketing as an inexpensive and handy way of collecting data. Blogs, review sites and so on are also a valuable source of information because posting their views and uploading their photos are what people do in the twenty-first century. We have therefore suggested that netnography can serve as another useful tool in data gathering in our efforts to better understand the world we live in. It is also clear that this is an area that is calling for future research.

The volume has also found that conventional modernist approaches to nationalism, as a critique to which banal and everyday nationalism approaches have been developed, have some explanatory power in the investigation of the relationship between food and nationalism. Various governments' concern with the nation's diet is often entwined with modernisation and with the rapid expansion of the state's power to intervene in people's life. The government thus becomes concerned with the nation's diet in its attempt to strengthen the county and uses institutions such as compulsory education and conscription to influence what people eat. In other words, food can be a tool of governance, in particular, in an authoritarian regime in order to propagate a certain idea of the nation in a top-down manner. In the current edition, we have also considered what the rise in popularity of veganism can tell us about the relationship between food and nationalism.

In modern society, food primarily comes across as something to be consumed by the majority of people. Therefore, insights from studies in marketing, tourism and trade are relevant to the volume in broadening this perspective. We have investigated the issue of branding in the case of the private sector actors, nation branding and gastrodiplomacy pursued by the nation-state and gastronationalism in the international arena. What we have found is that food is and has been used as a useful tool for promoting a particular image of the nation-state domestically but also internationally. The nation-state's claim of ownership and promotion of national foods also links in well with the increase in demands by consumers to receive more and better information about the food they purchase and consume, and the private sector's desire to add value and increase sales. Nevertheless, the state's 'ownership' of national food also leads, sometimes as an unintended consequence, to the homogenisation of the nation. One of the critiques of the inscription of food culture in UNESCO's intangible cultural heritage list focuses on this aspect: as the application is done by the member state, what might be a 'regional' practice would be presented in conjunction with the state that is applying for the inscription. That might lead to an 'appropriation' of a local practice as a national one, or it could be a source of tension among neighbouring states as seen in the case of Turkish' keşkek, and the kimchi wars, which are discussed in "Chapter Six: National Food in the International Context II—Gastronationalism and Populism". What is clear from our investigation is the usefulness of the 'food and nationalism' axis for understanding the various political process and policies involved and for demonstrating how they all relate to and influence one another.

In the current edition, we have endeavoured to fill some of the gaps left in the first edition. In reference to transnational movements and diasporas acknowledged in the conclusion of first edition as something missing in the volume, we have added a study of Bulgarians in the UK in their practice of maintaining/reshaping the Bulgarian nationhood through food practices in "Chapter Two: When Groups Participate in Defining the Nation". This is a first step in investigating diasporas and their relationship with nationalism/national identity through food. We have also added new sections on the importance of food security and food populism in "Chapter Six: National Food in the International Context II—Gastronationalism and Populism", which are partly a response to a number of developments since the publication of the first edition, in particular the rise of populism and Brexit.

We believe we have covered many lacunas in the first edition in the current edition. Still, we have not covered the impact of the Covid-19 pandemic on food and nationalism. We are aware many researchers are working on the impact of the pandemic, and some of their works are of relevance to our interest. Another important lacuna that we did not manage to address in this volume is that of climate change and the ways in which food and nationalism can enhance our understanding of responses to environmental issues and crises. These two crucial issues are certainly an agenda for future research.

Through its investigation, the current volume has highlighted that globalisation is an underlying factor that defines and redefines the relationship between food and nationalism. What is meant by globalisation here is a kind of social change through which connections between different parts of the globe increase, a process which has been going on since humans started to migrate from Africa and which has intensified from the mid-twentieth century with the rapid developments in technology. Globalisation is, in this sense, an essential condition of human life, not a novel phenomenon that emerged in the 1980s. Our investigation into food and nationalism has confirmed this view of globalisation. Individuals in modern societies are exposed to an increased range of food items and food cultures because of globalisation; people encounter foreign cuisines on a daily basis and know that some people in the world eat what they would not eat, or grow and plant what they would not. This is because globalisation, in the form of increased international trade, has brought a range of new food items, cuisines and culinary ideas and traditions to ordinary people's lives. As the exposure to foreign food items/cuisine/food culture increases, the value of the particular also increases as the means of differentiation or as the indication of quality. This then leads to re-arrangement of inter-group relationship. Hummus simultaneously becomes 'Arab' and 'Israeli' in what is dubbed as the 'hummus war'. The contestation over hummus or kimchi, as discussed in "Chapter Six: National Food in the International Context II—Gastronationalism and Populism", provide good examples of the tensions that arise from the interplay between the local, national and global, as a result of globalisation.

The significance of globalisation is not limited to trade and travel. Our investigation has suggested nationalism in relation to food is often engaged within an emergence of global ethical or normative frameworks. Even in the area of international trade in which CO and GIs are largely seen as tools for increasing exports of agricultural stuff (and attracting more tourists), they represent global standards, a set of ideas about what a particular good should be for the purpose of consumer protection. The principle that the consumer should be protected by increased transparency and better regulation by the nation-state or international organisations is a norm that is increasingly shared in many parts of the world. While this is associated with international trade, something that is very material, it has contributed to the building of global normative frameworks.

The presence of global ethical/normative frameworks is felt in other cases as well. For instance, the re-affirmation of the right to eat whale meat, dog meat or foie gras in the face of opposition based on the idea of animal rights, one of the emerging global norms, is justified in reference to respect for cultural rights, yet another global norm. In regard to global norms, the volume has found that international organisations play a complex role in relation to food and nationalism. UNESCO, whose mission is to preserve the diversity of cultures of the world as a universal good in its own right, has developed the idea of world heritage, which appears to be used as a means of nation branding by the member states; in other words, UNESCO is a venue for the nation-states to project their images externally. When it comes to the intangible cultural heritage list, however, UNESCO appears to be used by the nation-state and to a certain extent by the private sector as well, to engage with the domestic audience; the French and Japanese governments, both managed to have their respective cuisine inscribed in the list and are more concerned with tackling what they consider to be the decline of national culture, and UNESCO acts as an indisputable authority to authenticate the particular: national culture. In this sense, the nation-state is trying to make the most of the international/global authority an international organisation possesses in order to deal with nation-rebuilding.

The sometimes paradoxical role which international organisations play is also highlighted in the investigation of the EU's role in relation to GIs. On the one hand, the EU supports the GI system as a means of promoting free trade and strengthening consumer protection, both are universalistic orientations. In this sense the EU is acting as the enforcer of global standards for the good of humanities. However, the EU is also locked in a number of disputes with its trading partners because of its protection of GIs. In this regard, the EU is acting as the protector of the member states' interests, in other words, particularistic interests by emphasising the GIs as IP. The protection of IP is, in turn, a universalistic value; IP should be protected because it is the right thing to do. *The national* is again protected in reference to *the universal*. The same can also be seen in the example of GM foods and the struggle between the EU and the US over what should be the global standard for dealing with GM products.

Our investigation into food and nationalism has after all highlighted the complex interplay between the effects of globalisation and the world that is based on a nation-centric ideology. It has demonstrated that globalisation does not simply bring about the homogenisation of culture, but rather it adds more layers to the cultural landscape. What is clear from our volume is that this layering of culture can be analysed and untangled through the 'food and nationalism' axis, which brings together and highlights the ways in which the banal and everyday interact with *the national* and *the global*.

References

Abbas, Hussam and Nira Rousso. (2006) Lamb, Mint and Pine-Nuts: The Flavours of the Israeli-Arab Cuisine [in Hebrew]. Tel Aviv: Yedioth Aharonot.

Abufarha, Nasser (2008) 'Land of Symbols: Cactus, Poppies, Orange and Olive Trees in Palestine Identities', *Global Studies in Culture and Power*, 15(3): 343–368.

Abunimah, Ali 'Did you know? Palestine's Knafeh is now "Israeli" too?' 3 June (2014) http://electronicintifada.net/blogs/ali-abunimah/did-you-know-palestines-knafeh-now-israeli-too (last accessed 2 January 2021)

Abu-Ghosh, Nawal (1996) *The Arab-Israeli Cuisine* [in Hebrew]. Jerusalem: Keter.

Abu-Laban, Yasmeen (2020) 'Donut Nation: Tim Hortons and Canadian Identity', in Nieguth, Tim (ed) *Nationalism and Popular Culture*. London: Routledge: pp. 19–35.

Agarwal, Sanjeev and Barone, Michael (2005) 'Emerging Issues for Geographical Indication. Branding Strategies', *MATRIC Research Paper*, 05-MRP 9, Ames, Iowa: Midwest Agribusiness Trade Research and Information Center, Iowa State University.

Aguilera Bornand, Isabel (2019) 'Ethnicity, class, and nation in Chilean Cuisine', in Ichijo, Atsuko; Johannes, Venetia and Ranta, Ronald (eds) *The Emergence of National Food: The Dynamics of Food and Nationalism*. London: Bloomsbury: pp. 107–116.

Albala, Ken (2011) *Food Cultures of the World Encyclopaedia*. California: Greenwood.

Alloun, Esther (2020) 'Veganwashing Israel's dirty laundry? Animal politics and nationalism in Palestine-Israel', *Journal of Intercultural Studies*, 41(1): 24–41.

Almog, Oz (2000) *The Sabra: The Creation of the New Jew*. Berkley: University of California Press.

Amram, Azri (2021) 'Fifty shades of Kosher: negotiating kashrut in Palestinian food spaces in Israel', *Food, Culture & Society*: https://doi.org/10.1080/15528014.2021.1958285

Anderson, Benedict (1983) *Imagined Communities: Reflections on the Origin and Spread of Nationalism*. London: Verso.

Anderson, Benedict (1992)ations and Nationalism since 1780. Cambridge:*f Nationalism* (2nd ed.), London: Verso.

Andersson, Helen (2019) 'Recontextualizing Swedish nationalism for commercial purposes: a multimodal analysis of a milk marketing event', *Critical Discourse Studies*, https://doi.org/10.1080/17405904.2019.1637761

Andersson, Helen and Angela Smith (2021): 'Flags and fields: a comparative analysis of national identity in butter packaging in Sweden and the UK', *Social Semiotics*, https://doi.org/10.1080/10350330.2021.1968276

Appadurai, Arjun (1988) 'How to Make National Cuisine: Cookbooks in Contemporary India'. *Comparative Studies in Society and History*, 30(1): 3–24.

Araki, Masaya (2013) 'The confrontation between the nation-states regarding the codex standards of cheese and geographical indications: disputes over edam, emmental, gouda, parmesan and others' [in Japanese], *A.I.P.P.I*, 58(11): 766–779

Ariel, Ari (2012) "The Hummus Wars", *Gastronomica: The Journal of Food and Culture*, 12(1): 34–42.

Aron, William; Burke, William and Freeman, Milton M.R. (2000) 'The whaling issue' *Marine Policy*, 24: 179–191.

Aronczyk, Melissa (2008) '"Living the Brand": Nationality, Globality and the Identity Strategies of Nation Branding Consultants', *International Journal of Communications*, 2: 41–65.

Arthurs, Deborah (2012). 'The Best Frogspawn You'll Ever Drink!', *Dailymail Online*, 2.7.2012.

Ashkenazi, Michael and Jacob, Jeanne (2000) *The Essence of Japanese Cuisine: an Essay on food and Culture*. Philadelphia: University of Pennsylvania Press.

Ashley, Bob, Hollows Joanne, Jones Steve and Taylor Ben (2004) *Food and Cultural Studies*, London: Routledge.

Avieli, Nir (2005) 'Vietnamese New Year rice cakes: Iconic festive dishes and contested national identity', *Ethnology*, 44(2): 167–187

Avieli, Nir (2009) 'At Christmas we Don't Like Pork, Just Like the Maccabees', *Journal of Material Culture* 14(2): 219–241.

Avieli, Nir (2011) 'Dog meat politics in a Vietnamese town', *Ethnology*, 50 (1): 59–78.

Avieli, Nir (2013) 'Grilled Nationalism: Power Masculinity and Space in Israeli Barbeques', *Food, Culture and Society* 16(2): 301–320.

Avieli, Nir (2018) *Food and Power: A Culinary Ethnography of Israel*. Oakland: University of California Press

Bahar, Aykan (2015) 'Patenting' Karagöz: UNESCO, nationalism and multinational intangible heritage, *International Journal of Heritage Studies*, 21(10): 949–961.

Bahar, Aykan (2016) 'The politics of intangible heritage and food fights in Western Asia', *International Journal of Heritage Studies*, 22(10): 799–810.

Bailey, Jennifer (2008) 'Arrested development: The fight to end commercial whaling as a case of failed norm change', *European Journal of International Relations*, 14(2): 289–318.

Balabanis, George et al. (2001) 'The impact of nationalism, patriotism and internationalism on consumer ethnocentric tendencies', *Journal of International Business Studies*, 32: 157–175.

Bar-David, Moli (1963) *Folkloric Cookbook: Delights for Israeli Festivals* [in Hebrew]. Tel Aviv: Bar-David.

Barthes, Roland (2019) 'Towards a Psychobiology of Contemporary Food Consumption', in: Counihan, Carole, Penny Van Esterik and Alice Julier (eds.) *Food and Culture: A Reader*. New York: Routledge, pp. 13–20.

Beeson, Mark and Bisley, Nick (eds) (2013) *Issues in 21st Century World Politics (second edition)*, Basingstoke: Palgrave Macmillan.

Beeton, Isabella (1861) *Mrs Beeton's Book on Household Management*. London: S.O Beeton Publishing.

Belasco, James (2008) *Food: the Key Concepts*. New York: Berg.

Bell, David and Valentine, Gill (1997) *Consuming Geographies: We Are Where We Eat*. New York: Routledge.

Bergflodt, Sigurd et al. (2012) 'Nordic Food culture(s)—Thoughts and Perspectives by way of introduction, *Anthropology of Food*, 7 [Online]: https://doi.org/10.4000/aof.7296.

Bhabha, Homi K. (1997) *The Location of Culture* London: Routledge.

Billiet, Stijn (2019) Brexit and Fisheries: Fish and Chips Aplenty?, *The Political Quarterly*, 90(4): 611–619.

Billig, Michael (1995) *Banal Nationalism*. London: Sage.
Blok, Anders (2008) 'Contesting Global Norms: Politics of Identity in Japanese Pro-Whaling Countermobilization', *Global Environmental Politics*, 8(2): 39–66.
Blok, Ander (2011) 'War of the Whales: Post-Sovereign Science and Agonistic Cosmopolitics in Japanese-Global Whaling Assemblages', *Science, Technology, & Human Values*, 36 (1): 55–81.
Bock, Sheila (2021) 'Fast Food at the White House: Performing Foodways, Class and American Identity', *Western Folklore*, 80(1): 15–43.
Booth, Robert (2010). 'Taiwan Launches "Gastro-Diplomacy" Drive', *The Guardian*, 8.8.2010.
Borras, Saturnino M. Jr. (2020) 'Agrarian social movements: The absurdly difficult but not impossible agenda of defeating right-wing populism and exploring a socialist future', *Journal of Agrarian Change*, 20(1): 3–36.
Boscia, Stefan (2021) 'What are the UK-EU "sausage wars" in Northern Ireland and are they over?', *CityA.M*, 1, 7, 2021.
Bowen, Sarah (2010) 'Embedding Local Places in Global Spaces: Geographical Indications as a Territorial Development Strategy', *Rural Sociology*, 75(2): 209–243
Bowett, Julia and Hay, Pete (2009) 'Whaling and its controversies: Examining the attitudes of Japan's youth', *Marine Policy*, 33: 775–783.
Breuilly, John (1982) *Nationalism and the State*, Manchester: Manchester University Press.
Broude, T. (2017) 'From Chianti to Kimchi: Geographical Indications, Intangible Cultural Heritage, and Their Unsettled Relationship with Cultural Diversity', in I. Calboliand N. and L.Wee Loon (eds.), *Geographical Indications at the Crossroads of Trade, Development, and Culture: Focus on Asia-Pacific*, Cambridge: Cambridge University Press, pp. 461–484.
Brown, Mary Ellen (1984) *Burns and Tradition*. London: Macmillan.
Brown, Pete (2019) Pie Fidelity. Milton Keynes: Penguin Books.
Brubaker, Rogers (2004) *Ethnicity without Groups*. Cambridge: Harvard University Press.
Brumann, Christoph (2014) 'Shifting tides of world-making in the UNESCO World Heritage Convention: cosmopolitanisms colliding', *Ethnic and Racial Studies*, 37(12): 2176–2192.
Bueltmann, Tanja (2012) '"The Image of Scotland which We Cherish in Our Hearts": Burns Anniversary Celebrations in Colonial Otago', *Immigrants & Minorities: Historical Studies in Ethnicity, Migration and Diaspora*, 30(1): 78–97.

Buettner, Elizabeth (2002). Haggis in the Raj: Private and public celebrations of Scottishness in late imperial India. *Scottish Historical Review*, 81(2): 212–239.

The Cabinet Office of Japan (2006) *Basic Program for Shokuiku Promotion (abstract)*, available from http://www8.cao.go.jp/syokuiku/about/pdf/plan_ol_eng.pdf.

Calder, Angus and Donnelly William (eds) (1991) *Robert Burns: Selected Poetry*. London: Penguin, pp. 293–4.

Caldwell, Mellisa (2002) 'The Taste of nationalism: Food Politics in Postsocialist Moscow', *Ethnos: Journal of Anthropology*, 67(3): 295–319.

Catalinac, Amy and Chan, Gerald (2005), 'Japan, the West and the whaling issue: understanding the Japanese side', *Japan Forum* 17(1) 2005: 133–163.

Cenry, Philip (2013) 'Globalization and statehood', in Beeson, Mark and Nick Bisley (eds) *Issues in 21st Century Politics (second edition)*, Basingstoke: Palgrave Macmillan, pp. 30–46.

Cesaro, Christina M. (2000) 'Consuming Identities: Food and Resistance among the Uyghur in Contemporary Xinjiang', *Inner Asia*, 2(2): 225–238.

Chan, Kwok Shing (2007) '*Poonchoi:* the Production and Popularity of a Rural Festive Cuisine in Urban and Modern Hong Kong', in Cheung, Sidney C.H and Tan Chee-Beng (eds.) *Food and Foodways in Asia*, Abingdon: Routledge, pp. 55–66.

Chapple-Sokol, Sam (2013) 'Culinary Diplomacy: Breaking Bread to Win Hearts and Mind', *The Hague Journal of Diplomacy*, 8: 161–183.

Charlier, Christophe and Ngo, Mai-Anh (2012) 'Geographical indications outside the European Regulation on PGIs, and the rule of the free movement of goods: Lessons from cases judged by the Court of Justice of the European Communities', *European Journal of Law and Economy*, 34: 17–30.

Charters, Steve and Nathalie Spielmann (2014) 'Characteristics of strong territorial brands: The case of champagne', *Journal of Business Research*, 67(7): 1461–1467.

Chatterjee, Partha (1993) *The Nation and Its Fragments: Colonial and Postcolonial Histories*. Princeton, NJ: Princeton University Press.

Chen, Yujen (2022). 'The Taste of Colonialism? Changing Norms of Rice Production and Consumption in Modern Taiwan', in Ranta et al. (eds) 'Going Native'? Settler Colonialism and Food. London: Palgrave Macmillan: 65–84.

Chuck, Samantha A. Fernandes, and Lauri L. Hyers (2016) 'Awakening to the politics of food: Politicized diet as social identity', *Appetite*, 107: 425–436.

Chern, Wen; Ishibashi, Kiyoko; Taniguchi, Kiyoshi and Toyama, Yuki (2003) *Analysis of the Food Consumption of Japanese Households*, FAO ECONOMIC AND SOCIAL DEVELOPMENT PAPER 152, Rome: Food and Agricultural Organisation of the United Nations.

Cho, Hong Sik (2006) Food and Nationalism: Kimchi and Korean National Identity, *The Korean Journal of International Studies*, 4(1): 207–229.

Chuang, Hui-Tun (2009) 'The Rise of Culinary Tourism and its Transformation of Food Cultures: The National Cuisine of Taiwan', *The Copenhagen Journal of Asian Studies*, 27(2): 84–108.

Civitello, Linda (2006) *Cuisine and Culture: A History of Food and People*. Hoboken: Wiley.

Clapp, Jennifer (2006) 'Unplanned Exposure to Genetically Modified Organisms: Divergent Responses in the Global South', *The Journal of Environment & Development*, 15(1): 3–21.

Clapp, Jennifer (2012) *Hunger in the Balance: The New Politics of International Food Aid*. Ithaca: Cornell University Press.

Clapp, Jennifer (2013) *Food*. Oxford: Polity.

Cohen, Anthony (1996) 'Personal nationalism: A Scottish view of some rites, rights, and wrongs', *American Ethnologist*, 23(4): 802–815.

Collingham, Lizzie (2012) *The Taste of War: World War Two and the Battle for Food*. London: Penguin Books.

Cook, Ian and Philip Crang (1996) 'The World on a Plate: Culinary Culture, Displacement and Geographical Knowledges', *Journal of Material Culture* 1(2): 131–153.

Cormack, Patricia (2008) 'True Stories of Canada: Tim Hortons and the Branding of National Identity', *Cultural Sociology*, 2008, 2: 369–384.

Cornfled, Lilian (1949) *What to Cook with the Austerity Portions* [in Hebrew]. Tel Aviv: Dov Gutman Press.

Costello, Leesa; McDermott, Marie-Louise and Wallace, Ruth (2017) 'Netnography: Range of practices, misconceptions, and missed opportunities', *International Journal of Qualitative Methods*, 16: 11–17.

Counihan, Carole and Van Estrik, Penny "Introduction to the Second Edition". (2008) In: Counihan, Carole and Van Estrik (eds.) *Food and Culture: A Reader*. New York: Routledge.

Cowan, Jane (1991) 'Going out for coffee?: Contesting the grounds of gendered pleasures in everyday sociability', in Peter Loizos and Evthimoios Papataksiarchis (eds) *Contested Identities: Gender and Kinship in Modern Greece*, Princeton: Princeton University Press.

Craw, Charlotte (2008) 'The ecology of emblem eating: Environmentalism, nationalism and the framing of kangaroo consumption', *Media International Australia*, 127(1): 82–95.

Crew, Charlotte (2012) 'Gustatory Redemption? Colonial Appetites, Historical Tales and the Contemporary Consumption of Australian Native Foods', *International Journal of Critical Indigenous Studies*, 5(2): 13–24.

Curzi, Daniele and Martijn Huysmans (2021) The Impact of Protecting EU Geographical Indications in Trade Agreements, American Journal of Agricultural Economics, https://doi.org/10.1111/ajae.12226.

Cusack, Igor (2000) 'African Cuisines: Recipes for Nation-Building?', *Journal of African Cultural Studies*, 13(2): 207–225.

Cusack, Igor (2003) 'Pots, pens and "Eating out the body": Cuisine and the gendering of African nations', *Nations and Nationalism*, 9(2): 277–296.

Cusack, Igor (2004) '"Equatorial Guinea's national cuisine is simple and tasty": Cuisine and the making of national culture', *Arizona Journal of Hispanic Cultural Studies*, 8: 131–148.

Cwiertka, Katarzyna (2006) *Modern Japanese Cuisine: Food, Power and National Identity*, London: Reaktion Books.

Cwiertka, Katarzyna (2012) *Cuisine, Colonialism and Cold War: Food in Twentieth Century Korea*, London: Reaktion Books.

Cwiertka, Katarzyna (2015) *Modern Japanese Cuisine: Food, Power, National Identity*, London: Reaktion Books.

Dahl, Gudrun (1998) 'Wildflowers, Nationalism and the Swedish Law of Commons', *Worldviews: Environment, Culture, Religion*, 2: 281–302.

Daliot-Bul, Michal (2009) 'Japan Brand Strategy: The Taming of "Cool Japan" and the Challenges of Cultural Planning in a Postmodern Age', *Social Science Japan Journal*, 12(2): 247–266

Davis, Mitchell and Anne McBride (2008) 'The State of American Cuisine', The James Beard Foundation.

De Cillia, Rudolf, Reisigl, Martin and Wodak, Ruth (1999) 'The Discursive Construction of National Identities', *Discourse and Society* 10(2): 149–173.

DeSoucey, Michaela (2010) 'Gastronationalism: Food Traditions and Authenticity Politics in the European Union', *American Sociological Review*, 75: 432–455.

DeSoucey, Michaela (2016) *Contested Tastes: Foie Gras and the Politics of Food*, Princeton, Princeton University Press.

Díaz-Méndez, Cecillia and Gómez-Benito, Cristóbal (2010) 'Nutrition and the Mediterranean diet: A historical and sociological analysis of the concept of a "healthy diet" in Spanish society', *Food Policy*, 35: 437–447

Dugnoille, Julien (2014) 'From plate to pet promotion of trans-species companionship by Korean animal activists', *Anthropology Today*, 30(6): 3–7.

Dougnoille, Julien (2018) 'To Eat or Not to Eat Companion Dogs: Symbolic Value of Dog Meat and Human-Dog Companionship in Contemporary South Korea', *Food, Culture & Society*, 21(2): 214–232.

Edensor, Tim (2002) *National Identity, Popular Culture and Everyday* Life. Oxford: Berg.

Edensor, Tim (2006) 'Reconsidering national temporalities: institutional times, everyday routines, serial spaces and synchronicities', *European Journal of Social Theory*, 9(4): 525–45.

Edwards, Jason (2019) 'O, *The Roast Beef of Old England!* Brexit and Gastronationalism', *The Political Quarterly*, 90(4): 629–636.

Eghbariah, Rabea (2017) "The Criminilaztion of Za'atar and Akkoub: on Edible Plants Palestinian Cuisine and Israeli Plant Protection Laws." In Studies in Food Law, Tirosh, Yofi and Aeyal Gross (eds): 492–533. [in Hebrew]

Ehara, Junko (2014) 'Washoku as food culture and its implication to modern society', *Noson to Toshi wo Musubu (Connecting the Rural and Urban Areas)*, 64(7): 6–13.

Elgenius, Gabriella (2010) *Symbols of Nations and Nationalism: Celebrating Nationhood*. Basingstoke: Palgrave Macmillan.

Erkisen, Thomas Hylland (2001) 'Between Universalism and Relativism: a Critique of the UNESCO concept of Culture', in Cowen, Jane K, Marie-Benedicte Dembour and Rihard A. Wilson (eds) *Culture and Rights: Anthropological Perspectives*. Cambridge: the University of Cambridge Press, pp. 127–148.

Esenbel, Selçuk (1994) 'The anguish of civilised behaviour: The use of Western cultural forms in the everyday lives of the Meiji Japanese and the Ottoman Turks during the nineteenth century', *Japan Review*, 5: 145–185.

Eum, IkRan (2008) 'A Study on Current Culinary Culture and Religious Identity in the Gulf Region', *International Area Studies Review*, 11: 55–72.

European Commission (1998) 'Report of the Scientific Committee on Animal Health and Animal Welfare on Welfare Aspects of the Production of Foie Gras in Ducks and Geese', report available at: http://ec.europa.eu/food/fs/sc/scah/out17_en.html (accessed 18.1.2020).

Fabien-Ouellet, Nicolas (2019) 'The Canadian Cuisine Fallacy', in Ichijo, Atsuko., Johannes, Venetia and Ronald Ranta (eds) *The Emergence Of National Food: The Dynamics Of Food And Nationalism*. London: Bloomsbury, pp. 151–163.

Faiola, Anthony (2006) 'Putting the Bite On Pseudo Sushi And Other Insults: Japan Plans to Scrutinize Restaurant Offerings Abroad', *Washington Post*, Friday, November 24, 2006, available from: http://www.washingtonpost.com/wp-dyn/content/article/2006/11/23/AR2006112301158.html (accessed on 27 April 2015).

Fell, James and MacLarren, Donald (2013) 'The welfare cost of Japanese rice policy with home-good preference and an endogenous import price', *Australian Journal of Agricultural and Resource Economics*, 57: 601–619.

Ferguson, Priscilla Parkhurst (2006) *Accounting for Taste: The Triumph of French Cuisine*. Chicago: The University of Chicago Press.

Ferguson, Priscilla Parkhurst (2010) 'Culinary Nationalism', *Gastronomica* 10(1): 102–109.

Ferguson, Priscilla Parkhurst (2011) 'The Sense of Taste', *The American Historical Review*, 116(2): 371–384.

Fischler, Claude (1988) 'Food, self and identity', *Social Science Information*, 27(2): 275–292.

Fitting, Elizabeth (2006) 'The Political Use of Culture: Maize Production and the GM Corn debate in Mexico', *Focaal—European journal of anthropology*, 48: 17–34.

Forchtner, Benhard and Tominc, Ana (2017) 'Kalashnikov and cooking-spoon: Neo-Nazism, veganism and a lifestyle cooking show on YouTube', *Food, Culture & Society*, 20(3): 415–441.

Foster, Robert J. (1991) 'Making national Culture in the Global Ecumene', *Annual Review of Anthropology*, 20: 235–260.

Fox, Jonathan and Miller-Idriss, Cynthia (2008a) 'Everyday nationhood', *Ethnicities*, 8(4): 536–563.

Fox, Jonathan and Miller-Idriss, Cynthia (2008b) 'The "here and now" of everyday nationhood', *Ethnicities*, 8 (4): 573–576.

Francks, Penelope (1998) 'Agriculture and the state in industrial East Asia: the rise and fall of the Food Control System in Japan', *Japan forum*, 10(1): 1–16.

Francks, Penelope (2007) 'Consuming rice: food, "traditional" products and the history of consumption in Japan', *Japan Forum*, 19(2): 147–168.

Franks, Tim (2009) 'Jerusalem Diary: Hummus Wars', *BBC News*, 24.11.2009.

Fraser, Joy and Christine Knight (2019) 'Signifying Poverty, Class, and Nation through Scottish Foods: From Haggis to Deep-Fried Mars Bars', in Ichijo, Atsuko., Johannes, Venetia and Ronald Ranta (eds) *The Emergence Of National Food: The Dynamics Of Food And Nationalism*. London: Bloomsbury, pp. 73–84.

Freeden, Michael (1998) 'Is nationalism a distinct ideology?', *Political Studies*, 46(4): 748–765.
Fuchs, Alinor (2013) [in Hebrew] 'US Media: "Hummus is Taking over the Country"', *Mako*, 5.2.2013: http://www.mako.co.il/food-cooking_magazine/Article-b9e1106b0a06e31006.htm (accessed, 18.1.2020).
Gabaccia, Donna (1998) *We Are What We Eat*. Cambridge: Harvard University Press.
Gales, Nick; Leaper, Russell and Papastavroub, Vassili (2008) 'Is Japan's whaling humane?', *Marine Policy*, 32: 408–412.
Galili, Shooky. 2007. 'The Land of Hummus and Pita'. Available at: www.ynetnews.com/articles/0,7340,L-3401347,00.html (accessed 18.1.2020). [in Hebrew]
Garcia-Santamaria, Sara (2020) The Italian 'Taste': The Far-Right and the Performance of Exclusionary Populism During the European Elections, *Tripodos*, 49: 129–149.
Garon, Sheldon (1994) 'Rethinking modernization and modernity in Japanese history: A focus on state-society relations', *The Journal of Asian Studies*, 53(2): 346–366.
Gasparetti, Fedore (2012) 'Eating *tie bou jenn* in Turin: Negotiating Differences and Building Community Among Senegalese Migrants in Italy', *Food and Foodways*, 20(3): 257–278.
Garvin, Diana (2014) 'The Italian Kitchen as a Site for the Practice of Autarchy and Fascist Intervention', *Digest: a Journal of Foodways and Culture*, 3:1.
Gellner, Ernest (1983) *Nations and Nationalism*, Oxford: Basil Blackwell.
Gentilcore, David (2010) *Pomodoro!: A History of the Tomato in Italy*. New York: Columbia University Press.
Ghanem, As'ad (2001) *The Palestinian-Arab Minority in Israel, 1948–2000: A Political Study*. Albany: State University of New York Press.
Gheihman, Nina (2021) 'Veganism as a lifestyle movement', *Sociology Compas*, 15(5): https://doi.org/10.1111/soc4.12877.
Giddens, Anthnoy (1985) *The Nation-State and Violence (Vol. II of a Contemporary Critique of Historical Materialism)*. Oxford: Polity.
Gille, Zsuzsa (2011) 'The Hungarian Foie Gras Boycott: Struggles for Moral Sovereignty in Postsocialist Europe', *East European Politics and Societies*, 25(1): 114–128.
Gluck, Caroline (2011) 'The end of elsewhere: Writing modernity now', *American Historical Review*, 116(3): 676–687.

Golan, Tiki. 2008. 'What is the Most Israeli Dish?' [in Hebrew].*Akhbar Ha-'Ir*, May 5.

González Turmo, Isabel (2004) 'A methodology for analysing recipe books', *Social Science Information*, Vol 43(4):753–773.

The Government of Japan (2014) 'Proposed Research Plan for New Scientific Whale Research Program in the Antarctic Ocean (NEWREP-A)', a proposal submitted to the International Whaling Commission on 18 November 2014, available from http://www.jfa.maff.go.jp/j/whale/index.html (accessed on 30 March 2015).

Gray, Alan S (2012) *The Scotch Whisky: Annual Review of Industry*. Edinburgh: Sutherlands Edinburgh.

Greenfeld, Liah (1992) *Nationalism: Five Roads to Modernity*. Cambridge, MA: Harvard University Press.

Grew, Raymond (ed.) (1999a) *Food in Global History*. Boulder, Co: Westview.

Grew, Raymond (1999b) 'Food and global history', in Grew, Raymond (ed.) *Food in Global History*, Boulder, Co: Westview, pp. 1–29.

Guggenheim, Karl et al. (1991) 'The Beginning of the Study of Food and Nutrition in the Land of Israel', [in Hebrew] *Catedra*, 59: 144–160.

The Guardian (2015) 'Japan asked to prove its whaling is for scientific research', *The Guardian*, 19 June 2015, available from: https://www.theguardian.com/environment/2015/jun/19/japan-asked-to-prove-whaling-for-scientific-research (last accessed on 28 November 2020).

Gur, Janna. 2008. *Fresh Flavours from* Israel. Tel Aviv: Al Hashulchan Gastronomic Media.

Gurel, Burak, Kucuk, Bermal and Sercan Tas (2021) 'The rural roots of the rise of the Justice and Development Party in Turkey', in Scoones, Ian et al. (eds) *Authoritarian Populism and the Rural World*, London: Routledge, pp. 97–119.

Guy, Kolleen (2003) *When Champagne Became French: Wine and the Making of a National Identity*, Baltimore, MD, and London: Johns Hopkins University Press.

Gvion, Liora (2006) 'Cuisine of Poverty as Means of Empowerment: Arab food in Israel', *Agriculture and Human Values*, 23: pp. 299–312.

Gvion, Liora. 2012. *Beyond Hummus and Falafel: Social and Political Aspects of Palestinian Food in Israel*. London: University of California Press.

Gvion, Liora (2014) 'Intertwining Tradition with Modernity: The Case of Palestinian Restaurants in Israel' *Journal of Intercultural Studies* 35(4): 366–384.

Gvion, Liora (2019) 'Obliterating or Reviving the Nonexisting Nation', in Ichijo, Atsuko et, al. (eds) *The Emergence of National Food: The Dynamics of Food and Nationalism*. London: Bloomsbury, pp. 130–141.

Hajdu, Anna and Natalia Mamonova (2020) Prospects of Agrarian Populism and Food Sovereignty Movement in Post-Socialist Romania, *Sociologia Ruralis*, 4: 880–904.

Han, Kyung-Koo (2011) 'The "Kimchi War" in Globalizing East Asia: Consuming Class, Gender, Health and National Identity', in Kendall, Laurel (ed) *Consuming Korean Tradition in Early and Late Modernity Commodification, Tourism, and Performance*. Honolulu, University of Hawaii Press, pp 149–166.

Harada, Nobuo (2005) *Washoku and Japanese Culture: A Social History of Japanese Cuisine* [in Japanese]. Tokyo: Shogakukan.

Harris, Jessica B (2012) *High on the Hog: A Culinary Journey from Africa to America*. New York: Bloomsbury.

Hashimoto, Naoki (2015) 'Food culture of Japan, No. 5: How has washoku been developed' (in Japanese), *New Food Industry*, 57(3): 21–27.

Heazel, Michael (2004) 'Scientific uncertainty and the International Whaling Commission: an alternative perspective on the use of science in policy making', *Marine Policy*, 28: 361–374.

Heazel, Michael (2013) '"See you in court!": Whaling as a two level game in Australian politics and foreign policy', *Marine Policy*, 38: 330–336.

Hechter, Michael (1975) *Internal Colonialism: The Celtic Fringe in British National Development 1536–1966*, London: Routledge and Kagan Paul.

Heldke, L.M. (2003) *Exotic Appetites: Ruminations of a Food Adventurer*. New York: Routledge.

Heller, Chaia (2013) *Food, Farms, and Solidarity: French Farmers Challenge Industrial Agriculture and Genetically Modified Crops*. Durham: Duke University Press.

Helstosky, Carol (2003) 'Recipe for the nation: reading Italian history through La Scienza in Cucina and La Cucina Futurista', *Food and Foodways: Explorations in the History and Culture of Human Nourishment*, 11 (2–3): 113–140.

Helstosky, Carol (2004) 'Fascist Food Politics: Mussolini's Policy of Alimentary Sovereignty', *Journal of Modern Italian Studies*, 9(1): 1–26.

Hemstad, Ruth (2010) 'Scandinavuanism, Nordic cooperation, and "Nordic Democracy"', in Jussi Kurunmaki and Johan Strang (eds) *Rhetorics of Nordic Democracy*. Helsinki: Finnish Literature Society, pp. 179–193.

Higman B. W. (2012) *How Food Made History*. Chichester: Wiley-Blackwell.

Hinchliffe, Steve (2009) 'Connecting people and places', in Stephanie Taylor, Steve Hinchliffe, John Clarke and Simon Bromley (eds) *Making Social Lives*. Milton Keynes: The Open University, pp. 207–244.

Hine, Christine (2011) 'Internet research and unobstructive methods', *Social Research UPDATE, Issue*, 61: 1–4, available from https://sru.soc.surrey.ac.uk/SRU61.pdf (last accessed on 6 December 2021).

Hinnawi, Miriam. 2006. *Arab Cuisine from the Galilee* [in Hebrew]. Jerusalem: Academon.

Hirata, Keiko (2004) 'Beached whales: Examining Japan's rejection of an international norm', *Social Science Japan Journal*, 7(2): 177–197

Hirata, Keiko (2005) 'Why Japan Supports Whaling', *Journal of International Wildlife Law and Policy*, 8:129–149

Hirsh, Dafna (2011) 'Hummus is best When it is Fresh and Made by Arabs', *American Ethnologist* 38(4): 617–630.

Hirsch, Dafna and Ofra Tene (2013) 'Hummus: The Making of an Israeli Culinary Cult', *Journal of Consumer Culture*, 13(1): 25–45.

Hjalager, Anne-Mette, and Greg Richards, eds. (2002). Tourism and gastronomy. Vol. 11. London: Routledge.

Hobsbawm, Eric (1990) *Nations and Nationalism since 1780*, Cambridge: Cambridge University Press.

Hobsbawm, Eric and Ranger, Terence (eds) (1983) *The Invention of Tradition*, Cambridge: Cambridge University Press.

Holtzman, Jon D (2006) 'Food and memory', *Annual Review of Anthropology*, 35: 361–378.

Holtzman, Jon (2017) On Whale: Conundrums of Culture and Cetaceans as Local Meat, *Ethnos*, 82:2, 277–297.

Hobsbawm, E. J. (1993) *Nations and Nationalism Since 1780*. Cambridge: Cambridge University Press.

Horie, Nobuhiro (2004) 'Crop failure, price regulation, and emergency imports of Japan's rice sector in1993', *Applied Economics*, 36: 1051–1056

Horiuchi, Yusaku and Saito, Jun (2010) 'Cultivating rice and votes: The institutional origins of agricultural protectionism in Japan', *Journal of East Asian Studies*, 10 (3): 425–452.

The House of Representatives of Japan (2014) Minutes of the 186th Agriculture, Forestry and Fisheries Committee meeting on 16 April 2014 (in Japanese), available from http://www.shugiin.go.jp/internet/itdb_kaigiroku.nsf/html/kaigiroku/000918620140416010.htm. (accessed on 23 March 2015).

Hubbell, Amy L. and Jorien Van Beukering (2022) 'Sustaining the Memory of Colonial Algeria through Food', in Ranta et al. (eds) *'Going Native'? Settler Colonialism and Food*. London: Palgrave Macmillan, pp. 221–245.

Hurd, Ian (2012) 'Almost saving whales: The ambiguity of Success at the International Whaling Commission', *Ethics & International Affairs*, 26(1): 103–112.

Hutchinson, John (1987) *The dynamics of cultural nationalism: Gaelic revival and the creation of the Irish nation state*. London: Allen & Unwin.

Hutchinson, John (2005) Nations as Zones of Conflict. London: Sage.

Huysmans, Jef (2005) *What is Politics.*, Milton Keynes: the Open University.

Huysmans, Martijn and Swinnen, Johan (2019) 'No terroir in the cold? A note on the geography of geographical indications', *Journal of Agricultural Economics*, 70(2): 550–559.

Huysmans, Martijn (2020) 'Exporting protection: EU trade agreements, geographical indications, and gastronationalism', *Review of International Political Economy*: https://doi.org/10.1080/09692290.2020.1844272

Ichijo, Atsuko (2009) 'Sovereignty and nationalism in the twenty-first century: The Scottish case', *Ethnopolitics*, 8(2): 155–172.

Ichijo, Atsuko (2013) *Nationalism and Multiple Modernities: European and Beyond*. Basingstoke: Palgrave.

Ichijo, Atsuko (2019) 'What has the Brexit process done to Scotch whisky?', *Political Quarterly*, 90(4): 637–644.

Ichijo, Atsuko., Johannes, Venetia and Ronald Ranta (eds) (2019) *The Emergence of National Food: The Dynamics of Food and Nationalism*. London: Bloomsbury.

Imoo, Ken'ichiro (2014) 'A new business idea academy: how to develop strategic thinking' [in Japanese], *Shukan Toyo Keizai (Eastern Economy Weekly)*, No. 6505: 102–103.

Ingham, John (2013) 'Outcry over EU plot to seize control of our seabeds', The Express, 6.2.2013, available at: https://www.express.co.uk/news/uk/375851/Outcry-over-EU-plot-to-seize-control-of-our-seabed?comments=show-all (accessed 15.7.2021).

International Court of Justice (2014) 'Whaling in the Antarctic (Australia v. Japan: New Zealand intervening)', Press release, No. 2014/14, The Hague: International Court of Justice, available from http://www.icj-cij.org/docket/index.php?p1=3&p2=1&case=148&code=aj&p3=6 (accessed on 23 March 2015).

Ionescu, Ghita and Ernst Gellner (eds.) (1969) *Populism: Its Meaning and National Characteristics*. New York: Macmillan.

Ishii, Atsushi (2011) 'The "overview" of the whaling problem', in Ishii, Atsushi (ed.) *Explaining the 'Whaling Problem'* [in Japanese]. Tokyo: Shinhyoron, pp. 3–63.

Ishikawa, Yoshimi (1994) 'Rice, cherry blossoms and the Japanese' [in Japanese], *Sekai (The World)*, May 1994: 68–71.

Jacobs, Hersch (2009) 'Structural Elements in Canadian Cuisine', *Cuizine: The Journal of Canadian Food Culture*, 2(1): https://doi.org/10.7202/039510ar.

Japan Fisheries Agency (2012) 'Whales and whaling', Tokyo: Japan Fisheries Agency, available from http://www.jfa.maff.go.jp/j/whale/index.html.

Japan Pasta Association (2013) *Pasta Report, October 2013* [in Japanese], available from http://www.pasta.or.jp/association/report/index.html.

Japan Times (2018) 'Japan formally announces IWC withdrawal to resume commercial whaling', the *Japan Times*, 28 December 2018, available from: https://www.japantimes.co.jp/news/2018/12/26/national/japan-formally-announces-iwc-withdrawal-resume-commercial-whaling/ (last accessed on 28 November 2020).

Jena, Pradyot and Grote, Ulrike (2010) 'Changing Institutions to Protect Regional Heritage: A Case for Geographical Indications in the Indian Agrifood Sector', *Development Policy Review*, 28 (2): 217–236.

Johannes, Venetia (2019) *Nourishing the Nation: Food as National Identity in Catalonia*. Oxford: Berghahn.

Johnson, Michelle (2016) 'Nothing is Sweet in My Mouth: Food, Identity, and Religion in African Lisbon', *Food and Foodways*, 24(3–4): 232–254.

Jones, Rhys and Merriman, Peter (2009) 'Hot, banal and everyday nationalism: Bilingual road signs in Wales', *Political Geography*, 28: 164–173.

Jones, S R H (2003) 'Brand building and structural changes in the Scotch whisky industry since 1975', *Business History*, 45(3): 72–89.

Josling, Tim (2006) 'The War on *Terroir*: Geographical Indications as a Transatlantic Trade Conflict', *Journal of Agricultural Economics*, 57(3): 337–363.

Kania-Lundholm, Magdalena (2014) 'Nation in Market Times: Connecting the National and the Commercial. A Research Overview', *Sociology Compass*, 8(6): 603–613.

Keating, Joshua (2011) 'How Food Explains the World', *Foreign Policy*, 186: May/June, online addition.

Laura Kitchings (2022) 'Definitions of Hawaiian Food: Evidence of Settler Colonialism in Selected Cookbooks from the Hawaiian Islands (1896–2021)', in Ranta et al. (eds) *'Going Native'? Settler Colonialism and Food*. London: Palgrave Macmillan, pp. 127–146.

Kimura, Tets and Egege, Sandra (2018) 'Heroes and villains: a discourse analysis of Australian and Japanese whaling reports in newspapers', *Continuum*, 32(3): 322–334.

King, Michelle (2019) *Culinary Nationalism in Asia*. London: Bloomsbury.

Knafo, Saki (2013) 'Sabra's Quest to Push Hummus Mainstream is about Much More than Chickpeas', *Huffington Post*, 10.6.2013: http://www.huffingtonpost.com/2013/06/10/sabra-hummus_n_3391688.html (accessed 10 October 2014).

Knecht, Peter (2007) 'Rice: representations and reality', *Asian Folklore Studies*, 66: 5–25

Kohn, Hans (1944) *The Idea of Nationalism*. New York; NY: Macmillan

Kolsto, Pal (2006) 'National Symbols as Signs of Unity and Division', *Ethnic and Racial Studies* 29(4): 676–701.

Kolpas, Norman (2021) *Foie Gras: A Global History*. London: Reaktion Books.

Kozinets, Robert (2015) *Netnography Redefined, 2nd Edition*. London: Sage.

Kozinets, Robert (2020) *Netnography: The Essential Guide to Qualitative Social Media Research*. London: Sage.

Kramer, Hans M (2013) 'How "Religion" Came to Be Translated as Shukyo: Shimaji Mokurai and the Appropriation of Religion in Early Meiji Japan', *Japan Review*, 25: 89–111.

Kurin, Richard (2004) 'Safeguarding Intangible Cultural Heritage in the 2003 UNESCO Convention: a critical appraisal', *Museum International*, 56 (1–2): 66–77.

Kushner, Barak (2012), *Slurp! A Social and Culinary History of Ramen—Japan's Favorite Noodle Soup*. Folkestone, Kent: Global Oriental.

Khwaja, Shahira and Elkin, Peter (2021) 'A close look at the United Kingdom's post-Brexit GI regime', *World Trademark Review*, 25 January 2021, available from: https://www.worldtrademarkreview.com/brand-management/close-look-the-united-kingdoms-post-brexit-gi-regime (accessed 6.8.2021).

Kymlica, Will (1995) *Multicultural Citizenship*. Oxford: Oxford University Press.

Lane, Sylvan (2019) 'Trump to hit EU with new tariffs after WTO ruling', *The Hill*, 10.2.2019, available at: https://thehill.com/policy/finance/464103-trump-to-impose-tariffs-on-eu-aircraft-agricultural-exports-on-oct-18 (accessed 5.8.2021).

Lang, Tim and Michael Heasman (2015) *Food Wars: The Global Battle for Mouths, Minds and Markets*. London: Routledge.

Laqueur, Walter (2003) *A History of Zionism*. New York: Schocken Books.

Lee, Seow Ting and Hun Shik Kim (2020) Food fight: gastrodiplomacy and nation branding in Singapore's UNESCO bid to recognize Hawker culture, *Place Branding and Public Diplomacy*, 17: 205–217.

Leer, Jonathan (2016) 'The Rise and Fall of the New Nordic Cuisine', *Journal of Aesthetics and Culture*, 8(1): https://doi.org/10.3402/jac.v8.33494.

Leer, Jonathan (2019) 'Monocultural and multicultural gastronationalism: National narratives in European food shows', *European Journal of Cultural Studies*, 22(5–6): 817–834.

Leimgruber, Walter (2010) 'Switzerland and the UNESCO Convention on Intangible Cultural Heritage', *Journal of Folklore Research*, 47 (1–2): 161–196.

Li, Peter J. et al. (2017) Dog Meat Consumption in China: A Survey of the Controversial Eating Habits in Two Cities, *Society & Animals*, 26(6): 513–532.

Lien, Marianne Elizabeth (2004) 'The politics of food: An introduction', in Lien, Marianne Elizabeth and Nerlich, Brigitte (eds) *The Politics of Food*, Oxford: Berg, pp. 1–17.

Lien, Marianne Elizabeth and Nerlich, Brigitte (eds) (2004) *The Politics of Food*. Oxford: Berg.

Leitch, Alison (2003) 'Slow Food and the Politics of Pork Fat: Italian food and European identity', *Ethnos: Journal of Anthropology*, 68(4): 437–462.

Litani, Yehuda and Naim Araidi (2000) *Not by Hummus Alone: Hummus, Olive Oil, References* [in Hebrew]. Tel Aviv: Dinur and Modan.

Louer, Laurence (2007) *To Be an Arab in Israel*. London: Hurst & Company.

Lubrada, Balsa (2019) '"Homeland farming" or "rural emancipation"? The discursive overlap between populist and green parties in Hungary', *Sociologia Ruralis*, 60(4): 810–832.

Lundahl, Outi (2020) 'Dynamics of positive deviance in destigmatisation: celebrities and the media in the rise of veganism', *Consumption Markets & Culture*, 23(2): 241–271.

Lupton, Deborah (1994) 'Food, Memory and Meaning: the Symbolic and Social Nature of Food Events', *The Sociological Review* 42(4): 664–685.

Maeva, Mila (2017) 'Emigrant's Home and Preservation of Cultural Heritage (on Bulgarian Cases from the UK and Norway)'. in: Gergove, Lina et al. (eds) *Cultural Heritage and Migration*, Sofia: Paradigma, pp. 427–436.

Magee, Paul (2005) 'Foreign Cookbooks', *Postcolonial Studies* 8(1): 3–18.

Malešević, Siniša (2013) *Nation-States and Nationalisms: Organization, Ideology and Solidarity*. Cambridge: Polity.

Mamonova, Natalia and Jaume Franquesa (2020) Right-Wing Populism in Rural Europe: Introduction to the Special Issue, *Sociologia Ruralis*, 4: 702–708.

Mann, Michael (1993) *The Sources of Social Power II: The Rise of Classes and Nation-States, 1760–1914*. Cambridge: Cambridge University Press.

Mar'i, Abd el-Rahman (2013) 'Walla Bseder: A Linguistic Profile of the Israeli Arabs'. [in Hebrew]. Jerusalem: Keter.

Marks, Gil (2010). *Encyclopaedia of Jewish Food*. New Jersey: John Wiley and Sons.

Masterman, E. W. G. (1901) 'Food and its Preparation in Modern Palestine', *The Biblical World* 17(6): 407–419.

Matalon, Lorne (2008) "Mexico's Poor Seek Relief From Tortilla Shortage", *National Geographic*, 4.6.2008.

McGray, Douglas (2002) 'Japan's Gross National Cool', *Foreign Policy* (May/June).

Meigs, Anna (1997) 'Food as a Cultural Construction'. in: Carole Counihan and Penny Van Esterik (eds) *Food and Culture: A Reader*. New York: Routledge, pp. 95–106.

Mendez Cota, Gabriela (2016) *Disrupting Maize: Food, Biotechnology and Nationalism in Contemporary Mexico*. London: Rowman & Littlefield.

Meyer, Erna (1937) *How to Cook in Palestine* [in Hebrew and German]. Tel Aviv: WIZO.

Milanesio, Natalia (2010) Food Politics and Consumption in Peronist Argentina, *Hispanic American Historical Review*, 90(1): 75–108.

Millstone, Erik et al. (2019) Food Brexit and Chlorinated Chicken: A Microcosm of Wider food Problems, *The Political Quarterly*, 90(4): 645–653.

The Ministry of Agriculture, Forestry and Fishery of Japan (n.d.) *What is 'Shokuiku (Food Education)'*, available from http://www.maff.go.jp/e/pdf/shokuiku.pdf.

The Ministry of Agriculture, Forestry and Fishery of Japan (2006) Minutes of the first expert meeting on authentication of Japanese restaurants abroad [in Japanese], http://www.maff.go.jp/j/shokusan/sanki/easia/e_sesaku/japanese_food/kaigi/pdf/report.pdf accessed on 12 December 2010

The Ministry of Agriculture, Forestry and Fishery Of Japan (2007a) Minutes of the second expert meeting on authentication of Japanese restaurants abroad [in Japanese], http://www.maff.go.jp/j/shokusan/sanki/easia/e_sesaku/japanese_food/kaigi/pdf/report_1.pdf accessed on 12 December 2010

The Ministry of Agriculture, Forestry and Fishery of Japan (2007b) Minutes of the third expert meeting on authentication of Japanese restaurants abroad [in Japanese], http://www.maff.go.jp/j/shokusan/sanki/easia/e_sesaku/japanese_food/kaigi/pdf/report_2.pdf accessed on 12 December 2010

The Ministry of Agriculture, Forestry and Fishery of Japan (2011a) Minutes of the first meeting of the Working Group to Prepare for the Inscription of Japanese Food Culture in the Intangible Cultural Heritage List on 5 July 2011 [in Japanese)], available from: http://www.maff.go.jp/j/keikaku/syokubunka/pdf/110705_report.pdf.

The Ministry of Agriculture, Forestry and Fishery of Japan (2011b) Minutes of the second meeting of the Working Group to Prepare for the Inscription of

Japanese Food Culture in the Intangible Cultural Heritage List on 19 August 2011 [in Japanese], available from: http://www.maff.go.jp/j/keikaku/syokubunka/pdf/110819_report.pdf.

The Ministry of Agriculture, Forestry and Fishery of Japan (2011c) Minutes of the third meeting of the Working Group to Prepare for the Inscription of Japanese Food Culture in the Intangible Cultural Heritage List on 28 September 2011 [in Japanese], available from: http://www.maff.go.jp/j/keikaku/syokubunka/pdf/full.pdf.

The Ministry of Agriculture, Forestry and Fishery of Japan (2011d) Minutes of the fourth meeting of the Working Group to Prepare for the Inscription of Japanese Food Culture in the Intangible Cultural Heritage List on 4 November 2011 [in Japanese], available from: http://www.maff.go.jp/j/keikaku/syokubunka/pdf/gijiroku.pdf.

The Ministry of Agriculture, Forestry and Fishery of Japan (2013) *Washoku: Traditional Food Culture of the Japanese* [in Japanese], Tokyo: MAFF.

The Ministry of Agriculture, Forestry and Fishery of Japan (2015) *Towards 'Washoku' in the Future* [in Japanese], Tokyo: MAFF.

The Ministry of Foreign Affairs of Japan (2014) 'Statement by Chief Cabinet Secretary, the Government of Japan, on International Court of Justice "Whaling in the Antarctic (Australia v. Japan: New Zealand intervening)"', Tokyo: MOFA, available from http://www.mofa.go.jp/press/danwa/press2e_000002.html (accessed on 23 March 2015)

Mintz, Sidney W. (1986) *Sweetness and Power: The Place of Sugar in Modern History*. New York: Penguin Books.

Mintz, Sidney W. and Du Bois, Christine M. (2002) 'The Anthropology of Food and Eating', *Annual Review of Anthropology*, 31: 99–119.

Mkono, Muchazondida (2013) 'Using net-based ethnography (netnography) to understand the staging and marketing of "authentic African" dining experiences to tourists at Victoria Falls', *Journal of Hospitality & Tourism Research*, 37(2): 184–198.

Montanari, Massimo (2004) *Food is Culture*. New York: Columbia University Press.

Monterescu, Daniel and Ariel Handel (2019) 'Liquid Indigeneity: Wine, Science, and Colonial Politics in Israel/Palestine', *American Ethnologist*, 46(3): 313–327.

Monterescu, Daniel (2017) 'Border Wines: Terroir across Contested Territory', *Gastronomica*, 17(4): 127–140.

Moor, Margaret (1998) *The Ethics of nationalism*. Oxford: Oxford University Press.

Morishita, Joji (2006) 'Multiple analysis of the whaling issue: Understanding the dispute by a matrix', *Marine Policy*, 30: 802–808.

Morris, Carolyn (2013) 'Kai or Kiwi? Maori and "Kiwi" cookbooks, and the Struggle for the Field of New Zealand Cuisine', *Journal of Sociology* 49(2–3): 210–223.

Moss, Michael and Hume, John (2000) *The Making of Scotch Whisky: A History of the Scotch Whisky Distilling Industry*. Edinburgh: Cannongate.

Muller, Jan-Werner (2017) *What is Populism?*. London: Penguin Books.

Murata, Yoshihiro (2014) 'Washoku: UNESCO's intangible cultural heritage' [in Japanese], *Women's Forum (Josei no Hiroba)*, No. 422: 68–71.

Murray, Emmanuel V. (2007). 'Thailand-The Kitchen of the World: Origin and Growth of the Thai Food Industry & Lessons for India', *Cab Calling*. April-June: 16–26.

Muzhinji, Norman and Victor Ntuli (2021) 'Genetically modified organisms and food security in Southern Africa: conundrum and discourse', *GM Crops & Food*, 12(1): 25–35.

Nairn, Tom (1977) *The Break-Up of Britain: Crisis and Neo-Nationalism*. London: New Left Books.

Narayan, Uma (1995) 'Eating Cultures: Incorporation, Identity and Indian Food', *Social Identities* 1(1): 63–86.

Newling, Jacqui (2022) '"Uneasy lies the head that wears the crown"—lamb or kangaroo, which should reign supreme? The implications of heroising a settler colonial food icon as national identity', in Ranta et al. (eds) *'Going Native'? Settler Colonialism and Food*. London: Palgrave Macmillan, pp. 173–199.

Neuman, Nicklas and Jonathan Leer (2018) 'Nordic Cuisine but National Identities: "New Nordic Cuisine" and the gastronationalist projects of Denmark and Sweden', *Anthropology of Food*, 13: https://doi.org/10.4000/aof.8723.

Nirwandy, Noor and Ahmed Azran Awang (2014) 'Conceptualizing Public Diplomacy Social Convention Culinary: Engaging Gastro Diplomacy Warfare for Economic Branding', *Procedia—Social and Behavioral Sciences*, 130: 325–332.

NHK (2019) 'Why Japan withdrew from the IWC', *Backstories*, 10 February 2019, accessible from https://www3.nhk.or.jp/nhkworld/en/news/backstories/367/ (last accessed on 1 August 2020)

Nomura, Ko (2020) 'Antiwhaling groups in Japan: Their historical lack of development and relationship with national identity', *Journal of Environment and Development*, 29(2) 223–244.

Nordic Council of Ministers (2015). The emergence of a new nordic food culture: Final report from the program New Nordic Food II, 2010–2014.

The Nordic Council (n.d.) 'New Nordic Food Manifesto', available from: https://www.norden.org/en/information/new-nordic-food-manifesto (accessed on 13 August 2020)

Nye, Jospeh (1990) 'Soft Power' *Foreign Policy*, 80(Autumn): 153–171.

O'Connor, Kaori (2009) 'Cuisine, Nationality and the making of a National Meal: the English Breakfast', in: Carvalho, Susana and Gemenne, Francois (eds.) *Nations and their Histories: Constructions and Representations*. London, Palgrave Macmillan, pp. 157–171.

O'Sullivan, Feargus (2017) 'France's Kebab Crackdown', 10.7.2017, Bloomberg, available at: https://www.bloomberg.com/news/articles/2017-07-10/france-is-cracking-down-on-kebab-vendors (accessed 15.7.2021).

Oh, Minjoo and Jackson, Jeffrey (2011) 'Animal rights vs. cultural rights: Exploring the dog meat debate in South Korea from a world polity perspective', *Journal of Intercultural Studies*, 32(1): 31–56.

Ohnuki-Tierney, Emiko (1993) *Rice as Self: Japanese Identities through Time*, Princeton, NJ: Princeton University Press.

Ohnuki-Tierney, Emiko (1999) 'We eat each other's food to nourish our body: The global and the local as mutually constituent forces', in Raymond Grew (ed.) *Food in Global History*, Boulder, CO: Westview Press, pp. 240–72.

Okamura, Jonathan Y. (2010) 'From running amok to eating dogs: a century of misrepresenting Filipino Americans in Hawai'i', *Ethnic and Racial Studies*, 33(3): 496–514.

Onishi, Mutsuko and Yamamoto, Etsuko (2014) 'Interview: Food culture of whale meat (1)' [in Japanese], *Shokuseikatsu Kenkyu* (Studies in Food Life), 34(2): 69–77.

The Organization to Promote Japanese Restaurants Abroad (2007) Annual Report: 2006 [in Japanese], available at http://jronet.org/wordpress/wp-content/uploads/2015/01/report_of_activities_h19.pdf (accessed on 27 April 2015).

Orlove, Benjamin (1997) 'Meat and Strength: The Moral Economy of a Chilean Food Riot', *Cultural Anthropology*, 12(2): 234–268.

Orlove, Benjamin and Schmidt, Ella (1995) 'Indigenous and Industrial Beer in Peru and Bolivia', *Theory and Society*, 23(2): 271–298.

Ottolenghi, Yotam and Sami Tamimi (2012) *Jerusalem*. London: Ebury Publishing.

Oum, Young (2005) 'Authenticity and Representation: Cuisines and Identities in Korean-American Diaspora', *Postcolonial Studies*, 8(1): 109–125.

Özkirimli, Umut (2005) *Contemporary Debates on Nationalism: A Critical Engagement*. Basingstoke: Palgrave Macmillan.

Palmer, Catherine (1998) 'From Theory to Practice: Experiencing the Nation in Everyday Life', *Journal of Material Culture*, 3: 175–199.

Panayi, Panikos (2008) *Spicing Up Britain: The Multicultural History of British Food*. London: Reaktion Books.

Panayi, Panikos (2014) *Fish & Chips: A History*. London: Reaktion Books.

Peace, Adrian (2010) 'The whaling war: Conflicting cultural perspectives', *Anthropology Today*, 26(3): 5–9.

Peretz-Rubin, Pascal (1987) *Israel Flavours* [in Hebrew]. Ramat Gan: Ruth Sirkis Publishers.

Perry, Charles (2010) 'The Taste for Layered Bread among the Nomadic Turks and the Central Asian Origins of Baklava', in: Sami Zubaida and Richard Tapper (eds) *A Taste of Thyme: Culinary Cultures of the Middle East*. London: I.B. Tauris Parke, pp. 87–91.

PETA (2014) 'Foie Gras: Cruelty to Ducks and Geese': http://www.peta.org/issues/animals-used-for-food/factory-farming/ducks-geese/foie-gras/ (accessed 20.4.2015).

Phillipson, Jeremy and David Symes (2018) '"A sea of trouble": Brexit and the fisheries question', *Marine Policy*, 90: 168–173.

Pilcher, Jeffrey M. (1996) 'Tamales or Timbales: Cuisine and the Formation of Mexican National Identity, 1821–1911', *The Americas*, 53(2): 193–216.

Pilcher, Jeffrey M. (1998) *Que Vivan Los Tamales! Food and the Making of Mexican Identity*. Albuquerque: University of New Mexico Press.

Podberscek, Anthony (2009) 'Good to pet and eat: The keeping and consuming of dogs and cats in South Korea', *Journal of Social Issues*, 65(3): 615–632.

Poon, Shuk-Wah (2014) 'Dogs and British colonialism: The contested ban on eating dogs in Colonial Hong Kong', *The Journal of Imperial and Commonwealth History*, 42 (2): 308–328.

Porciani, Ilaria (2019) 'Food Heritage and Nationalism in Europe', in Porciani Ilaria (ed) *Food Heritage and Nationalism in Europe*, London: Routledge, pp. 3–32.

Pratt, Jeff (2007) 'Food Values: The Local and the Authentic' *Critique of Anthropology* 27(3): 285–300.

Prescott, Craig; Pilato, Manuela and Bellia, Claudio (2020) 'Geographical indications in the UK after Brexit: An uncertain future?', *Food Policy*, 90: https://doi.org/10.1016/j.foodpol.2019.101808.

Prideaux, Jillian (2009) 'Consuming Icons: Nationalism and Advertising in Australia', *Nations and Nationalism* 15(4): 616–635.

Prieto-Piastro, Claudia (2021) *Eating In Israel: Nationhood, Gender and Food Culture*. London: Palgrave Macmillan.

Quinn, Ben (2019) 'Kipper rules Boris Johnson blamed on EU are actually British, says Brussels', *The Guardian*, 18.7.2019.

Rabikowska, Marta (2010) 'The ritualisation of food, home and national identity among Polish migrants in London', *Social Identities*, 16(3): 377–439.

Rabin, Alinoar (2012) *Nazareth A Fascinating Culinary City*. Jerusalem: Keter.

Ram, Uri (2008) *The Globalization of Israel: McWorld in Tel Aviv, Jihad in Jerusalem*. Routledge: Oxon.

Ranta, Ronald (2015) 'Food and Nationalism: From Foie Gras to Hummus', *World Policy Journal* 32(3): 33–40.

Ranta, Ronald (2018) 'Gentrification, vegans, and the death of historic London pie shops', The Conversation, 9th October 2018.

Ranta, Ronald (2019) 'Dissonance on the Brexit Menu: What does Britain Want to Eat?', *Political Quarterly*, 90(4): 654–663.

Ranta, Ronald (2020) 'Pie and Mash: A Victorian Anachronism in Modern Cosmopolitan Britain?', Dublin Gastronomy Symposium.

Ranta, Ronald and Daniel Monterescu (2022) 'Decolonising Israeli Food? Between Culinary Appropriation and Recognition in Israel/Palestine', in Ranta et al. (eds) *'Going Native'? Settler Colonialism and Food*. London: Palgrave Macmillan, pp. 147–171.

Ranta, Ronald and Nevena Nancheva (2019) 'Eating Banitsa in London: Re-inventing Bulgarian foodways in the context of Inter-EU migration', *Appetite*, 139(1): 67–74.

Ranta, Ronald and Prieto-Piastro, Claudia (2019) 'Does Israeli food exist?: The multifaceted and complex making of a national food', in Ichijo, Atsuko; Johannes, Venetia and Ranta, Ronald (eds) *The Emergence of National Food: The Dynamics of Food and Nationalism*, London: Bloomsbury, pp. 119–129.

Ranta, Ronald and Yonatan Mendel (2014) 'Consuming Palestine: Palestine and Palestinians in Israeli Food Culture', *Ethnicities*, 14 (3): 412–435.

Ranta, Ronald and Yonatan Mendel (2016) *From the Arab Other to the Israeli Self: Palestinian Culture in the Making of Israeli National Identity*. London: Routledge.

Ranta, Ronald, Alex Colás, and Daniel Monterescu (eds) (2022) *'Going Native'? Food and Settler Colonialism*. London: Palgrave Macmillan.

Raviv, Yael (2002a) 'National Identity on a Plate', *Israel-Palestine journal of Economics, Politics and Culture*, 8(9): 164–172.

Raviv, Yael (2002b) 'Recipe for a Nation: Cuisine, Jewish Nationalism, and the Israeli State'. PhD diss. New York University, US.

Raviv, Yael (2003) 'Falafel: A National Icon', *Gastronomica: The Journal of Food and Culture*, 3(3): 20–25.

Raviv, Yael (2015) *Falafel Nation: Cuisine and the Making of National Identity in Israel*. Lincoln: University of Nebraska Press.

Rawlinson, Francis (2019) *How Press Propaganda Paved the Way to Brexit*. London: Palgrave Macmillan.

Regev, Motti and Edwin Seroussi (2004) *Popular Music and National Culture in Israel*. Berkeley: University of California Press.

Rippon, Matthew (2014) 'What is the geography of Geographical Indications? Place, production methods and Protected Food Names', *Area*, 46(2): 154–162.

Rockower, Paul (2010) "The Gastrodiplomacy Cookbook", Huffington Post, 14.9.2010.

Rockower, Paul (2011) 'Projecting Taiwan: Taiwan's Public Diplomacy Outreach', *Issues and Studies*, 47(1): 107–152.

Rockower, Paul (2014) 'The State of Gatrodiplomacy', *Public Diplomacy*, 11: 11–15.

Roden, Claudia (1999) *The Book of Jewish Food: An Odyssey from Samarkand and Vilna to the Present Day*. London: Penguin Books.

Romagnoli, Marco (2019) 'Gastronomic heritage elements at UNESCO: Problems, reflections on and interpretations of a new heritage category', *International Journal of Intangible Heritage*, 14: 158–171.

Rogers, Ben (2003) *Beef and Liberty: Roast Beef, John Bull and the English Nation*. London: Vintage.

Rozin, Orit (2006) 'Food, Identity, and Nation-Building in Israel's Formative Years', *Israel Studies Forum*, 21(1): 52–80.

Russell, Ian (2007) 'Competing with ballads (and whisky?): The construction, celebration, and commercialization of North-East Scottish identity', *Folk Music Journal*, 9(2): 170–191.

Sakamoto, Rumi and Allen, Matthew (2011) 'There's something fishy about that sushi: how Japan interprets the global sushi boom', *Japan Forum*, 23(1): 99–121.

Scher, Philip (2010) 'UNESCO Conventions and Culture as a Resource', *Journal of Folklore Research*, 47 (1–2): 197–202

Scholliers, Peter (2001) 'Meals, Food Narratives, and Sentiments of belonging in Past and Present', in Scholliers, Peter (ed) *Food, Drink and Identity: Cooking, Eating and Drinking in Europe Since the Middle Ages*. Oxford: Berg, pp. 1–22.

Scholze, Marko (2008) 'Arrested Heritage, The Politics of Inscription into the UNESCO World Heritage List: The Case of Agadez in Niger', *Journal of Material Culture*, 13(2): 215–231.

Scoones, Ian et al. (eds) (2021) *Authoritarian Populism and the Rural World*. London: Routledge.

Scotch Whisky Association (2009) 'A Defining Moment For Scotch Whisky', a statement by the Chairman of The Scotch Whisky Association, Paul Walsh, Edinburgh: Scotch Whisky Association.

Scotch Whisky Association (2011a) *Scotch Whisky and Tourism: A Report by 4-consulting*, Edinburgh: Scotch Whisky Association.

Scotch Whisky Association (2011b) Scotch Whisky Association: Briefing for the new Scottish Parliament, Edinburgh: Scotch Whisky Association.

Scotch Whisky Association (2011c) Annual Review 2011, Edinburgh: Scotch Whisky Association.

Scotch Whisky Association (2012a) *A Century of Protecting and Promoting Scotch Whisky*, Edinburgh: Scotch Whisky Association.

Scotch Whisky Association (2012b) *Scotch Whisky and Scotland's Economy: A 100 Year Old Blend*, Edinburgh: Scotch Whisky Association.

Scotch Whisky Association (2013a) *Question and Answers*, Edinburgh: Scotch Whisky Association.

Scotch Whisky Association (2013b) *Annual Review 2013*, Edinburgh: Scotch Whisky Association.

Scotch Whisky Association (2014a) 'Frank and constructive debate', statement published on 10 July 2014 available from http://www.scotch-whisky.org.uk/news-publications/blog/frank-and-constructive-debate/#.VGn0_MmAXhk accessed on 17 November 2014.

Scotch Whisky Association (2014b) 'Scottish referendum 2014', a statement issued on 19 September 2014, available from http://www.scotch-whisky.org.uk/news-publications/blog/scottish-referendum-2014/#.VGnzs8mAXhk accessed on 17 November 2014.

Scotch Whisky Association (2014c) 'The Smith Commission on Devolution: Submission by The Scotch Whisky Association', published on 31 October 2014, available from http://www.scotch-whisky.org.uk/news-publications/news/swa-response-to-smith-commission/#.VIGOiMmiu-Y accessed on 17 November 2014.

Segev, Tom (1998) *1949: The First Israelis*. New York: First Owl Books.

Sengupta, Jayanta (2010) 'Nation on a Platter: the Culture and Politics of Food and Cuisine in Colonial Bengal', *Modern Asian Studies*, 44 (1):81–98.

Shaffer, Marguerite (2001) *See America First: Tourism and National Identity, 1880–1940*. Washington: Smithsonian Institution Press.

Shafir, Gershon (1996) *Land, Labor and The Origins of The Israeli-Palestinian Conflict, 1882–1914*. Berkeley and Los Angeles: University of California Press.

Shima, Kazuo (2019) 'On the withdrawal from the IWC' (in Japanese), *Gyogyo to Gyokyo*, 2: 14–21.

Shiratori, Sanae (2014) 'Washoku now inscribed as World Heritage is a work of art with perfect nutrition and taste' [in Japanese], *Karento (Current)*, 8333: 72–75.

Shoham, Hizky (2021) 'The Israel BBQ as national ritual: Performing unofficial nationalism, or finding meaning in triviality', *American Journal of Cultural Sociology*, 9: 13–42.

Simmons, Amelia (1798) *American Cookery*. Hartford: Simeon Butler.

Simonsen, Kim (2019) 'Gastro Scandinavism: the Branding of New Nordic cuisine as a Discursive Space for Forging New identities', in Cecilia Cassinger, Andrea Lucarelli and Szilvia Gyimothy (eds) *The Nordic Wave in Place Branding: Poetics, Practices, Politics*. Cheltenham, Edward Elgar Publishing, pp. 175–190.

Simpson-Miller, Brandi (2022) *Food and Identity in Nineteenth and Twentieth Century Ghana: Food, Fights, and Regionalism*. London: Palgrave.

Sirkis, Ruth (1975) *Popular Food from Israel*. Tel Aviv: Zmora Bitan Modan-Publishers.

Sitwell, William (2016) *Eggs or Anarchy*. London: Simon & Schuster.

Skey, Michael (2009) 'The national in everyday life: A critical engagement with Michael Billig's thesis of *Banal Nationalism*', *The Sociological Review*, 57(2): 331–346

Skey, Michael (2011) *National Belonging and Everyday Life: The Significance of Nationhood in an Uncertain World*. Basingstoke: Palgrave.

Smith, Andy (2008) 'Territory and the regulation of industry: Examples from Scotland and Aquitaine', *Regional and Federal Studies*, 18(1): 37–53.

Smith, Andy (2010) 'Industries as spaces for the politics of territory: The case of Scotch whisky', *Regional and Federal Studies*, 20(3): 389–407.

Smith, Anthony D (2008) 'The limits of everyday nationhood', *Ethnicities*, 8(4): 563–573.

Smooha, Sammy (1989) *Arabs and Jews in Israel. Vol 1: Conflicting and Shared Attitudes in a Divided Society*. Boulder: Westview Press.

Smythe, Elizabeth (2014) 'Food sovereignty, trade rules, and the struggle to know the origin of food', in Peter Andrée, Jeffrey Ayers, Michael Bosia and Marie-Josée Massicotte (eds) *Globalization and Food Sovereignty: Global and Local Change in the New Politics of Food*, Toronto: University of Toronto Press, pp. 288–318.

Sneijder, Petra and te Molder, Hedwig (2009) 'Normalizing ideological food choice and eating practices. Identity work in online discussions on veganism', *Appetite*, 52: 621–630.

Sobral, Jose M (2019) 'Salt Cod and the Making of a Portuguese National Cuisine', in Ichijo et al. (eds) *The Emergence of National Food*. London: Bloomsbury, pp. 17–27.

Spierling, Menno (2007) 'Food, Phagophobia and English National Identity', in: Wilson, Thomas M. (ed.) *Food, Drink and Identity in Europe*. Amsterdam: Rodopi, pp. 31–48.

Spillman, Lynette P. (1997) *Nation and Commemoration: Creating National Identities in the United States and Australia*. Cambridge: Cambridge University Press.

Standaert, Michael (2020) 'China signals end to dog meat consumption by humans', *The Guardian*, 9 April 2020, available from https://www.theguardian.com/environment/2020/apr/09/china-signals-end-to-dog-meat-consumption-by-humans (last accessed on 1 August 2020).

Stoett, Peter (1999) 'Whaling: Confrontations continue', *Environmental Politics*, 8(2): 153–156.

Suh, Jeongwook and MacPherson, Alan (2007) 'The impact of geographical indication on the revitalisation of a regional economy: a case study of "Boseong" green tea', *Area*, 39(4): 518–527.

Suisankai (2019) 'Bryde's whales are in fact delicious!: the Liberal Democratic Party hosts the "tasting of commercially caught whale meat"' [in Japanese], *Suisanakai*, November 2019: 16–17.

Sunanta, Sirijit (2005). 'The Globalization of Thai Cuisine', Paper presented at the Canadian Council for Southeast Asian Studies Conference, York University, Toronto, October 14–16, 2005.

Suntikul, Wantanee (2019). 'Gastrodiplomacy in tourism', *Current Issues in Tourism*, 22(9): 1076–1094.

Sutton, David (2001) *Remembrance of Repasts: An Anthropology of Food and Memory*. Oxford: Berg.

Sutton, David (2017) 'Comment: Reflections on meat-eaters, vegetarians, and vampires', *Ethnos*, 82(2): 298–307.

Takeda, Hiroko (2008) 'Delicious Food in a Beautiful Country: Nationhood and Nationalism in Discourse on Food in Contemporary Japan', *Studies in Ethnicity and Nationalism*, 8(1): 5–30.

Tal, Nitzan (2022) '"A Manly Amount of Wreckage": South-African Food Culture and Settler Belonging in Ivan Vladislavic's Double Negative', in Ranta et al. (eds) *'Going Native'? Settler Colonialism and Food*. London: Palgrave Macmillan, pp. 203–220.

Tapsfield, James (2016) The Brexit battle takes waves, 17.6.2016, Daily Mail: https://www.dailymail.co.uk/news/article-3642793/The-Brexit-battle-takes-waves-Nigel-Farage-Bob-Geldof-lead-rival-flotillas-bizarre-clash-Thames.html (accessed 15.7.2021).

Tavakoli, Rokhshad and Wijesinghe, Sarah (2019) 'The evolution of the web and netnography in tourism: A systematic review', *Tourism Management Perspectives*, 29: 48–55.

Tene, Ofra (2002) *Thus You Shall Cook! Readings in Israeli Cookbooks* [in Hebrew]. MA thesis., Tel Aviv University.

Terrio, Susan J. (1996) 'Crafting Grand Cru Chocolates in Contemporary France', *American Anthropologist*, 98(1): 67–79.

The Organization to Promote Japanese Restaurants Abroad (JRO) (2007) Annual Report: 2006 (in Japanese), available at http://jronet.org/wordpress/wp-content/uploads/2015/01/report_of_activities_h19.pdf accessed on 27 April 2015

Tominc, Ana (ed) (2022) *Food and Cooking on Early Television in Europe*. London: Routledge.

Tosato, Andrea (2013) 'The Protection of Traditional Foods in the EU: Traditional Specialities Guaranteed', *European Law Journal*, 19 (4): 545–576.

Treitel, Corinna (2009) 'Nature and the Nazi diet', *Food and Foodways*, 17:3, 139–158.

Trubek, Amy (2008) *The Taste of Place: A Cultural Journey into Terroir*. Berkeley: University of California Press.

Tyrrell, Alex (2011) '"No common corrobery": the Robert Burns Festivals and identity politics in Melbourne, 1845–59', *Journal of the Royal Australian Historical Society*, 97(2): 161–180.

Tyrrel, Alex, Hill Patricia and Kirkby Diane (2007) 'Feasting on National Identity: Whisky, Haggis and the Celebration of Scottishness in the Nineteenth Century', in: Kirkby, Diane and Luckins, Tanja (eds.) *Dining on Turtles: Food Feasts and Drinking in History*, London: Palgrave Macmillan, pp. 46–63.

UNESCO (2010) 'Gastronomic Meal of the French': http://www.unesco.org/culture/ich/index.php?lg=en&pg=00011&RL=00437 (accessed 20.4.2015).

United Nations' World Tourism Organisation (2012). *Global Report on Food Tourism*.

Vadi, Valentina (2016) 'Food wars: food, intangible cultural heritage and international trade', in Westra, L et al. (eds.) *The common good and ecological integrity: human rights and the support of life*, London: Routledge, pp. 49–60.

Valaskivi, Katja (2013) 'A brand new future? Cool Japan and the social imaginary of the branded nation', *Japan Forum*, 25 (4): 485–504.

Vered, Ronit (2013) 'Wine from the Land of those Expelled from Iqrit' Ha'aretz, 4.12.2013, [in Hebrew] http://www.haaretz.co.il/gallery/recipes/dining/.premium-1.2182221 (accessed 15.2.2015).

Vered, Ronit (2014) 'Knafeh, the Short Version of the Conflict', Ha'aretz, 30.7.2014, [in Hebrew] http://www.haaretz.co.il/gallery/recipes/dining/.premium-1.2392440 (accessed 15.2.2015).

Volcic, Zala and Mark Andrejevic (2016) *Commercial Nationalism: Selling the Nation and Nationalizing the Sell*, Basingstoke: Palgrave.

Wada, Ichiro (2014) 'The ICJ's ruling on the "whaling problem" and future of whaling for the scientific purpose' [in Japanese], *Suisan Shuho* (Fishery Weekly), 1865: 33–40.

Wada, Ichiro (2017) 'My view on the current situation of the whaling problem and how to deal with it' [in Japanese], *The Fishing and Food Industry Weekly*, 1897: 17–21.

Wakefield, Sarina (2012) 'Falconry as heritage in the United Arab Emirates', *World Archaeology*, 44(2): 280–290.

Wallendorf, Melanie and Arnould, Eric J. (1991) '"We Gather Together": Consumption Rituals of Thanksgiving Day', *Journal of Consumer Research*, 18(1): 13–31.

Wanat, Zosia and Eddy Wax (2020) 'Coronavirus reheats Europe's food nationalism', 5.7.2020, *Politico*, https://www.politico.com/news/2020/05/17/coronavirus-reheats-europes-food-nationalism-262251 (accessed 15.7.2021).

Wang, Dong (2010) 'Internationalizing heritage: UNESCO and China's Longmen Grottoes', *China Information*, 24(2): 123–147

Watson, J.J and K. Wright (2000), 'Consumer ethnocentrism and attitudes toward domestic and foreign products', *European Journal of Marketing*, 34(9/10): 1149–1166.

Weber, Eugene (1976) *Peasants into Frenchmen: The Modernisation of Rural France, 1870–1914*. Redwood City, CA: Stamford University Press.

Welch, David (2004) 'Nazi Propaganda and the *Volksgemeinschaft*: Constructing a People's Community', *Journal of Contemporary History*, 39(2): 213–238.

Welz, Gizela (2013) 'Halloumi/Hellim: Global markets, European Union regulation, and ethnicised cultural property', *The Cyprus Review*, 25(1): 37–54.

Whale Library (n.d.) 'Whaling statistics', http://luna.pos.to/whale/sta.html accessed on 3 April 2015.

White, Wajeana, Albert A. Barreda, and H. E. İ. N. Stephanie (2019) 'Gastrodiplomacy: Captivating a Global Audience Through Cultural Cuisine-A Systematic Review of the Literature', *Journal of Tourismology*, 5(2): 127–144.

Wilk, Richard R. (1999) 'Real Belizean Food: Building Local Identity in the Transnational Caribbean', *American Anthropologist*, 101(2): 244–255.

Wilk, Richard R. (2006) *Home Cooking in the Global Village: Caribbean Food Buccaneers to Ecotourists*. London: Bloomsbury.

Wilson, Rachel (2011) 'Cocina Peruana Para El Mundo: Gastrodiplomacy, the Culinary National Brand, and the Context of National Cuisine in Peru', *Exchange: the Journal of Public Diplomacy*, pp. 13–20

Wilson, Thomas (2005) 'Drinking cultures: Sites and practices in the production and expression of identity', in Wilson Thomas (ed.) *Drinking Cultures: Alcohol and Identity*, Oxford: Berg, pp. 1–21.

World Tourism Organization (2012) 'Global Report on Food Tourism'. Madrid: UNWTO.

Wrenn, Corey Lee (2019) 'The Vegan Society and social movement professionalization, 1944–2017', *Food and Foodways*, 27(3): 190–210.

Wright, Wynne, and Alexis Annes (2013) 'Halal on the menu?: Contested food politics and French identity in fast-food', *Journal of Rural Studies*, 32: 388–399.

Yack, Bernard (2001) 'Popular sovereignty and nationalism', *Political Theory*, 29(4): 571–536.

Yack, Bernard (2012) *Nationalism and the Moral Psychology of Community*. Chicago, IL: Chicago University Press.

Yasuda, Ryo (2006) 'Globalism and nationalism in the anti-whaling problem', in Nomura, Toru and Yamamoto, Jun'ichi (eds) *The Present of the Global, National and Local* [in Japanese], Tokyo: Keio University Press, pp. 237–262.

Yiftachel, Oren (2006) *Ethnocracy: Land and Identity Politics in Israel/Palestine*. Philadelphia: University of Pennsylvania Press.

Yormirzoev, Mirzobobo, Teuber, Ramona and Li Tongzhe (2019), 'Food quality vs food patriotism: Russian consumers' preferences for cheese after the food import ban', *British Food Journal*, 121(2): pp. 371–385.

Youatt, Rafi (2012) 'Power, Pain, and the Interspecies Politics of Foie Gras', *Political Research Quarterly*, 65(2): 346–358.

Zamir, Tzachi (2004) 'Veganism', *Journal of Social Philosophy*, 35(3): 367–379.

Zerbe, Noah (2004) 'Feeding the Famine? American food aid and the GMO debate in Southern Africa', *Food Policy*, 29: 593–608.

Zhang, Juyan (2015) 'The Foods of the Worlds: Mapping and Comparing Contemporary Gastrodiplomatic Campaigns', *International Journal of Communications*, 9: 568–591.

Unattributed Newspaper/Magazine Articles

BBC Travel (2020) How kimchi rekindled a decades long feud, 18.12.2020, BBC, available at: https://www.bbc.com/travel/article/20201217-how-kimchi-rekindled-a-decades-long-feud (accessed 15.7.2021)

Calcalist, 'A New Front in the War: Osem against Strauss in the US; The Hummus War', 3.8.2008 [in Hebrew].

Canadian Newswire, "Dairy Farmers to Canadian Ice Cream Lovers ... Beware of imposters", 22.7.2010.

The Economist, 'Thailand's gastro-diplomacy: like the cuisine, like the country', 21.2.2002.

The Economist (2005) The Kimchi Wars: South Korea and China duel over pickled cabbage 19.11.2005. Available at: https://www.economist.com/asia/2005/11/17/the-kimchi-wars (accessed 15.7.2021)

The Economist, "An Emotive Issues: A Good-Humoured War Over Food", 12.11.2009.

The Economist, Just add Spice: A Gastronomic Revolution', 29.1.2014.

The Economist, 'Cooking up a Business Cluster', 22.2.2014.

The Guardian, Say bye bye to parmesan, muenster and feta: Europe wants its cheese back, 11 March 2014

Websites:

Burns Country, http://www.robertburns.org/suppers/.

Codex Alimentarius International Food Standards: http://www.codexalimentarius.org/about-codex/en/

Cookpad, http://cookpad.com/.

European Commission on GIs: http://ec.europa.eu/trade/policy/accessing-markets/intellectual-property/geographical-indications/.
IEHCA: http://www.iehca.eu/IEHCA_v4/iehca.html.
Intangible Cultural Heritage: http://www.unesco.org/culture/ich/index.php?pg=00001.
Japanese Culinary Academy: http://culinary-academy.jp/.
The Japan Pasta Association, http://www.pasta.or.jp/index.html.
Kabe-no-ana restaurant, http://www.kabenoana.com/index.html.
MAFF on dietary culture: http://www.maff.go.jp/j/keikaku/syokubunka/index.html.
The official Thai Select website: http://www.thaiselect.com/main.php?filename=index.
Organization to Promote Japanese Restaurant Abroad: http://jronet.org.e.rl.hp.transer.com/about/.
Starbucks: http://www.starbucks.co.uk/menu/beverage-list.
Taiwan Festival: http://www.taiwanfestival.co.uk/.
Thai e-Book: http://thailand.prd.go.th/ebook2/kitchen/intro.html.
Thai Select US: http://www.thaiselectusa.info/pages/restaurant/580#.XvNzjFVKjcs, https://www.nationthailand.com/noname/30353720.
UKCISA: http://www.ukcisa.org.uk/Info-for-universities-colleges%2D%2Dschools/Policy-research%2D%2Dstatistics/Research%2D%2Dstatistics/International-students-in-UK-HE/.
UNESCO: http://en.unesco.org/.
Washoku Japan: http://washokujapan.jp/.
WHO on GM food: https://www.who.int/news-room/questions-and-answers/item/food-genetically-modified.
WTO on GIs: https://www.wto.org/english/tratop_e/trips_e/gi_background_e.htm.

Index[1]

A

Agriculture, 6, 117, 119, 124, 135, 136, 154, 156, 203
AllRecipes, 34
Animal cruelty, 190, 190n5, 192
Animal welfare, 196, 197, 199, 200
Argentina, 158, 159, 159n2, 202
Association of Lebanese Industrialists (ALI), 165, 167
Austerity, 44, 123, 125–128
Australia, 12, 61, 83, 84, 159n2, 179, 182, 188, 202
Australia Day, 12, 62, 83
Autarky, 113, 129
 See also Self-sufficiency
Authenticity, 4, 17, 34, 53, 67, 81, 92, 136, 147, 152, 164, 167, 170, 173, 231

B

Banal flagging, 81
Banal nationalism, 6–8, 11, 13, 19, 30, 77, 78, 92–101, 235
Banitsa, 62–64
BBQ, 2, 12, 62
Beef, 2, 16, 56, 85, 159, 159n2, 193, 198
Belgium, 196, 227
Biotechnology, 201, 202
Boseong green tea, 225
Brexit, vii, 2, 16, 18n3, 22, 23, 138, 155, 159–163, 208, 228, 235, 237
Britain/Great Britain, 3, 16, 56, 59, 86, 87, 90, 96, 97, 134, 159, 229
British beef, 16, 92

---

[1] Note: Page numbers followed by 'n' refer to notes.

© The Author(s), under exclusive license to Springer Nature Switzerland AG 2022
R. Ranta, A. Ichijo, *Food, National Identity and Nationalism*, Food and Identity in a Globalising World, https://doi.org/10.1007/978-3-031-07834-7

273

Index

British food, 20–21, 58, 90, 138, 160, 161
Bubble tea, 141, 141n1
Bulgaria, 63, 164n5, 196
Bulgarian diaspora in the UK, 20, 63
Burns Supper/Burns Night, 20, 59–61, 63

C

Canada, 82, 83, 202, 227
Caribbean food, 90
Catalonia, 15
Champagne, 56, 223
Cheese, 63, 70, 90, 92, 135, 138, 154, 160, 166, 167, 169, 170, 225–227
Chef's Table, 4, 85
Chile, 52, 97, 159n2, 169
China, 37, 138–141, 144, 154, 168, 169, 189–191, 193
Chocolate, 79, 157, 235
Christmas food, 63, 86
Civilisation, 197
Civilisation and improvement, 110
Codex Alimentarius International Food Standards (the Codex standards), 223, 226
Coffee, 79, 80, 82, 234
Colonialism, 113, 188
Commercial nationalism, 78, 81, 82
Conscription, 37, 108, 109, 127, 129, 236
Consumerism, 74n3
Consumer protection, 224, 234, 238, 239
Cookbooks, vi, 3, 4, 7, 14, 33, 73, 84, 113, 122, 123, 125, 128, 128n5, 129

Cookpad, 38–40, 44, 45
'Cool Japan' initiative, the, 149–151
Corn, 13, 31, 203
Cornish pasty, 88, 89
Cosmopolitanism/cosmopolitan values, 199, 209, 209n2
Counter-cuisines, 3, 11
Country of origin (CO), 80, 95, 238
Court of Justice of the European Communities, the, 227
Covid-19 Pandemic, v, 2, 155, 192n6, 237
Cuisines of resistance, 11, 12
Cultural diplomacy, 52, 132–135, 138–140, 152, 164
Cultural heritage, 73, 154, 164, 169, 192, 196, 197, 201, 203, 219, 222, 233
Cultural imperialism, 185, 192, 193, 204
Cultural nationalism, 81, 150, 218, 221, 231
Cultural rights, 18, 192, 193, 204, 211, 239
Cyprus/Cypriot, 18, 169, 170

D

Danish food, 146
Denmark, 142, 143, 145, 146
Diago, 96
Diasporas, 6, 20, 57, 62, 75, 118, 119, 122, 123, 125, 137, 237
Diet, 12, 16, 21, 22, 41, 86, 87, 93, 105–131, 156, 184, 185, 188, 192, 198, 199, 204, 207, 212n6, 216, 218, 233, 236
Dog meat eating, 189–193, 199, 204

E

England/English, 2, 8, 13, 16, 20, 31, 56, 59, 78, 85–92, 108, 125, 198, 212n6
'Enrich the country, strengthen the military,' 108, 114
Ethics/ethical, v, 19, 22, 80, 142–145, 169, 177–205, 221, 238, 239
European Union, the, 17, 18n3, 22, 92, 159, 211, 228, 229
Everyday nationhood/nationalism, 5, 6, 27, 29, 30, 35, 36, 39, 42–45, 50, 54, 55, 77, 78, 105, 107, 200, 207, 235, 236

F

Faeroe Islands, 142
Falconry of the UAE, 214
Fascist Italy, 113, 114
Fast food, 71, 82, 157, 195, 220
Feta cheese, 18, 165, 227
Finland, 142, 145
Fish and chips, 85, 86, 92
Fishing, 143, 145, 154, 156, 160, 162, 163, 197
Foie gras, 23, 178, 194–197, 199, 202, 204, 220, 239
Food aid, 19, 134, 202
Food and Agricultural Organization (FAO), 223
Food and national events, 62
Food and religion, 14
Food and the military, 15, 112
Food Control System (Japan), 115
Food education, 212
Food labelling, 7, 17, 79
Food marketing, 7, 21, 74, 131, 133, 134, 166

Food packaging, 161
Food war, 22, 155, 162, 164–170
Foreign food, 14, 15, 19, 27, 40, 58, 90, 234, 238
France, 56, 62, 134, 194–197, 202, 210n5, 212, 217, 219–221, 225, 227
Free trade, 154, 162, 223, 224, 226–231, 234, 239
French food, 134, 135, 202, 220

G

Gastrodiplomacy, vi, 16, 21, 22, 105, 106, 131–152, 164, 194, 212, 221, 223, 234, 236
Gastronationalism, 4, 7, 16, 17, 21, 22, 66n1, 105, 106, 142, 153–173, 221, 223, 227, 228, 236–238
Gastronomic meal of the French, the, 210, 212, 218–222
Gastronomy, 27, 133, 146, 194, 195, 219, 221
Genetically modified (GM) food/crops, 178, 201–203, 240
Geographical indications (GIs), 18n3, 23, 87, 97, 102n7, 154, 208, 222–230, 238, 239
Germany/German, 16, 31, 72, 107–114, 169, 170, 180, 210n5, 227
Ghana, 3, 15, 107
Globalisation, 7, 11, 17, 21, 65, 71, 77, 86, 93, 102, 117, 146, 152, 157n1, 164, 169, 170, 172, 173, 191, 197, 205, 220, 221, 229, 230, 238, 240
'Global Thai' initiative, the, 136, 138

Greece/Greek, 18, 63, 164n5, 165–167, 227
Greenland, 142, 146

H

Haggis, 59–61, 92
Halal meat, 72, 195
Halloumi/hellim, 169, 170
Healthy eating, 4
Heisei Rice Riots, 116, 117
Herbs, 40, 68, 69
Heritage, 16, 17, 23, 69, 81, 96, 133, 137, 153, 155, 156, 166, 167n6, 170, 196, 202, 209, 210, 214, 222, 230
Hong Kong, 190, 191
Human rights, 17–19, 23, 211
Hummus, 17, 22, 64, 66–67, 70, 74, 75, 155, 164–168, 167n6, 238
Hummus wars, the, 66n1, 165–167, 169, 238
Hungary, 158, 164n5, 196, 197

I

Iceland, 142, 145, 181
Icelandic food, 145
Imperialism, 108, 188, 189
India, 3, 14, 58, 61, 225
Indian food, 4, 58
Intangible cultural heritage, vi, 18, 23, 150, 169, 195, 196, 208–212, 214, 215, 216n10, 217–219, 221, 222n13, 229, 230, 237, 239
Intellectual property (IP), 149, 224, 227, 229–231, 239

International Criminal Court (ICC), the, 207
International Whaling Commission (IWC), 179–182
Israel, 3, 20, 21, 64–75, 107, 108, 117, 119, 123, 125, 126, 128, 159n2, 164–166, 164n5, 189, 199, 200
Israelisation, 64, 65, 71–75
Israel's Independence Day, 12, 62
Italian food, 37, 38, 113
Italy, 3, 14, 18, 31, 62, 92, 108–114, 157n1, 227
See also Fascist Italy

J

Japan, 3, 31, 97, 107, 168, 179, 212
See also 'Cool Japan' initiative, the; Meiji Japan
Japanese style pasta, 19, 20, 27, 35–51
Japan Pasta Association, the, 38–40, 42, 48
Jewish food, 57, 69, 165
Johnson, Boris, 161, 161n4

K

Kaiseki, 216, 217, 219
Kangaroo, 5, 83, 84
Kimchi, 17, 22, 32, 41, 155, 164, 167–169, 238
Knafeh, 70
Korea, 37, 97, 107, 167, 193, 204
See also South Korea

L

Lebanon, 7, 165–168
Local economy, 225, 226
Local food, 3, 143, 154

M

Mad cow disease, 16
Maize, 203
Masterchef, 4, 85
Meat eating, 110, 111, 114, 129, 159n2, 178–188
Mediterranean diet, 18, 106, 142
Meiji Japan, 41n7, 106n1, 108–111, 114, 135
Melbourne, 61
Mentaiko, 40, 40n4, 41, 45, 46
Mexico/Mexican, 3, 8, 31, 107, 203, 210, 225
Migration, 2, 11, 60, 126
Ministry of Agriculture, Forestry and Fishery of Japan (MAFF), the, 147, 148, 148n2, 150, 212n6, 214–217, 216n10, 219, 220
Mizrahi Jews, 127
Morocco/Moroccan, 18, 35
Mussolini, Benito, 113

N

National heritage, 70, 155, 208
National interest, 152, 153, 172, 197, 224, 228, 229
Nation/national branding, v, 6, 7, 80, 81, 132, 138, 150, 164, 209, 214, 218, 234, 236, 239
Natto, 38, 40, 40n4, 47, 48
Nazism, 111–113, 200, 210
Neoliberalism, 106, 208, 229, 230
Netnography, 20, 27, 51–54, 235, 236
'New' Jew, the, 119–123, 129, 233
New Nordic Cuisine (NNC), 22, 132, 141–146, 152
New Zealand, 60, 61, 77, 179, 182
Non-cuisines, 2
Nordic Council, 142, 144, 145
Nordic cuisine, 143
Norm(s)/normative, vii, 7, 17, 22, 23, 80, 119, 155, 156, 164, 177–205, 207, 212, 221, 224, 234, 238, 239
North American Free Trade Agreement (NAFTA), 203
Norway, 142, 143, 145, 163, 180, 181, 184
Nutella, 157, 157n1
Nutrition, 8, 9, 33, 113, 117, 121, 122, 128, 143, 164, 212n6, 216

O

Ontological security, 49
Organic, 3, 56, 80, 81, 112
Organisation for 'Tozteret Ha'aretz,' 124
Organization to Promote Japanese Restaurants Abroad (JRO), the, 148, 149

P

Palestine, 21, 68, 69, 108, 118–128
Palestinianisation, 64, 65, 67–70
Pasta, 19, 27, 31, 37–42, 37n3, 45–48, 50, 113

Peron, Juan, 158, 159
Peru/Peruvian, 138, 222
Pie, 13, 20, 78, 85–93, 101, 102
Piebury, 87, 92
Piecaramba, 87
Pied Noir, 62
Pieminister, 87, 90, 91
Plants, vi, 41, 68, 69, 111, 187, 238
Political economy, 5, 18, 29, 112, 128
Poonchoi, 57
Populism, 4, 6, 16, 17, 21, 22, 66n1, 105, 106, 153–173, 221, 228, 237, 238
'Protected Geographical Status' the, 17

Q
Quebec, 15

R
Recipes, vi, 27, 69, 86, 113, 125, 187
Regional food, 3, 89, 90, 143, 144
Representative list of the Intangible Cultural Heritage of Humanity, the, 36, 210, 212, 213, 218
Restaurants, 7, 16, 28, 32, 37, 38, 52, 53, 66, 67, 69n2, 72–74, 78, 79, 84, 87, 90–92, 101, 136, 137, 140, 142, 144–151, 166, 167, 185, 191, 192, 215, 217

Rice, 2, 12, 21, 31, 37, 41, 47, 48, 51, 109–111, 113–117, 129, 136, 225
Rural economy, 197, 224

S
Salvini, Matteo, 157
Scandinavia, 142
Schnitzel, 72
Scotch whisky, 59, 60, 78, 93–102, 160, 225, 228
Scotch Whisky Association (SWA), the, 94–102, 94n6, 228
Scotland, 15, 59–61, 94–102
Scottish National Party (SNP), the, 98, 100
Self-determination, 177, 204
Self-sufficiency, 107, 111–113, 121, 123, 129, 158, 216
  See also Autarky
Senegalese food, 62
Settler colonialism, 199
Shokuiku (food education), 212, 212n6
Slow food movement, the, 3, 92
Soft power, vi, 131–135, 139, 150, 164, 209, 214, 217
South Africa, 62, 159n2
Southern Africa, 202, 203
South Korea, 168, 169, 189, 191, 225
  See also Korea
Sovereignty, 4, 18, 19, 130, 138, 154, 158, 160–162, 177, 178, 197, 200, 202, 203, 208, 212, 230

Soy sauce, 32, 37, 40, 40n4, 41, 47, 48, 50
Supermarket, v, 67, 79, 79n1, 87, 89, 101, 164, 235
'Sushi police,' 147–151
Sustainability, 144, 145, 188
Sweden, 18, 81, 142–144
Swedish food, 18, 45, 81

T

Taiwan, 138–141, 151
Tequila, 223, 225, 226
Terroir, 3, 4, 6, 56, 142, 143, 154, 156, 159, 164n5
Thailand/Thai, 8, 16, 79, 132, 135–137, 141, 147, 151, 189
Thai Select, 136, 137
Thanksgiving, 13
Tim Hortons, 82, 83
Tokugawa Japan, 109
Tourism, 6, 22, 52, 53, 59, 81, 96, 133, 140, 141, 144, 145, 147, 165, 209, 225, 228, 229, 236
Tozteret Ha'aretz, 124, 125
Trade, 6, 17, 23, 80, 83, 87, 102, 115, 117, 133, 144, 154, 159, 162, 167, 169, 201–203, 208, 209, 222–231, 234, 236, 238, 239
Trade agreement, 154, 162, 169, 201, 227, 229
Transnational, 1, 2, 22, 143, 145, 237
Trump, Donald, 2, 22, 154, 155, 157
Tsena (Israel's austerity measures), 126

Turkey, 13, 72, 77, 107, 157n1
Turkish coffee, 8

U

UK-EU relations, 160, 161
UNESCO, vi, 18, 23, 36, 150, 169, 195, 196, 208–212, 214–222, 216n10, 222n13, 229, 230, 237, 239
United Kingdom (UK), the, 7, 18n3, 22, 78, 79, 79n1, 81, 85–88, 90, 92, 95–97, 100–102, 138, 140, 141, 149, 155, 160, 162, 163, 180, 181, 201, 228, 229, 235, 237
United Nations (UN), the, 139, 208
United States (Us), the, vi, 3, 32, 33, 82, 135, 137, 144, 150, 154, 158, 159, 159n2, 165, 181, 201–203, 226, 227, 240
Universal values, 23, 209, 230, 231

V

Veganism, 23, 178, 198–200, 205, 236
Vegetarianism, 112, 200
Vietnam, 57, 135, 189
Vietnamese, 2, 12
Vietnamese New Year rice crackers, 12

W

Washoku, 36, 41, 150, 212–219
Washoku Association of Japan (Washoku Japan), 214

Whale meat eating, 23, 178–193
Whaling, 179–188, 199
Wine, 3, 4, 56, 70, 134, 154, 164n5, 234
Women's International Zionist Organisation (WIZO), 122
Working-class, 52, 67, 86, 87, 159
World Health Organization (WHO), the, 169, 201, 223
World heritage, 209, 210, 218, 221, 239
World Trade Organization (WTO), the, 97, 102, 116, 223, 224, 228
World War I (WWI), 111, 112
World War II (WWII), 16, 85n3, 86, 110, 111, 111n2, 114, 129, 138, 158, 180, 184, 185, 188

Z

Zionism/Zionist movement, 21, 118–129
Zone of conflict, 55, 142

The manufacturer's authorised representative in the EU is Springer Nature Customer Service Centre GmbH, Europaplatz 3, 69115 Heidelberg, Germany. If you have any concerns regarding our products, please contact ProductSafety@springernature.com

Printed and bound by CPI Group (UK) Ltd, Croydon, CR0 4YY

25/03/2026

02078205-0001